120
Dramatic
Story Sermons
for Children's Church

120
Dramatic
Story Sermons
for Children's Church

Marianne Radius

 BakerBooks

A Division of Baker Book House Co
Grand Rapids, Michigan 49516

Published by Baker Books
a division of Baker Book House Company
P.O. Box 6287, Grand Rapids, MI 49516-6287

First printing, May 1985. Fourth printing, September 1995

Previously published under the titles *The Tent of God* and *Two Spies on a Rooftop* by
William B. Eerdmans Publishing Company.

Printed in the United States of America

ISBN 0-8010-7730-3
Library of Congress Catalog Card Number 68-30984

For

MY HUSBAND

who walked with me on the journey of this book

Preface

If I were not afraid of frightening my readers away by so formidable a term, I might call this an Old Testament biblical theology for young readers. For I have tried to show both the gradual unfolding of God's revelation of Himself and the awakening religious understanding of God's people. God does not change. He is the same yesterday, today, and forever. But God's people are always on a journey, both individually and as a body. We grow from babes in Christ to spiritual maturity — though our progress sometimes seems to be a slipping back one step for every two we stumble forward. And the people of God as a whole learn through history, as God gradually unfolds before their eyes His cosmic plan of redemption.

All of this starts, to be sure, in the garden, where God Himself is present. But even there a journey is required, a spiritual journey from innocence to maturity. At this very beginning of our lives we took the wrong fork of the road or, as the theologian so vividly puts it, we fell. All the rest of human history can be summed up as the struggle to climb back.

The Old Testament is so full of tents that you might almost call it one great campground. At first glance this might seem unimportant. After all, man's first shelter was a tent, and so it is natural that later generations should recall the tent with a nostalgic fondness. But if we look more closely, we observe that the tent is intended to be a symbol.

It is a symbol first of all of the journey, of the fact that we have here no abiding city, but are only passing pilgrims on our way to a better world. And then it is a symbol of intimate living together. Anyone who has ever been on a camping trip will recognize how appropriately it describes such living together.

God also had a tent, built at His own command, according to the pattern He showed to Moses on the mountain. The startling fact that the first sanctuary built by God's people was a tent is obscured for us by the translation "tabernacle," though "tent of meeting" might be a better name. Obviously, while the Israelites wandered in the wilderness, the house of God had to be movable. But here, too, there is a deeper spiritual meaning. God's tent is a symbol of His amazing love and condescension, a sign that He wished to live among His people in a house like theirs. And, even more, it is a sign that God shared the wanderings of His wayward people, for He Himself tells us that He "walked among them in a tent." Even this does not exhaust its meaning. For God continued to "walk among" His people in a tent for nearly three hundred years after the people lived in houses. When David wished to build Him a house of cedar, God replied that He would walk in a tent until His people had peace from their enemies. Thus the tent of God becomes a symbol of the fact that the journey of God's people is not solitary, nor is it purposeless. God Himself accompanies us as we travel. Indeed, He directs our journey, He creates in our hearts the wish to return to Him, and the power to travel along this otherwise quite impassable road. All of this culminates in the incarnation, when God actually *becomes* man, and walks the dusty roads of Palestine. The Old Testament ends with the amazing event of God assuming not a tent of fine embroidered linen, but the tent of human nature. "And the Word became flesh, and camped among us, and we beheld his glory."

—MARIANNE RADIUS

Contents

	Preface	7
1.	The Many-Storied Journey	13

I
THE BEGINNING OF THE JOURNEY

2.	In the Beginning	19
3.	In His Image	21
4.	The Paradise of God	24
5.	The Story of Two Brothers	26
6.	The Time of Testing	30
7.	The Great Rain	33
8.	The Bow in the Cloud	37
9.	The Day God Laughed	39

II
THE HOMESICK PILGRIMS

10.	The Man Who Had to Leave Home	45
11.	"Love Seeketh Not Its Own"	48
12.	The God Who Sees and Hears	51
13.	Visitors from Another World	53
14.	The Rain of Fire	56
15.	Our Guide and Our Protector	59
16.	Stronger Than Death	61
17.	God Plans a Wedding	65
18.	The Plot That Failed	68

19.	The Gate of Heaven	71
20.	Bitter Lessons	74
21.	Holding Onto God	76
22.	The Two-Way Promise	79
23.	God's Mystery Plan	81
24.	Sold Into Slavery	85
25.	The Hole	87
26.	As We Forgive	90
27.	Where He Leads Me	93
28.	The Wanderers	97
29.	Standing on the Promises	99
30.	The Trailblazer	102

III
THE TENT OF GOD

31.	In the Hands of God	107
32.	A Letter from a Mother	110
33.	More Than All the Treasures of Egypt	112
34.	The Reluctant Messenger	115
35.	Who Is God?	119
36.	God Accepts a Substitute	122
37.	Through the Deep Waters	125
38.	Trust and Obey	128
39.	God Is My Banner	130
40.	The Mountain of God	133
41.	The Broken Promise	135
42.	The Tent of God	138
43.	"The Pattern I Showed You"	142
44.	Slow to Believe	145
45.	"I Wish That I Were Dead!"	148
46.	The Choice Belongs to God	150
47.	God Will Provide a Lamb	153
48.	An Angel in the Road	155
49.	What's in It for Me?	158
50.	Moses Is Satisfied	161

IV
THE HEART OF THE TENT

51.	Two Spies on a Rooftop	167
52.	Crossing the River	170

53. What Do These Rocks Mean? — 172
54. The Walls Came Tumbling Down — 175
55. God Assigns a Test — 178
56. Old Clothes and Moldy Bread — 180
57. The People at the Oak Tree — 183
58. God Hears the Cries of His People — 186
59. "Show Me a Sign!" — 189
60. We Do Not Fight Alone — 191
61. God Welcomes the Stranger — 194
62. God Turns Tears to Laughter — 197
63. Dedicated to God — 200
64. One Man Against a Thousand — 202
65. "The Philistines Are Upon You!" — 205
66. The Lesson of Suffering — 207
67. Hannah Gives Her Son Back to God — 210
68. God Calls a Child to Service — 213
69. The Israelites Kidnap God — 215
70. The Dead God Meets the Living God — 218
71. The Stone That Points Two Ways — 221
72. God Chooses a King — 223
73. Saul Makes a Good Beginning — 226
74. The Test of Obedience — 228
75. God's Arithmetic — 231
76. "Send for the Youngest!" — 234
77. In the Name of the Lord of Hosts — 237
78. The Education of a King — 239
79. "The Lord Watch Between Me and Thee!" — 241
80. The Lesson of Waiting — 244
81. A Woman's Good Advice — 247
82. The Wages of Sin — 249
83. The Circle of God's Mercy — 252
84. David Learns About God's Holiness — 254
85. The House That Lasts Forever — 257
86. The Bitter Fruit of Envy — 259
87. The Man Who Was Nearly Perfect — 263

V
THE FORK IN THE ROAD

88. "Long Live King Solomon!" — 269
89. What Do You Want Most? — 272

12

90.	The House of God	275
91.	The Sign of the Golden Temple	277
92.	Solomon in All His Glory	280
93.	Torn Into Pieces	284
94.	Jeroboam Reaps a Bitter Harvest	286
95.	The Secret Place of God	289
96.	The Widow's Story	292
97.	The Fire of God	294
98.	The Still, Small Voice	298
99.	God's Last Message to Ahab	301
100.	Elisha Picks Up Elijah's Coat	304
101.	God Wakes the Dead	306
102.	The Witness	309
103.	The Free Gift	312
104.	Protected by Chariots of Fire	315
105.	The Man Who Laughed at God	317
106.	The Terrible Judgment of God	320
107.	The Man Who Ran Away from God	322
108.	Who Is My Neighbor?	325
109.	The God Who Answers Prayer	328
110.	Josiah Discovers a Great Treasure	331
111.	The King Who Burned His Bible	333
112.	The Weeping Preacher	336
113.	The Death of the City	338
114.	The Strange Leading of God	342
115.	The Lost Dream	345
116.	Seven Times Hotter	347
117.	The King Who Ate Grass	350
118.	The Scales of God	352
119.	"Who Stopped the Mouths of Lions"	355
120.	"If I Perish, I Perish!"	358
121.	The Sure Promise of God	360
122.	The Great Shout of Laughter	363
123.	The Living Tent	365

1
The Many-Storied Journey

Perhaps at one time or another you have gone on a camping trip. You put up your tent. You collect wood and build a fire. At night you unroll your sleeping bag, and spread it on the ground. In the morning you roll it back up again. When I see your tent pitched beside a lake or in the woods, I know you do not plan to stay there permanently. You are on a journey.

In this book I want to tell you about a journey. Or, perhaps I ought to say I want you to come along with me on this journey. For though this trip was first made by people who lived long ago, we cannot be content just to read about what happened to them. Each of us has to retrace the steps they made, and make the journey for himself.

This journey was made by many different people, who traveled in many different ways. Some rode on donkeys or camels. Some sailed in boats. But most of them walked, setting one weary foot ahead of the other. But whether they traveled north or south, east or west, whether they rode in state or just plodded mile after mile, they all traveled on more than one level.

In the center of the city where I live there is a giant highway interchange, where several main roads meet. This interchange is several stories high. The roads shoot off in many different directions, at many different levels. It is so complicated that you cannot map it out in your mind's eye. You can only follow carefully the signs pointing to the

place where you wish to go, trusting blindly that the road will take you to your destination.

This many-storied highway intersection is something like the journey I wish to tell you about. For the people in my story travel on many different levels at once. They go from one place to another, walking or riding. At the same time their whole life might be called a journey, every day one more step between life and death. At still another level they must travel from being a newborn babe in Christ to spiritual maturity. This level of the journey is a gradual, slow, sometimes painful learning to trust in God, to set aside what I myself want to do and do instead what God wants. It is a day-by-day dying of my old sinful desires, while the glorious new man in Christ comes gaspingly to life. And finally, at still another level, this is the journey of all the people of God through history, from the day we were thrust out of the garden which was our only true home, to the day we reach at last that glorious city which God is preparing for all who love and trust Him.

Journeys and tents naturally belong together. All the first travelers lived in tents. And even later, when they had houses of sun-baked brick or wood, they still liked to remember the tents they had once lived in, and to talk about them. But there was still another reason why the tent was something special to these travelers. These people never traveled alone. At every level of their many-storied journey they were accompanied by God Himself. Indeed, God planned their journey, and directed its every step, so that the whole journey was not a random wandering from place to place, but a carefully mapped route to a destination. And while the people themselves lived in tents, God commanded them to make a tent for Him too, so that in the very center of the camp the people could aways see the tent of God, the sign that God journeyed with His people.

Our journey starts in a garden, where God Himself is present with the man and the woman He has made.

I
THE BEGINNING OF
THE JOURNEY

For we are strangers before thee, and sojourners, as all our fathers were: our days on the earth are as a shadow, and there is no abiding (I Chronicles 29:15).

2
In the Beginning

Genesis 1

Long ago, longer ago than you can remember, your mother was a girl, your father was a boy. Like you, each of them lived at home with his own parents, your grandparents. Like you, each of them went to school, helped around the house, and spent many happy hours in play. Before that, longer ago than even they can remember, your two grandfathers were boys, your two grandmothers were girls. They lived at home with their parents, your great-grandparents. They, too, went to school, helped around the house, and spent many happy hours in play. And your great-grandparents — there were eight of them — were once children too. So you could go back, if you wanted to, till you got to the very first father of all and the very first mother.

That very first mother was called Eve; that very first father was called Adam. They were the first people that ever lived, and the Bible tells us that they were never children at all. You see, because they were the first, they had no loving parents to teach and help them. And so God made them grown-up right away.

Adam and Eve were not frightened when they found themselves all alone in the world. For God, before He made Adam and Eve, had made a beautiful home for them. He had made the earth for them to live on, the blue sky to stretch above their heads, the sun to give them warmth and light, and the grains and fruits to provide all sorts of delicious foods.

When you make a table, you have to have boards and nails and glue. When you sew a doll's dress, you have to have cloth. When you bake a cake, you need flour and sugar and eggs. But when God made the world, He did not need any materials to shape and cut and form into our world. God made the earth out of nothing at all. God's word is so powerful that He has only to speak, and whatever He names immediately is there.

God started His wonderful work of making by creating a great shapeless mass. This mass was all mixed up. The sky and the earth were mixed together. The water and the dry land were all confused. Everything was dark. Above this shapeless mass hovered the Spirit of God. The Holy Spirit brooded above the mass as a bird broods over her eggs, warming them into life and growth.

Where the Spirit of God is, there darkness cannot last. And so it seems quite natural that the very next thing that God made was light. "Let there be light!" God said, and there the light was! God saw that the light was good. He called the light *day,* and the darkness *night*. That was the first day of God's making.

The next day God divided the clouds and the sky from the earth. God called the sky *heaven*. That was the second day of God's making. The third day God said, "Let the waters be gathered together into one place, and let the dry land appear!" And even as God spoke, that very thing happened. There were little brooks, and rivers, and lakes, and oceans. And rising above the water there was dry ground. "Let the earth grow green with grass and plants and trees," God said. And everywhere the brown dirt was covered with the beautiful green of grass and leaves and fruit trees. And God saw that it was good. That was the third day of God's making.

On the fourth day, God made the sun and the moon and the sparkling stars. "Give light," He commanded them, "and divide the night from the day, the summer from the winter, and one year from another year." And God saw that it was good. That was the fourth day of God's making. And God said, "Let the lakes and the rivers be filled with fish, and the sky with birds." Even as God spoke, there appeared all sorts of fish in the water, and the sky was filled with birds flying to and fro. That was the fifth day of God's making.

On the sixth day, God made all kinds of animals, big ones and little ones, those that live in the dark forest, and those that live in the open fields. Now the home that God was preparing was finished. It had everything in it the first father and the first mother needed.

But the most important part of God's making was still to come. For God did not make all this just for the joy of looking at it, as you and I might paint a picture and hang it on our wall to decorate a room. No, God had something quite different in mind. The dark aisles of the forest, the ocean waves breaking on the beach, the silver moon, the dazzling sun which warmed the earth into growth, the birds which soared in the sky, the deer which seemed almost to fly as they ran from place to place — all these were beautiful, and all of them were good. But not one of them could answer when God talked to them. Not one of them could be God's friend.

Of course, God did not need a friend. God was not lonely. You see, there are three persons in God — the Father, the Son, and the Holy Spirit. And between these three persons there is a wonderful fellowship of love, of talking and working together. No, God did not need a friend. But God, who is the source of all the love and goodness there is — God so overflowed with love and goodness that He wanted to make someone who could share this love. If I may use the figure (stepping oh so carefully and reverently, because I am speaking about the great God), God's love was so great it could hardly be contained. It spilled over the top of the cup. And so God put this love into words that everyone could understand. He made a man to share in His love, His goodness, even to share in His work.

3

In His Image

Genesis 2

*t*he whole new world stood on tiptoe, waiting. This was the most exciting moment of the most exciting week. For six days God had been busy making. He had made many wonderful things. But why had

He made all these wonders? For whom was the new world being prepared?

The shining new rivers could not talk, of course. But if they could have talked, they might have asked, "Who is going to swim in my quiet pools? Who is going to drink the sparkling water of my springs?" And the newly made green trees, who was going to rest beneath their shady leaves? Who was going to bite into their delicious, juicy fruit? Who was going to milk the cows and the goats and make cheese and butter from the milk? Who was going to warm himself on chilly nights with the wool off the sheep's back? Who? Who? And the angels of God, in heaven, they were watching. They were marveling at what God had made. They, too, must have wondered; they too must have asked each other, Who?

The final moment had come. God Himself was going to answer this *Who*. God was going to make that creature for whom all this other making was only a preparation, only a home, a place to live and to work. God was going to make the man. And God picked up a handful of dirt, and out of the dirt He made a man. What? All these wonders for a creature made of dirt? Yes, and that was not the half of it. For that man, made out of the dust of the ground, was — wonderful to say! — like God, his Maker. God made the man in His own image. He breathed into the nose of the dirt man He had made, and in that very instant man became a living soul. Like God, he could talk, and he could laugh, and he could remember, and he could think. Like God, he could tell the difference between right and wrong. He could hope, and he could pray. Like God, he had a soul that would live forever. But most of all, like God, he could love.

God had worked for six days. The seventh day He did not work. On the seventh day God rested. He was not tired; He did not need to sleep. He used this seventh day to think about and to enjoy the things He had made. And then God decided that the man should be like Him in *this* way too. He would not have to work all the time. After he had worked six days, he, too, should have the seventh day to rest, to think about and to enjoy the things God had done for him. God gave a special blessing to the seventh day, because it was the day God had rested from His work of making.

Then God brought all the animals, one by one, before Adam. Think what a parade that must have been! There came the lordly lion, the timid rabbit, the giant elephant so large that the ground shook when he moved, the little mouse who skittered through the grass, the horse, the cow, and many, many more. Not one of these creatures had a name as yet. It was part of Adam's work to name them. Adam looked at each one, and he saw just what each animal was really like. To every animal he gave a name that told what it really was. And that became the name of that animal from then on. But none of the animals was suited to be a companion to Adam. For Adam was made in God's image, with a living soul, and the animals were not. Adam was alone. He was the only man; there was no one to share his experiences with him.

"It is not good that the man should be alone," God said. "I will make someone to help him and to share his life." God put Adam to sleep, a deep, dreamless sleep. God took a rib from the side of Adam, and from that rib He made a woman. He brought the woman to Adam.

When Adam saw the new companion God had made for him, he exclaimed, "This woman is part of me, for she was taken out of me!" God married them there in the lovely garden, and He spoke the words which are still said at every wedding, at the wedding of your father and mother too: "Therefore shall a man leave his father and his mother and live with his wife, and the two of them shall be one."

Then God gave the man and the woman a wedding present, a gift fit for a king. He gave them the whole earth, the home that God had so marvelously prepared for them. "Have children," God said, "and fill up the earth, and care for it. Learn about it, and rule over it." And God blessed the man and the woman.

So Adam and Eve lived in their new home. Every day they learned new things about God's wonderful world. They saw the sun rise in the east, and set again in the west. They watched the moon grow larger every night, and then again grow smaller. They learned how to care for the trees, and what the animals were like. And in the evening God Himself walked in the garden, and there He gave to Adam and Eve the most precious gift of all the many hundreds of gifts He had given them — the gift of the friendship of God. This was the crowning joy of their lives. Adam and Eve could walk and talk with God. They were very happy.

4

The Paradise of God

Genesis 3

*T*here was a hedge around it, and inside this hedge was the loveliest sight man has ever seen. For this garden had been planted by God Himself, and He arranged it so that every view delighted the eye. The trees had been chosen for the beauty and fragrance of their flowers as well as the luscious taste of their fruits. Among the trees grew the golden, ripening grain, and through it all wound the river, to drink, to bathe in, or just to watch as the fish leaped high out of the water, and the birds soared effortlessly overhead.

They called the garden Paradise, or, sometimes, just the Garden of God. The hedge was not there to shut out thieves or wild animals — for all the animals, even the lion and tiger, were friendly, and roamed through the lovely garden at will. No, the hedge was just to mark off the garden from the rest of the earth. All the earth had been given to man as his home. But Paradise was a very special place. It was the place where the great God of heaven and earth came down to meet the man, the place where God invited the man to meet his Maker. In the early evening, when the first cool breeze began to blow, God walked in the garden, and there He talked to the man and woman as a man talks to his friends. And this, of course, was the crowning touch to the beauty of that most beautiful of all places. There was love in the garden, and the friendship of God Himself.

In the middle of the garden were two special trees. The tree of life was a symbol of that wonderful, unending life which only God can give. Whoever loved and obeyed God would be allowed to eat the fruit of this tree, and he would then live forever. The second tree was a testing tree. It was called the tree of the knowledge of good and evil. God had showered down upon man His goodness and His love. He had heaped up to overflowing the gifts He had given them. Did Adam and Eve love and trust God in return? God would try them out. He would give them a command. If they obeyed God, it would prove that they loved Him. They would then be allowed to eat the fruit of the tree of life, and to live in the wonderful garden in perfect happiness forever.

"You may eat the fruit of all the trees in the garden," God told Adam and Eve, "with one exception. You must not eat the fruit of the tree of the knowledge of good and evil." God did not give them any reason why they must not touch the fruit of this tree. He did not explain His command. He wanted them to obey Him simply because they loved and trusted Him, even though they did not understand why He had made this command.

There was one person who did not like the lovely garden and the happy couple who lived there. This person was Satan. Once Satan had been one of God's angels. But long before all this, Satan had rebelled against God, and he had been thrown out of that happy place where all is love and light because God is there. Ever since then Satan had hated God. He could not stand the sight of the happy couple in the garden. He wanted them to be as unhappy as he himself was.

Satan did not approach Adam and Eve as he was, so that they would turn away in horror. No, he came disguised as a snake, and he spoke first of all to Eve. "Did God really say you may not eat any of the fruit in the garden?" he asked her. "No," Eve said, "God has given us all the fruit, except the one tree, the tree of the knowledge of good and evil. If we eat the fruit of that tree, He says that we will die."

"You will not die," Satan answered. "God knows that if you eat the fruit of that tree, you will become like God Himself. That is why He does not want you to eat it." Would Eve believe what God had said? Or would she believe Satan? This was a test of her love and her trust in God. She looked at the tempting fruit of the tree. It was beautiful. Surely, it would taste delicious too. She would love to become like God! She forgot God's command. She reached out her hand, and picked the fruit, and ate it. She gave some to Adam, and he ate it too.

That evening, when Adam and Eve heard God walking in the garden, they did not run to meet Him. They hid themselves instead. They were ashamed, and they were afraid. God called to them. "Where are you?" He said. Slowly, reluctantly, they came forward. "I heard Your voice, and I hid myself, because I was afraid," Adam said. "Have you eaten the fruit of the tree which I commanded you not to touch?" God asked. Adam quickly found an excuse. "The woman You gave me," he said, "she gave me some of the fruit, and I ate it." "What have you done?" God said to Eve. She had an excuse too. "The snake fooled me," she said. Each of them blamed someone else, but each was really responsible for his own sin.

No longer could the man and the woman live in the beautiful garden. Nor could they eat the fruit of the tree of life. Only those who love and trust God can eat of that tree. Only they will live forever. Instead of a happy family, now there was jealousy, and quarreling, and anger, and sickness, and pain. There was loneliness and sorrow and death. No longer was it easy to raise enough food to eat. Even the ground showed the sad results of Adam's sin. Where once fruit trees had grown, now there were thorns and thistles. There were terrible storms and droughts. The animals were wild and dangerous.

Adam and Eve had to leave the garden where once God had walked and talked with man. The righteous God cannot associate with sinners. God set His cherubim at the gate of the garden, and he carried a flaming sword that turned constantly this way and that way, to close the entrance to God's Paradise.

But God did not forsake the man and the woman in their sin. He gave them a promise. They would have trouble all their life. At last they would die. But God promised He would send a Saviour to help them. Adam and Eve did not know who this Saviour would be. They had to trust blindly in the promise of God. But you and I know who the Saviour is. He is Jesus Christ, the Son of God, who came down to our troubled earth on Christmas Day, to pay for all our sins.

5
The Story of Two Brothers

Genesis 4

At first there was only one child in the family, and those of you who are only children can understand what this means. Not that he had much of a chance to be lonely. Either his father or his mother was with him nearly all the time; and the three of them, being the only people there were in all God's great world, clung together.

Perhaps they spoiled him a little bit. He was the first baby they had ever seen — the first baby there had ever been, for that matter, since both his father and his mother had been made by God as grown-ups from the start. They were endlessly delighted by his cute ways as he learned to walk, and then to talk, and, as he grew into boyhood, followed them around trying to imitate whatever he saw them do.

There was another reason why this child, their first-born, was precious to Adam and Eve. For the promise of God that somehow (they did not know how) He would come to their rescue, this promise was to be fulfilled through their children. And so, when Eve first held her baby son in her arms, she cried out, "I have gotten a man! It is God who helped me do this!" Did she hope that baby Cain was the Saviour God had promised to send? If she did, she was sadly mistaken. For Cain would bring his father and mother only tears, not joy. He would give them the first horrifying glimpse of what they had done when they turned their backs on God.

And then God sent them another baby boy. They called this second son Abel. Now there were two children in their home. The boys could play together. They could explore the fields and the woods together. Cain, who was a little the older, could teach Abel some of the things he had already found out. At least, this is the way it ought to have been.

An older child, who has been the center of all his parents' love and attention, does not always welcome a younger brother or sister. Was this the way Cain felt? Was he jealous of the new baby? He need not have been. For in a father's and in a mother's heart there is room for ten or even more children, each one occupying his own special place which no other child could ever fill.

However that may be, the two boys were quite different from each other. Adam was a farmer. Cain and Abel helped him in the fields, and their father taught them all he knew. Cain especially liked to care for the growing crops. He worked in the fields. Abel had a way with animals. He looked after the sheep. But there was another, more important difference between the two boys. Abel loved God, and trusted in His promise. Cain did not. He was quite sure that he could look out for himself. He did not need God.

Life was hard for all of them now that they had been driven out of the beautiful garden. They had to work long hours to scrape a bare living from the ground. They got very tired. Sometimes they were sick. They spoke angry words to each other, and quarreled bitterly. And so,

struggling, tired, heartsore, sometimes afraid, always lonely and home-sick for the wonderful garden where they had walked with God, they planted and harvested their crops. Always they clung desperately to the promise of God. They did not understand how God would restore them to His precious friendship. They did not know when it would happen. They had only the promise, but that was enough for them. Some day they were going to walk and talk with God again.

And so the boys grew up. One year, after the harvest, each of them brought an offering of thanks to God. Cain brought some of the grain from his fields. But it was *only* a gift of grain; there was no real thanks in his heart. Abel brought a little lamb from his flock. He offered the lamb to God with true thankfulness and trust in God's promise. He knew that he was sinful and did not deserve God's blessings. God can see every man's heart. He is not interested in your gifts unless you bring them with a thankful and a trusting heart. God accepted Abel's gift, but He did not accept Cain's. When Cain saw that Abel's gift was accepted, but his was not, his face grew dark with anger.

"Why are you angry?" God said to Cain. "If you bring an offering in the right spirit, it will be accepted too. Do not allow these angry thoughts to fill your mind. Sin is like a wild animal. It is always waiting to jump on you and choke you." Cain did not listen to God's warning. He called to Abel. "Let us go out into the fields," he said. So the two brothers went out to look at the fields. When they were out of sight of their parents, Cain jumped on Abel and killed him. No one had seen what he did. No one? God had seen!

"Where is your brother?" God asked Cain. "I don't know," Cain lied. "Am I my brother's keeper?" "Your brother's blood is crying out to me from the ground," God said. "Because you have done this, from now on the earth will not grow crops for you when you cultivate it. You must leave home, and wander alone over the earth." Now Cain was frightened. Not sorry for his crime. Just afraid of the punishment. "My punishment is greater than I can bear," he said to God. "Who-ever sees me will kill me." "I will put a sign on you," God said, "and anyone who raises his hand against you will be paid back seven times."

So that is the story of the first two children who were ever born. Abel was dead, and his murderer was his own brother. So quickly, so terribly, had the sin of Adam and Eve grown. Later God gave Adam and Eve another son to take the place of Abel. They called the new baby Seth, and he is the father of all the people after him who trust in God, of you and me, too.

You see, God is right. Sin is like a wild animal just waiting to jump on you and choke you. On you, and on me. There is only one way in all the world you can escape from this wild beast. It is to trust your whole life to the care of your Saviour, Jesus. He has paid for all your sins by His death. He, and He alone, can help you conquer the sin in your own heart.

6

The Time of Testing

Job 1, 2

Once upon a time, long, long ago, in the far-off mists of history, there lived a man who was very rich, and his name was Job. He owned thousands of sheep, and thousands of camels, and hundreds of oxen. And, of course, he had many, many servants to care for these great flocks of cattle.

Job was rich in his family too. He had seven sons and three daughters. And among all ten of his children there was no jealousy or quarreling. Every day, as the seven boys grew older, they got together for dinner at night, going in turn from each one's house to the other's, and always they invited their sisters to come too. What feasting there was at these gatherings, what happy talk and laughter!

"How hard it is," Jesus once said, "for a rich man to get into heaven!" But Job had found the way. This is where he was richest of all. He had built up for himself treasures in heaven. He did not trust in his flocks of sheep, in his loaded barns. No, he trusted only in the loving God who had given him all this wealth. He loved his children, naturally, but even more he loved the heavenly Father who had entrusted these children to his care. Every week he offered special sacrifices to God for his children. "Perhaps," he said to himself, "my children have sinned in their hearts." For Job knew that God can read the secrets of the heart.

While his children feasted, and Job sacrificed to God, God Himself held court, seated upon the great white throne in heaven. One by one each of His servants, the angels and the archangels and the cherubim and the seraphim, came down the golden streets and bowed before the King of kings in worship. And then each one reported what he had been doing, and each one received orders as to what he must do next.

Among this great crowd of shining messengers there was a stranger, one with a dark face and an ugly garment. Oh, he was not completely strange here, for he himself had once been one of the angels of light. But ever since he had been thrown out of heaven because of his rebellion, there was just one consuming passion left in his twisted, deformed heart — to make others like himself, exiled, homeless rebels, lost forever in the terrible darkness of hell.

"Where do you come from?" God asked Satan. And Satan answered, "From walking up and down the earth." "Have you noticed my servant Job?" God asked. "There is no one else like him on earth, a good man, who fears God, and turns away from wickedness." Satan laughed a devilish laugh. "There is good reason why Job fears God," he said sarcastically. "You have built a hedge around him. You have made him rich. Put out Your hand, and take away some of the things You have given him, and You will soon see how much he trusts in You!"

Is it true? Do you and I trust God only for what we can get out of Him? Is it only when He showers our lives with blessings, when He makes the path before us bright with sunshine, that we offer our thanks? God would try Job. Not to please Satan. No, rather to teach even this godly man Job that there is something more precious than sheep and camels and even children. And so God said to Satan, "Try him out! I will allow you to test his faith."

It was the first day of the week. All ten of Job's children were feasting at their oldest brother's house. That very morning their father had offered the customary weekly sacrifice for them. Suddenly a messenger burst in upon him, dusty and out of breath. "Your oxen were plowing, and raiders fell upon them and stole them, and killed all the servants! I only have escaped to tell you!" Before he was through speaking, another man came running: "Lightning from heaven has burned up all your sheep, and all your shepherds too! I alone have escaped to tell you!" Scarcely had he spoken, when another burst into the house: "Three bands of Chaldeans have stolen all your camels, and murdered all the drivers! I only have escaped to tell you!" Even as he spoke, one last, terrible message arrived: "Your sons and daughters were eating in their oldest brother's house, and a fearful wind blew the house down on top of them! They are all dead!"

Then Job stood up. He tore his coat in his terrible grief. He shaved the hair off his head, as men did in those days when they were heart-broken. And then he lay down on the ground and worshiped God. "The Lord gave, and the Lord has taken away," he said; "blessed be the name of the Lord!"

I wonder if you can imagine the fury of Satan when he saw Job's faith? Then Satan said to God, "A man will give everything he has, if only he can save his life. But put forth Your hand now, and touch his bone and his flesh, and see if he will not say, 'I will have nothing more to do with a God who allows those who trust him to suffer so!'" God answered, "He is in your hand. Only spare his life." Now Satan attacked Job with boils, from the bottom of his feet to the very top of his head. Job sat down upon the heap of ashes outside the door of his house, and scraped his painful sores with a piece of broken pottery. His wife said to him, "Let us have no more of this absurd talk about a God! Defy Him to His face, and then give up and die!" Job said, "You speak foolishly. Are we to receive good things from God, and not troubles?"

Job's friends came to see him, to offer him advice and comfort. When they saw the scarcely human figure sitting on the ash heap, they did not recognize him. All of them wept, and they tore their clothes, and for seven days and seven nights they sat beside Job without speaking, for they saw how great his grief was. At last they tried to speak words of comfort, but it was poor comfort they brought.

"You must have sinned terribly," one of them said, "that God should send you so fearful a punishment!" And another suggested, "It is because you have extorted your riches from the poor; this is just what happens to wicked men!" And a third said, "God has not yet begun to punish you as much as you have deserved. Confess your wickedness, and perhaps He will still have mercy!"

"Have pity on me, my friends!" Job begged. "Why do you add to my suffering? I can only say that I trust my life to my Saviour. Some day, even after I am dead, I am certain that I will see God with my own eyes."

Were these terrible trials a punishment for Job's sins, as his friends thought? Job *was* a sinner, as all men are. But Job trusted in God, and because of this trust, Jesus was going to bear the punishment of Job's sins. No, Job's troubles were lessons, painful lessons, but lessons that would bear rich and happy fruit. For it is only when everything we have depended on collapses, when every person we trust is gone, that we begin to taste the marvelous faithfulness of our God. In the end God gave back to Job everything He had taken away: his sheep, and oxen, and camels, and seven sons and three beautiful daughters. But the greatest gift God gave him was something far more precious than all of these. It was the sure knowledge that God would never forsake him, that whatever happened to him came from the loving hand of God. Job had tried God, and found Him faithful.

7

The Great Rain

Genesis 6, 7

Noah built a boat in his back yard. This does not seem strange to us. Lots of people build boats in their garages, or even in their basements. And when they have finished the boat, they lift it onto a two-wheeled trailer and tow it to the nearest lake. The strange thing about Noah's boat was its size. No trailer ever made could have moved this boat; and even if a trailer could have been found, there was no lake anywhere near where Noah lived that could have floated it. Noah's boat was about as long as the city block on which I live. It was seventy-five feet wide, and as high as a five-story building. The *Mayflower,* which brought the Pilgrims across the wild Atlantic Ocean to Plymouth Rock, was only about one-fifth the size of Noah's boat.

It took Noah a hundred and twenty years to build this boat. At first he worked all alone, cutting down the trees, dragging them to his yard, joining them together carefully, sealing the joints with pitch.

Later God gave him three sons, who helped as soon as they grew big enough to lend a hand. But the three of them were his only helpers. Plenty of his neighbors came to watch. But they did not help. They only came to laugh at the crazy man who built a boat bigger than anyone had ever heard of, and who built it, of all places, on dry land!

Noah kept on working even while his neighbors mocked him. For Noah knew that this boat was a matter of life or death for him and for all his family. God had spoken to Noah. "The earth is filled with violence," God said. "Every imagination of man's thoughts is wicked. I am going to destroy these wicked men with a flood. Build a boat in which you and your family and one pair of each of the animals can be saved alive." For Noah alone, of all the men on earth, still trusted and loved God.

God could have saved Noah in some less toilsome way than a boat which took a hundred and twenty years to build. He could have snatched him up to heaven, or covered him from the waters with His almighty hand. Nothing is impossible for God. But God chose this way, and I can think of at least two reasons why He did. The long, difficult building of the ark, log by log, was a test of Noah's faith, just as suffering was a test of Job's faith. It was quite a different test than Job's, but one just as hard. Noah was not a superman of faith. He was a sinner, weak, trembling, stumbling, doubting, just as you and I are.

How many times in that hundred and twenty years he must have wondered in his heart whether his neighbors were right! Whether he was really crazy after all! Whether God had actually spoken to him or he had just imagined it all! His neighbors went on marrying, feasting, fighting, killing. Not Noah! Noah clung to God's promise.

There was another reason why God let Noah work so long on his boat. While he worked, Noah preached to his careless neighbors. Over and over he told them about the flood God was going to send. Over and over he warned them to change their wicked ways, to trust in God instead of in their own right arm. But the people only laughed. "Just where do you think you are going with a boat that size?" they asked him. "If you were to put it in the river here, the water would all overflow, and you would be left stuck in the mud!" Another suggested, "Noah is going sailing on dry land!" And still another man turned away scornfully, saying, "They are all crazy. Don't pay any attention to this talk of floods!"

"You can laugh at us," Noah said, "but no man can laugh at God. Put away your wicked, violent deeds, and pray to Him for forgiveness. For the day is surely coming when He will punish those who do not trust in Him." "Yes, that is what you said last year — and the year before," the neighbors answered. "But it all turned out to be a false alarm. That promise you talk about — it is so very old. No one now

living remembers hearing God say it. Nothing is going to change. Things will go on forever just the way they are now!" And the neighbors had gone back to their wicked lives, to stealing and lying and killing one another.

At last the boat was finished. God spoke again to Noah. "Come into the boat," He said, "you and all your family, and all the animals." God did not say *"Go* into the boat!" He said *"Come,"* as if God Himself was already there, as indeed He was going to be there with them all that long, terrifying voyage. The animals went in first, two by two, coming from the fields and forest of their own accord, each called by the secret call of God. The cow and the horse came, the dog and the cat, the fierce lion and the even fiercer tiger (their fierceness gentled by the power of God), the timid little mouse, the deadly rattlesnake, the great ostrich, and the ruby-throated humming bird no bigger than the end of your thumb. And many, many more than I can name. Last of all Noah himself went in, he and his wife, and his three sons, and their wives. And then God Himself shut the door and sealed it tight and safe.

And then it began to rain. It rained for forty days and forty nights without stopping. The water got deeper and deeper, and the ark floated on top of it. Finally even the tops of the mountains were covered. Every man on earth except Noah's family drowned. Each one had now to appear before the very God he had mocked — to appear, and to answer for his wicked life. It is a fearful thing for a sinful man to fall into the hands of the living God!

What a desolate sight Noah now looked out on! Nothing but water everywhere, not the clear, flowing water of a river or ocean, but the sullen, muddy, polluted water of destruction. Here and there an uprooted tree floated, or a broken piece of some building, or even the decaying body of a drowned animal. For five months after it had stopped raining, the ark floated aimlessly on this horrible water.

If God is a terrifying Judge to those who have defied Him, you will not find there could be a more tender Father than He is to those who trust in Him. Not for one moment, night or day, did God take His eyes off Noah and the ark. Every second His almighty arm was stretched out to protect and to reassure His child. We know this for certain because God Himself wrote it down in the Bible.

8

The Bow in the Cloud

Genesis 8, 9

It was more than five months since Noah had seen the ground. No fields and hills, no grass and trees, no sunshine even — nothing but the grey, heaving mass of water stretching as far as the eye could see. Did Noah despair? Was he afraid? I am sure that no day of all those months passed that Satan did not whisper in his ear: "Don't you see? God has forgotten you! You will drown, like all the rest. Or, what is worse, you will starve and the day will come when your family, driven mad with hunger, will turn on each other, killing and devouring human flesh." And Noah must have cried out in his own heart, "Has God forgotten me?" It is a cry every one of us speaks in anguish at some time or other in his life. No, God has not forgotten. He did not forget Noah. He does not forget you in your bitterest moment, either. But *His* timetable is not *our* timetable. His purposes are not our purposes. It is patience we must learn, and trust, fixing our eyes not on the floodwaters all around us, but instead on the face of Jesus, who sits even now at the right hand of God, ruling our lives.

There was plenty of work to do, and that helped to keep up their spirits. There were only eight of them all together — Noah, his wife, their three sons, and their wives. The animals who were with them in the boat took a lot of time. They had to be fed and watered, and their stalls had to be kept clean, the cows and goats had to be milked, and on many days there were new baby animals to be cared for. And God blessed their work. Not one of the animals God had entrusted to their care died.

Had God forgotten them? No, God remembered them, moment by moment, day by day, week by week. God sent a wind to blow over the waters, and slowly the water began to go down. Of course, Noah and his family could not see what was happening. There was nothing in sight against which they could measure the water. And then one day, as they went about their work, feeding and caring for the animals, something startling happened. The ark bumped something underneath. The whole boat shuddered. All the family came running to peer through the window. There was another great creaking bump, and suddenly they stopped dead still. They were grounded! They had stuck fast on the topmost peak of Mt. Ararat, the highest mountain in that part of the world. They stumbled about, dizzy with the motionless floor beneath their feet. For so long they had walked on a heaving surface that they had forgotten how to walk on steady ground.

Now they had something they could measure the water against. Every spare moment they came to look out; they compared notes with each other; and in each of their hearts a great swell of praise and thanks to God went up, even as they went busily about their chores. They felt as if they had been born a second time, and so, in a very real sense, they had.

A little later the tops of the lower mountains around them appeared. It was nearly nine months now since they had come into the ark. That day Noah opened the window, and let the raven fly free. The raven was a strong bird. He could fly back and forth for hours without rest. When night came, he had not returned. The next day Noah let the gentle dove out. The dove was not strong like the raven. She could not find any place to perch where she could rest. She flew back to the ark, and Noah reached out his arm and took her in. A week later he let her out again. This time she came back at night with a tiny twig of the olive tree in her beak, and the twig had budded into small, grey-green leaves. How they stared at those leaves, handling them gently, as if they were the greatest treasure in all the earth! A week later Noah let the dove out a third time. This time she did not return to the ark.

Then Noah loosened the roof of the ark and took it off. Now the blessed sun shone in on them with light and warmth. The ground as far as they could see was dry. But still they waited. They waited for God to tell them it was time to come out. And God spoke to them, even as He had called them to come in. It was a year and ten days after the beginning of the great rain that they at last stepped out onto dry ground.

What was the first thing Noah did after this? Did he race in excited circles, laughing and shouting for joy? No, his first thought was to thank God. He collected stones and built an altar. And on this altar he offered a sacrifice of thanksgiving to the God who had remembered him in his desperate need.

God made a solemn promise to Noah, and to all his children; and that includes you and me too. "Never again," He said, "will I destroy the whole earth with a flood. As long as the earth continues, seedtime and harvest, and cold and heat, and summer and winter, and day and night shall not cease. And I will give you a sign to reassure you when once again you see the dark storm clouds above your heads. I will set my rainbow in the very clouds that frighten you. When you see the rainbow, you can know for sure that I am remembering my solemn promise.

"Go out now, and have many children, so that the whole empty earth is peopled again. I will put the fear of you into the hearts of all the animals, so that they do not fall upon you and tear you to pieces. All of them are yours to use and to eat. If any one of them kills one of you, that animal will have to answer to me. And if any man kills his fellow man, he shall be killed in his turn. For I made each of you in my own image, and therefore your lives are sacred."

Well, that was long ago. The memory of it has grown dim, so that you and I no longer tremble when we see dark rain clouds over our heads. God has kept His promise so faithfully for so many thousands of years that we can no longer even imagine a flood that would destroy the whole earth. But there are still many dreadful calamities that terrify us, and God's promise applies to all these as well. So when you see the rainbow glimmering in the clouds, take heart! It is a visible sign that God still remembers His solemn promise. This earth is in God's hands. Until the final judgment day, God's appointed judgment day, seedtime and harvest, and cold and heat, and summer and winter, and day and night shall not cease.

9
The Day God Laughed

Genesis 11

There were still people alive who remembered the terrible flood. But they were getting old. The young folk did not pay much attention any more to their endless talk about needing God and trusting in His promises. Who needed God? They were young and strong. Their life was ahead of them. They planned to look out for themselves.

Of course, it is true, there were some things a man could not handle by himself. But if they all got together, and pooled their strength and their ideas, that could be taken care of nicely.

That was how it occurred to them to build a city. Before this they had been farmers. A farmer has to have land to grow things on, and so they had spread out. Now they would stick together and build themselves a strong city. Who knows, if those other people, the ones who lived before the flood, had only had the sense to band together, perhaps they would not have drowned after all!

And then someone suggested a tower. A tower that would be a protection against enemies — and against a flood! A tower that would mark their great skill and daring, that would remind all people who came after them of their glory and their fame. A tower so high that it would reach right up to heaven itself!

They were dazzled by this idea. They worked as long as daylight lasted, day after day, digging clay, making bricks, bringing in heavy loads of tar from the pits to the north. Brick after brick, the tower rose higher and higher. It looked as if they were really right. They could actually reach to heaven itself, so great was their daring and their skill.

And what was God doing all this time? Do you know what I think He was doing? He was laughing at those foolish men who could not have drawn one breath or spoken one word without His help! Those foolish men who thought that they were their own masters, that they were going to get to heaven by their tower! Yes, God sometimes laughs. He laughs when He sees weak, sinful men banding together and setting themselves up to be like God.

God came down from heaven to see what the men were doing. He looked at the city, and He looked at the tower. Was it wrong to build a city? No, it was not wrong. It was not wrong to build a high tower, either. It was trying to get along without God that was wrong. It was banding together to prove to God that they did not need Him that was wrong. It was doing just whatever they liked, no matter what God commanded, no matter who else got hurt, instead of asking God to help them to live according to His commands. That was what was wrong.

After the flood God had made a promise. He had promised that

never again would He destroy all men by a terrible flood. And He had given men another promise too, even longer ago, that He Himself would conquer sin and provide a way by which sinful men could be saved. God was going to keep these promises. And that meant that God had to check the power of sin before it once again became so terrible.

The building site hummed with activity. Some brought in loads of clay from the pits. Others shaped the clay into bricks. The carriers took them up the steps of the tower to the top where the builders were working.

"I am ready for more bricks," the builder said to his carrier. The boy stared at him in astonishment, his mouth hanging open. He could not understand a word the builder said. "Bricks! More bricks!" the builder said impatiently. "I don't understand what you are saying," the carrier answered. Now it was the builder's turn to stare. "Speak up!" he shouted. "Don't talk gibberish!" Neither one could understand what the other said. The boy ran frightened down the steps, and the builder stamped angrily after him. He went up to the supervisor.

"This boy has lost his wits," he said. "I can't understand a word he says." The supervisor stared in amazement at the builder. "Are you trying to make a fool out of me?" he said. "Speak so you can be understood!" The builder turned pale. He couldn't understand the supervisor either.

"Is this some kind of a joke?" he asked. Others heard the angry voices and came running. Some suggested one thing, and some another. But not a single one of them could understand any other one. They seemed to be speaking different languages. They *were* speaking different languages. God had changed their languages. There were as many languages as there were workers. Angry shouts were followed by fist fights. Soon there was no one left working on the tower.

The next morning saw a strange sight. From each of the gates of the city people were streaming. Each man was followed by his own wife and children, carrying as much as they could of their property. Each family group went in a different direction. They looked back on the others with angry and suspicious looks.

They never finished building the city. They never finished building the tower either. For God had scattered them over all the face of the earth. Yes, that is what happened to the people who thought they were smart enough and strong enough to look out for themselves. That is what will happen to everyone who does not trust in God. God has only to laugh, and they will be scattered abroad like dust before the wind.

II
THE HOMESICK PILGRIMS

They desire a better country, that is, a heavenly: wherefore God is not ashamed of them, to be called their God; for he hath prepared for them a city (Hebrews 11:16).

10
The Man Who Had to Leave Home

Genesis 12

*e*very night they pitched their tents, cooked their supper, and lay down on the ground to sleep. Every morning they took the tents down again, packed up the few belongings they had been able to bring along, and went on. Their feet were rough and calloused from the long marches. Their skin was caked with the dust of travel. They had been on the way for years already, and still no end of the journey was in sight.

Once, long ago, Abraham had had a house of his own. It was a low white house made of sun-baked bricks. Its windows opened not on the street but on a private courtyard where fig trees grew, and a a little fountain splashed to cool the air on hot days. Ur was a prosperous town, and Abraham's home was comfortable. His furniture was beautifully carved, his walls were hung with embroidered silk, his dishes and cups were beautifully decorated. Besides all these blessings, this was a home where love was present. His wife, Sarah, was very beautiful, and although she had not given him the son he longed for, still his courtyard rang with childish laughter. For his nephew, Lot, whose father had died while he was still young, was almost like a son to Abraham.

But even with all this, Abraham was not happy. The people of Ur worshiped many gods — moon gods, sky gods, rain gods. Abraham's family worshiped them too. But somehow, in his heart, there echoed a faint memory of another time when men knew only one God, the true God, and when that God had walked and talked with men. Where had this memory come from? Not from his neighbors who remorselessly raised their knives to kill their own children in order to please their false gods. No, the haunting memory in Abraham's heart could only have come from the Holy Spirit Himself. For He alone can teach us what is false and what is true.

God had a special plan for Abraham, a plan that includes even you and me. He was going to reawaken that faint memory that was all that was left in the world of knowledge about the true God. He was going to separate one family from their heathen neighbors. He was going to teach that family the precious truth about Himself. And so the life-saving promises could be handed down from one generation to another, until at last they came even to you and me, who also had ancestors who once worshiped many gods. And then from you and me be handed on still further to other men and women, boys and girls, perhaps not yet born, but still included in God's amazing plan.

One day God spoke to Abraham. "Leave your country, and your relatives," He said. "Start out on the road which I will show you as you go. I am going to bless you, and make a great nation out of your children. All men will receive a blessing through you."

It was not easy for Abraham to leave behind his familiar home and all his relatives. It was even harder to set out when he had no idea where he was going. And if he had not trusted God, the promise that God would make a great nation out of his children would have seemed laughable. Abraham did not have a single child, and he was already seventy years old.

But Abraham did trust God. He left his pleasant home. He took his aged father, Terah, his wife Sarah, and his nephew Lot, and started out, not knowing where he was going. And you and I have to do the same thing. For this is the way God deals with all His children. He shows us the way to go just one step at a time. This is because He wants us to go forward trusting in Him. You are still young. You cannot possibly guess what work God has prepared for you, or where He wants you to serve. But you can know that if you trust your life to His direction, He will lead you.

Abraham and Sarah and Lot and Terah traveled a long, long way. At last they came to Haran, far to the north of Ur. They stayed there for a time. Terah was really too old for such a hard life. He fell sick in Haran, and died. Abraham buried his father. And then sadly, but still trusting in God, he went on, following where God directed him. For he had his eyes fixed on a home more beautiful than the house he had left in Ur, on a city far more dazzling than the one he had left behind him. Abraham wanted to live in those mansions Jesus is preparing for all who trust Him, in that city where the sun does not need to shine because God Himself is there and is the light of all His children. Abraham had had just a little glimpse of the wonderful friendship of God. He was hungry to know more of it.

He traveled south and west now, and came at last to Canaan. He was seventy-five years old. For years he and his family had lived in tents made of black goats' skins. Through strange lands, by roads Abraham had never seen before, among unfriendly people who spoke languages Abraham could not understand, all this way, all these years, God had led him. Canaan was just one more strange country to Abraham. He did not dream it was to become his new home.

One day they came to a grove of oak trees. The shade was pleasant in the hot afternoon. They put up their tents beneath the trees. That night God spoke to Abraham again. "I am going to give this country to your children," He said.

Nothing seemed less likely. Abraham had no child at all, and as year passed disappointing year, the hope that he might still have one grew more and more absurd. Still Abraham believed the promise of God, even though everything seemed to prove it was impossible. The next day he gathered rocks together and built an altar. And here, beneath the oak trees of Shechem, he offered a sacrifice to the faithful God who had led him all these years, just as his great ancestor Noah had done long before. Perhaps some day you can see for yourself that sacred spot where God spoke to Abraham, and Abraham answered, dedicating his whole life to God. But even if you never cross the sea to Palestine, right now and here you can offer to God the sacrifice of a life that trusts in the promises of the God who leads us.

11
"Love Seeketh Not Its Own"

Genesis 13

a boy whose father has died has a lost feeling in his heart. And our God, who is Himself the great Father, feels a tender yearning love for such lost children. We know this because the Bible is filled with special promises to the fatherless. God will be their helper, their protector, their father.

What is more, God especially commends them to *our* love and care. We may be His hands, His voice, to show His love to these unhappy children. If there is a boy or a girl among your friends, or in your class at school, who has lost his father or his mother, then God is offering you the chance to become, as it were, a mirror which reflects His love in the way you treat that boy or girl, the way you speak to him. This is a great responsibility.

When Lot's father died, God gave this chance to Abraham. Abraham took the boy into his own house. And as Abraham's love gradually healed the lost feeling in Lot's heart, so Lot softened the grief in Abraham's heart. Lot had no father; Abraham had no son. They comforted each other.

When God called Abraham to leave his home and his family, Abraham took along not only his aged father, but also his fatherless nephew. God had entrusted both to his care. Both were his responsibility.

Lot grew up on this journey. It was a hard school, but it taught many lessons a boy could never have learned in an easier course of study. The very hardships and loneliness of the journey drew the four travelers close together. When they got as far as Haran, they rested a while. When they went on, there were only three of them left. Abraham's aged father had died in Haran.

Those long years of intimate association were the most important thing that ever happened to Lot. For as they traveled they shared more than hardships and loneliness. Abraham talked to his nephew about the promises of God. You and I do not become Christians just because our uncle, or our father, or our mother is a Christian. We have to pass by the judgment seat of God single file. Each of us must answer for himself. Just the same, it is a great blessing to grow up in a Christian home. Lot, too, learned to trust in the promises of God. He trusted God, but there still lingered in his heart the memory of the luxury of Ur. Life there had been so pleasant, so sociable!

Now Lot was a grown man. He had a wife and children of his own. He was a rich man, too. Abraham had shared with his nephew the great flocks of cattle God had given him. The two of them owned so many sheep and camels and oxen it was hard to find enough pasture to go around. Sooner or later it was bound to happen. Abraham's shepherds and Lot's shepherds quarreled about pasture rights. And quarreling quickly leads to fighting.

This is why the two men, once adopted father and son, now more like two brothers, climbed to the mountaintop that morning. Abraham's steps were slow, and his eyes were sad. His life seemed to be one painful parting after another. Lot climbed easily. He was young, and eager to be off on his own at last.

They reached the top of the mountain, and stood looking at the land spread out beneath them. "We must not fight," Abraham said. "We are brothers. You choose. If you wish to go to the left, I will go to the right. Or if you choose the right hand, I will take the left." Lot did not even notice the sadness in his uncle's voice. He forgot how many kindnesses Abraham had shown him. He forgot that God had promised the land to Abraham, not to Lot. He looked to the east. There, far below them, he saw the silver ribbon of the Jordan River. It was beautiful country, so fertile and well watered that it resembled that garden God Himself had planted long ago in Paradise.

"I choose the Jordan valley," Lot said. And off he went, with scarcely a backward look at his uncle, to move his tents, his cattle, all his servants. Why did he choose the Jordan valley? Partly, I suppose, because it was so rich and beautiful. Cattle grazed on those lands would grow fat and tender. But there was also another reason. In the center of that plain lay the cities of Sodom and Gomorrah. Rich cities, where every comfort and luxury was available, cities that, no doubt, reminded Lot of his own birthplace, Ur. And as so often happens, alas, where there is great wealth, there is also great wickedness.

Lot knew the cities were wicked. But, oh, they were so beautiful! They drew him with an almost irresistible fascination. Every day as he moved from place to place to find fresh grass for his herds of cattle, he set up his tent a little nearer to Sodom. At last he moved his family into Sodom entirely, and left the shepherding to his servants.

Abraham was left alone on the mountaintop. Never had he felt so lonely as at that moment. Yet he was not really alone. For even as he stood there watching the eager departure of his nephew, God spoke to him. "Lift up your eyes," God said, "and look as far as you can see to the north and the south and the east and the west. Everything you

see I am going to give to you and to your children. Can you count the grains of sand on the seashore? If you can, then you will be able to count the number of your children. Do not stand here on the mountaintop looking after Lot. I want you to walk through the whole land, from one end of it to the other. I am going to give all of it to you."

"To you and to your children!" But, alas, Abraham was now a very old man. Soon it would be impossible for him to have any children. Impossible? Impossible, perhaps, for man, but nothing is impossible for God. Abraham believed God could do what was impossible, that He would surely do whatever He promised. He went down the mountain. He moved his tent to Hebron. He built an altar there, and offered a sacrifice of thanksgiving to God.

12
The God Who Sees and Hears

Genesis 16

God appeared many times to Abraham. Over and over He made the same promises. "You will have so many children's children," God said, "that they will be like the stars in the sky. No one will be able to count them. Your children will own this country. All men will be blessed through you."

But Abraham did not own any land at all. He did not have any children either, not a single one. It was now many years since God had first made this promise. Abraham and Sarah were getting to be old people.

Why did God wait so long to do what He had promised? He wanted Abraham's faith to grow strong. He wanted him to learn to trust only in God, not in his own strength. This often happens in our lives too. God promises us something, but it does not happen right away. There may be many reasons why God delays. Usually we do not know these reasons — just as Abraham did not know why God did not do as He had promised. But there is one thing of which we can be absolutely sure. God will keep His promises, every one of them. There is nothing in the whole world so sure as this. Abraham's own life teaches us that this is true.

One day Sarah said to Abraham, "God has not given me any children. Perhaps you ought to take a second wife. Perhaps God will fulfill His promises in this way. See, here is my maid, Hagar. Take her as your second wife."

So Abraham took Hagar as his second wife. Hagar was just an Egyptian slave girl. She had no rights of her own. She could not say what she would do, or where she would go. She could not even say whom she would marry. She had to do as she was commanded. And this was a convenient arrangement for Sarah. For if Hagar had a son, Sarah could adopt this son as her own.

But Hagar did not object to becoming Abraham's second wife. And when she discovered God was going to give her the baby He had not given to Sarah, she was elated. No longer did she speak respectfully to her mistress. No longer was she quick to obey Sarah's commands. Though she did not dare to say so openly, in her heart she despised the aging wife who had not been able to give her husband the son he longed for. Hagar quite forgot that it was God's goodness that she was going to have a baby. There was a look of contempt in her eyes when, slowly, grudgingly, she waited on her mistress.

Sarah was angry. She blamed her husband for what had happened. She said to Abraham, "You have wronged me. I gave you my maid as your second wife, but now that she is expecting a baby, she despises me. May the Lord judge between you and me!"

"She is still your slave girl," Abraham answered. "You can punish her in any way you wish." So Sarah treated Hagar harshly. Hagar had been so happy and so proud. But not any more. Now she was frightened. She felt all alone. No one, she thought, cared whether she lived or died. Not Sarah. Not Abraham either. She ran away. Her own family, her friends, lived far to the south, in Egypt. It was much farther away than Hagar could possibly have escaped. But she was drawn by her memories of home. She wandered through the wild desert which lay between Canaan and Egypt. At last, exhausted, she came to a well. She sat down to rest.

No one cared what happened to Hagar? Yes, there was someone who cared. God cared. He saw her sitting by that well of water. He saw the deep despair in her heart. He sent His angel to her. "Hagar,

Sarah's maid," the angel said to her, "where have you come from, and where are you going?"

"I am running away from my mistress," Hagar answered. The angel said to her, "Go back to your mistress, and obey her commands. You are going to have a son. You must call him Ishmael, which means *God hears,* because the Lord has seen your trouble, and He has heard your cries. Your children's children will be so many that no one can count them all."

Hagar had lived many years in Abraham's house. She had often heard about the God whom Abraham trusted, and about the promises He had made to Abraham. But she had never dreamed that this God cared about what happened to an Egyptian slave girl. She was quite overwhelmed that God should speak to her. She said in her amazement, "Thou art a God who sees!" And then she added to herself, "Have I really seen God, and yet remained alive?"

She turned around and went back to the place where Abraham's tent was pitched. Once again she became an obedient servant in that home. Not long afterwards God sent her the son He had promised. Abraham called the baby Ishmael, as the angel had commanded.

Abraham was eighty-six years old when Ishmael was born. As you can imagine, the little boy was a favorite of all the family. Perhaps they spoiled him a little bit. Even Sarah, though she did not like Hagar much, was fond of Ishmael. And Abraham loved him not only as his only, long-awaited son, but also as the fulfillment of God's promise.

13

Visitors from Another World

Genesis 18

Pamela bounced up and down on the sofa like a jumping jack. She ran to the front window to look out for perhaps the tenth time, and then went back to the dining room to be sure she had set the table just right. At that moment the doorbell rang. Pamela rushed to open it, to be the first to hug Grandma and her two cousins from out East. Mother came from the kitchen, and Daddy from the den. In a minute the living room was full of laughter and happy talk.

Having company is always fun. Sometimes company comes unexpectedly. You open the front door and there stands your best friend. "Mother and Daddy had to go out of town to see a sick friend," she says. "Can I stay for supper?" Your mother smiles. "Of course," she answers. "You know you are always welcome."

But suppose you open your front door, and you see three men you have never seen before standing on your porch. Would you ask them to come in and stay for supper? I wonder. But Abraham did!

It was a hot afternoon. Abraham sat just beside the door of his tent, enjoying the shade of the large oak trees overhead. As he looked off into the distance, he saw three men approaching. He ran to meet the strangers. "Sit down for a while in the shade," he begged them. "I will get some water and wash your feet, which must be dusty and tired from your journey. And I will make something for you to eat." Abraham knew what it was like to travel, how hot and dusty you become, and how your feet hurt when you have walked all day.

The three men came up to the tent door and sat down. Abraham hurried into the tent. "Take some flour," he said to Sarah, "and make some little cakes for our guests. I will kill a calf and roast it, so that they may eat." So Abraham and Sarah prepared food, and the three men ate it. Three men? These were not men. One of them was God Himself. The other two were angels. Yes, I know, God does not have a body. But that afternoon God appeared to Abraham as a man; He ate and talked with him at the tent door.

Why did God do this? Well, why do your grandmother, your cousins, your best friend, come to your house to eat? You know the answer. It is because they love you. They like to talk to you, to share your life, to be near you. Of course, God did not need Abraham in the way your best friend needs you. But He loved Abraham. He wanted to share Abraham's life, to talk to His friend (yes, the Bible says that Abraham was God's friend!). He wanted Abraham to know for sure that God directs and controls everything that happens in our lives.

On this visit God had two special messages. Sarah stood just inside the tent door, behind the visitors, listening and watching. "Where is Sarah?" God asked. "She is in the tent," Abraham answered. "Next year, at about this time," God said, "I will certainly return to you, and Sarah shall have a son." When she heard this, Sarah laughed in her heart. "How could I have a baby?" she said to herself. "Why, I am eighty-nine years old, and Abraham is ninety-nine!"

"Why did Sarah laugh?" God asked. "Is anything too hard for God?" Suddenly Sarah realized that this was no ordinary visitor. She was afraid. "I did not laugh!" she said out loud. "O yes, you did laugh," God said. For God knows even our most secret thoughts.

The three visitors stood up to leave. Abraham walked with them a little distance, to bring them on their way. The two angels went on ahead. Then God said, "I will not hide from you, Abraham, what I am about to do. You must tell it to your children's children, so that they, too, may take warning. The sin of the cities of Sodom and Gomorrah has become so great that it is like a great cry ascending to My throne." Abraham's heart sank. He knew all too well that Sodom was full of dreadfully wicked people. Perhaps he remembered the Flood, and what had happened to the wicked then.

"Will You destroy the good people together with the wicked?" Abraham asked God. "There may be as many as fifty good men in Sodom."

"If I find as many as fifty," God answered, "I will spare the whole city for their sake." Abraham spoke again. "Suppose there are forty-five?" And God answered, "If I find forty-five I will not destroy the city."

Then Abraham said, "What if there are only forty?" And God replied, "I will not do it for the sake of the forty." Abraham spoke again: "Do not be angry with me! Suppose there are thirty?" And God said, "I will not do it, if I find thirty." Again Abraham dared to speak. "Perhaps there will be twenty." God answered, "I will not do it for the twenty's sake."

Then Abraham spoke one last time. "Maybe you will find ten." And God said, "I will not destroy Sodom if I find ten good men there." How patiently our God listens to His children's prayers! Then God went on His way, and Abraham went back to his tent, hoping against hope that there were ten good men in Sodom.

Perhaps you wish that you had lived when Abraham did, that God would appear to you as a man you could see, would knock at your door, sit at your table, share your food. I should like to tell you something about this. God *has* appeared to you as a man. That is just exactly what we mean when we say that Jesus is the very Son of God, come into this world to die for our sins. Yes, and come into this world to show us what God is like, how much He loves us, how near He is to everything we do, how surely He controls and directs everything that happens to us. He will in very truth share your meals, and everything else you do. For He Himself tells us that He stands at the door of our heart, knocking; and that if we open the door, He will come in and eat supper with us.

14
The Rain of Fire

Genesis 19

If you stand on this mountaintop, you can see the whole valley, and the lake as well. The Lake of Death is what they call it, or, sometimes, the Dead Sea. It is easy to see why. Other lakes have blue water, transparent, reflecting the sky, washing in waves onto the beach. This water lies oily and sullen, motionless, the color of lead. There is the smell of death in the air too, and even the sound of death. No fish break the surface of the water to feed. No birds fly overhead. No little animals slip through the grass or climb the trees. Indeed, there is no grass, no trees, only a tangle of brush where one or two small streams enter the lake. The shore rises from the water in sheer, rocky cliffs; and where there are narrow beaches, they are littered with chunks of asphalt and sulphur, and pillars of salt.

You shiver as you look, in spite of the sweltering heat. Somewhere near where you stand, you remember, Abraham and Lot looked over this same valley, and the scene *they* saw was so beautiful that it reminded them of the garden God Himself had planted long ago in Paradise. Today four cities lie buried beneath those leaden waters. In all those cities not ten men could be found who loved and trusted God. Not ten, not even five, but only one. And that one was Lot, Abraham's nephew.

Missionaries sometimes live in the middle of heathen cities, but Lot had not gone to Sodom as a missionary. He had been drawn there by the city's wealth, its luxury, its excitement. He was tired of living as a lonely wanderer in a tent.

It is not wrong to be rich, to love excitement; even luxury is not necessarily wrong. But Sodom was much more than a wealthy city. It was also a wicked city, one of the most wicked in the whole world. The rich lived their lives of luxury, and they treated the poor with heartless cruelty. One and all, rich and poor, the men of Sodom were conceited, proud, lawless, violent. The streets of Sodom were filled with crime. Lot knew all this. And in his heart Lot loved and trusted God. But he wanted to share the pleasures of Sodom too. And so he left his cattle to his shepherds, and he moved his family into a house in Sodom.

Lot did not find living in Sodom as pleasant as he had expected. The wickedness he saw all around him bothered his conscience. He was troubled by the way his neighbors lived. Sometimes he spoke to his neighbors about all this. Reluctantly, without ever having wanted this to happen, he became a missionary after all. He spoke to the people of Sodom not because he wanted to, but because the Holy Spirit would give him no peace until he did. You may even have experienced something like this in your own life. There is something you ought to do, and you know it; or something you have done wrong you cannot bring yourself to admit. You choke the thought down. You refuse to admit it. Until at last the Holy Spirit so troubles your conscience that you yield to His insisting, you stop running away from God, you do what is right, and at last you find peace again.

And so God made a missionary out of Lot without Lot ever having planned it this way. And the words Lot spoke to his neighbors were the very voice of God. Not only that — they were the last word from God they would ever hear. God calls, and calls, and calls men to repent. But not forever. There is a day when even God's patience comes to an end. For every man there is a last call, a day of final reckoning; and you can never be sure when that day has come, when the day of mercy is past, and the day of judgment has arrived.

The men of Sodom did not bother themselves with gloomy thoughts like these. They were too busy having a good time. They laughed at Lot's solemn warnings. "Be quiet, you!" they said rudely. "Remember, you are only a guest in our city. You have no call to criticize."

That was how things were when the angels left God and Abraham on the mountaintop, and came to Lot's house in Sodom. "God is going to destroy this wicked city," they told Lot. "Take your wife and your daughters, and leave. Otherwise you will all be killed." Lot could hardly bear to leave his comfortable home, and all the excitement of living in Sodom. His wife was even more reluctant to go. And so, because God had mercy on Lot, the two angels took him and his wife and his two daughters by the hand, and hurried them out of the city. "Run for your life!" they told him. "Do not stop till you come to the mountains. And whatever you do, do not look behind you."

And then God rained fire down from heaven on the wicked city, and its three sister cities, all equally wicked, until all the buildings, all the luxurious homes, all the gold and silver and precious jewels, all the people (every one of whom had refused over and over God's offer of mercy) — everything was burned to the ground. And the lake rushed in and covered the ruins, and no man has ever seen those cities since.

Lot and his two daughters ran for their lives. Behind them came Lot's wife. She did not run as fast as the others because her heart was back there in Sodom. She looked back with longing eyes to all the pleasant things she had left behind. And as she did so, the fire raining down from heaven fell on her, and she was turned into a pillar of salt.

That was how God saved Lot. I do not mean saved him from the burning city, though that was the mercy of God too. But that was how God saved Lot from those worldly possessions that were entangling his soul. Lot loved the things he owned, and the pleasure they brought him. He loved them too much. So God removed these things from Lot's life before they could choke to death Lot's love for God and his trust in Him.

15
Our Guide and Our Protector

Genesis 21

For fourteen years Ishmael had been the only child in the family. He did not miss brothers and sisters because he had never known what it was like to have them. He rather enjoyed being the center of his parents' attention. Of course, his mother, Hagar, was only an Egyptian slave girl. But his father was Abraham himself. And even Sarah, Abraham's first wife, thought of Ishmael as her own adopted son. It was Sarah who had suggested Abraham take a second wife in the first place.

Abraham and Sarah had waited eleven years for God to send them the son He had promised. They tried to go on believing, they wanted to go on believing, but every year that passed made the promise seem more impossible. "Perhaps," Sarah had said to Abraham, "God expects you to take a second wife. After all, the promise was to you, not to me. You should marry my slave girl, Hagar. If she has a son, I can always adopt him. You better do it soon, before it is too late."

And so Abraham and Sarah hurried to make God's promise come true. Abraham married Hagar, and soon there was a baby boy in their tent. Sarah loved Ishmael almost as much as his own mother did, and both Abraham and Sarah expected that God would fulfill all His wonderful promises in Ishmael. For as year passed year, and Abraham and Sarah became older and older, any other plan seemed more and more ridiculous.

Ishmael grew up happy and secure in the love of his father and his two mothers. But God's ways are not our ways, and God's thoughts are different from our thoughts. It really is not possible to hurry God. He has His own reasons and purposes and times. God had a plan for Ishmael's life, but Ishmael was not the child of the promise.

Ishmael was thirteen years old when God appeared at the door of Abraham's tent and said, "Next year, at this time, you and Sarah will have a baby son." Even Abraham found this hard to accept. He loved Ishmael very much. "Oh, that Ishmael might live before You!" he said to God. And God promised, "I will bless Ishmael too. He will be the father of twelve princes, and of a great nation. But the son born to you and Sarah will be the one to inherit My special promises."

It is always exciting when a new baby is born in the family. But can you imagine the excitement when Sarah at last had a baby? Abraham had waited till he was a hundred years old for this, and Sarah had waited till she was ninety to hold this tiny son in her arms. She was so overcome with joy that she said, "God has filled my heart with laughter. Everyone who hears about this will laugh for joy with me." And so they called the baby Isaac, which means *laughter*.

When a new baby is born, the older children have to share Mother and Father with the new baby. Especially at first they may feel left out. Everyone comes to see the new baby; they all bring him presents. Mother is so busy that she has little time for the older children. But let me tell you a secret — if you have not already found it out for yourself. This does not last long. Very soon the new baby can walk and talk and feed himself. And there is plenty of room in Mother's heart for two children, or, for that matter, for a dozen. In Father's heart, too. And I am sure you know that God's heart is never so full that He forgets a single one of His children.

When Isaac was about two years old, Abraham made a great feast of thanksgiving. Many guests came to wonder at the miracle child, born long after it was possible for his parents to have a baby. Sarah was busy entertaining them. But as she came around the corner of the tent, what should she see but Ishmael and Isaac. They were not playing together. Instead, Ishmael was teasing, mocking, tormenting his little brother. All the bitterness and jealousy and disappointment in his heart was spilling out on Isaac.

Sarah was very angry. "Send Ishmael and Hagar away," she said to Abraham. "The son of the slave girl shall not share the inheritance with my son!" How could Abraham do this? It tore his heart apart to send his oldest son away. But God comforted him. "Do not feel badly," God said. "Do as Sarah said. Isaac is the heir to the promises. But I will bless Ishmael too, because he is your son." Abraham got up early the next morning. Sadly he took some bread and a jug of water, and gave them to Hagar. He sent Ishmael and Hagar away. (Do not grieve, Abraham, because you cannot watch over your son. God will guide his steps and watch him for you!)

Hagar and Ishmael wandered aimlessly in the desert. The sun was hot. Soon the water in the jug was gone. Ishmael was so exhausted by the heat that he could not go any farther. He lay down under one of the little scrub bushes. Hagar went a little way off, and sat down to weep tears of bitterness and despair. She would not leave her son, but she could not bear to watch him die. Neither one of them remembered the God who directs our lives. And Hagar — how could she have forgotten that once before she had wandered in this desert in deep despair, and that God had seen and heard her anguish, and had answered her in her trouble?

Neither of them remembered God, but God remembered them. He heard the moans of the exhausted Ishmael. His angel called to Hagar out of heaven: "What is the matter with you, Hagar? God hears Ishmael's voice. Get up! Take Ishmael by the hand, and raise him up, too. God is going to make a great nation out of your son." And God opened Hagar's eyes, and she saw a well of water right near where she had sat down. She hurried to fill her bottle. She gave Ishmael a drink.

God was with Ishmael, just as He had promised. Ishmael grew up in the wilderness. He became an expert shot with bow and arrow. Later his mother found him a wife from Egypt, which was where she had grown up herself. From Ishmael are descended the great nations of the Arabs who still, to this day, wander, fierce and fearless, through the very desert where Hagar heard the voice of God.

16
Stronger Than Death

Genesis 22

Is anything too hard for God?" Once Abraham and Sarah would have hesitated before answering this question. Once Sarah laughed when God said an eighty-nine-year-old woman was going to have a baby. But not any more. Now Sarah and Abraham laughed for very joy, because they had seen with their own eyes that nothing is too hard for God to do. And the baby Isaac, he whose name meant *laughter,* he, too, laughed back at the happy faces of his parents.

Yes, you might call Isaac a miracle baby. He was a sign that God would surely fulfill all His promises, no matter how impossible this might seem. And this tiny, laughing baby, who curled his rosy fingers around his father's gnarled knuckles, was a sign in another sense too. For of all the wonderful promises God made to Abraham, Isaac was the only one which came true in Abraham's lifetime. "Some day your children will own this country," God had said. But Abraham did not own a single acre, not one field, not even a small lot in town where he could build a house for his family. He still lived in a tent, a home-less wanderer from place to place. "Your children's children will out-number the stars in the sky, the grains of sand on the beach," God promised. The promise had been made years, decades ago, but Isaac was still the only child in Abraham's tent. "All men will be blessed through you." This was the most mysterious of all the promises. How? When? Where? Abraham did not know. But Isaac was the living, breathing sign that God could be trusted. Somehow in Isaac all God's promises would come true.

Abraham had waited a hundred years to hold this child in his arms. He had waited twenty-five years for God to fulfill His promise. But from these long years of waiting he had learned something about the power and the faithfulness of God he could never have learned in any other way. He was quite content now to see the other promises only as a distant hope. He did not need to hold the reality, the fulfillment, in his hands, where he could touch, and examine, and test it. Never again would God have to remind him, "Nothing is impossible for God!"

And the laughing Isaac is a sign to you and me as well. A reminder that God's promises are forever sure. That even though we may not see the fulfillment today, or tomorrow, or even next year, yet we can trust our God. Never again will we doubt His power. Never again? Not we? Not Abraham either?

And then God tested Abraham, to see whether he had really learned the hard lesson of trust — trust in God's power, trust in God's faith-fulness. "Abraham!" God said. Abraham answered obediently, "Here I am." Then God commanded, "Take your son, your only son, whom you love, even Isaac, and go to the land of Moriah, and sacrifice him to Me on a mountain I will show you."

Abraham was stunned. The heathen idols he had left behind him in Ur demanded the sacrifice of little children on their altars. But never had Abraham's God made such a request. This wonderful, laughing boy, for whom he had waited twenty-five years, whom he so treasured in his heart, the person he loved most in all the world, next to God Himself — how could he raise his own hand to kill him?

But it was even worse than this. For all God's promises were bound up in this boy. God Himself had said so. If Isaac died, how could God's promises ever come true? It would be impossible! Impossible? Even as the word framed itself in Abraham's mind, he remembered God's own words: "Is anything too hard for God?" Had not God given this very child to a man and woman already almost dead, they were so old? Is anything, anything at all, too hard for God? Is not Isaac himself the living sign that nothing is?

The next morning Abraham got up early. He cut wood for the sacrifice. He called two of his servants. And so Abraham and Isaac and the servants set out for the land of Moriah. He did not tell anyone where he was going, or what he was going to do. They traveled three days. At last they saw in the distance the mountain God had spoken of. Abraham said to his servants, "You wait here. The boy and I will go up the mountain and worship God, and then come back to you again."

Isaac carried the wood. Abraham carried the burning coals to light the sacrifice, and the knife to kill his son. Together they climbed the mountain. Isaac said to Abraham, "My father!" Abraham answered, "Here I am, my son." Isaac said, "I see the fire, and the wood, but where is the lamb for the sacrifice?" Abraham said, " will provide the lamb Himself." His old hands trembled, b was firm. Was Isaac to be the lamb? That was what G ed. Abraham did not know. He could not understa lindly to his faith. "God *will* provide."

At last they reached the top of the mountain. Abraha ilt an altar. He arranged the wood on the stones. He took a rope a bound his only, beloved son. He placed him on the altar. He raised his knife to kill his son. "Nothing," he said over and over to his breaking heart, "nothing is impossible for God."

At that very instant the angel of God called to Abraham out of heaven, "Abraham! Abraham!" And Abraham said, "Here I am." "Do not harm the boy," the angel said. "For now I know that you really trust God, since you have not kept back your only son from Him." Then Abraham saw behind him a ram, its horns tangled in the thicket.

He caught the ram, and offered him as a sacrifice to God, in the place of his son.

Yes, that day God tested Abraham, and Abraham met the test. Hoping against hope, he believed that nothing is too hard for God to do. Not even to bring Isaac back from the dead. And in one sense we might even say that Abraham did receive his son back from death itself. Abraham was certain that what God had promised, He was also able to perform.

Are you glad that you were not Abraham that day on Mt. Moriah? Glad that God does not put your faith to such a terrible test? Stop a minute, and think! Isn't this exactly what God asks you to believe too? *Nothing is impossible for God. God is stronger even than death.* "I am the resurrection and the life," Jesus says to us. "He that believeth on me, though he die, yet shall he live; and whosoever liveth and believeth on me, shall never die." The story of Abraham sacrificing Isaac, and the story of our blessed Saviour rising from the grave — these stories were written down so that you and I might know that our God *is* stronger than death, and that, believing, we also might share in that life which never ends.

17
God Plans a Wedding

Genesis 24

*E*very large ranch needs a foreman, someone to supervise the care of the cattle, and to assign the hands to whatever most needs doing. This was true of Abraham's household too, for Abraham owned thousands of animals, and had hundreds of servants to look after them. His foreman was Eliezer. Eliezer had worked for Abraham for so many years, and had proved himself so trustworthy, that Abraham left all his affairs in his charge.

Years ago Abraham had even intended to leave all his property to Eliezer. This was before either Ishmael or Isaac was born. If he could not have a son of his own, there was no one to whom Abraham would rather give his cattle, his silver and gold, than to this faithful servant who had been with him so long that he seemed more like a friend than like a hired hand.

And so it was quite natural that Abraham turned to Eliezer when the important matter of Isaac's marriage had to be settled. Isaac was thirty-seven years old when his mother, Sarah, died. He was still not married. He had loved his mother very much, and her death left him feeling sad and lonely. Abraham himself was now a hundred and forty years old. He did not expect to live much longer. He realized that he must do something about finding a wife for his son. The people who lived nearby were all heathen people. They worshiped idols. It was important that Isaac should not marry one of them. Isaac must marry someone who loved and trusted God. The most important thing about anybody's marriage is that it should be in the Lord.

Abraham called Eliezer. "I want you to go to Haran," he said, "where my family are living. You must bring back a wife for Isaac." Eliezer was doubtful about how this would work. "Perhaps," he said, "this woman will not be willing to leave her home, to come to a strange country and marry a strange man. What must I do then? Must I take Isaac back to Haran?"

"No, no!" Abraham said. "Isaac must on no account go back to Haran! God called me away from Haran to this land. The God of heaven, who promised to give this country to my children, He will send His angel to guide you on this journey."

So Eliezer set out. He took ten camels and loaded them with rich gifts for the new bride. Abraham had become a wealthy man, and it was only proper that he should send rich gifts to his son's bride. Eliezer was a man who trusted God. He knew that God directs all our lives. He was sure God had already chosen a wife for Isaac. But how was he to discover this woman? He did not know. But he did know where to go for help. He prayed.

"O Jehovah," he prayed, "the God of my master Abraham, today, I pray Thee, show kindness to my master Abraham. Here I stand by the fountain of water, and soon the women from Haran will be coming to get water. Let it be that the girl to whom I say, 'Give me a drink,' and she answers, 'Drink, and I will draw water for your camels also,' let this girl be the one Thou hast chosen for Isaac."

Does God answer such prayers? Yes, He hears and answers. "Before they call, I will answer," He promises. "And while they are yet speaking, I will hear." While Eliezer was still praying, before he had even finished, a beautiful young girl came to the fountain. She filled her pitcher with water. The servant said to her, "Give me a drink." And she answered, "Drink, and I will draw water for your camels also." Eliezer stared at her in amazement, hardly able to believe God had answered his prayer so soon. Then he took a golden ring from his baggage, and two golden bracelets, and gave them to the girl.

"What is your name?" he asked her. "Is there room for me to stay at your father's house?" The girl answered, "My name is Rebekah. I am the granddaughter of Nahor. We have plenty of room at our house, and food for you and your camels." When Eliezer heard this, he bowed his head, and said, "Blessed be the God of my master Abraham, who has not forgotten His lovingkindness, but has led me to the house of my master's brother, Nahor!" For Rebekah and Isaac were actually cousins.

Rebekah ran home to show the bracelets and the ring to her mother. When Eliezer and the camels arrived at her home, Rebekah's family welcomed them, and offered Eliezer something to eat. But he would not eat until he had told them why he had come. He explained about Abraham, and about Isaac, the son of the promise, who had been born when his parents were already old people. He told them how he had prayed at the well, and how Rebekah had come in answer to his prayer. "Will you let her go with me, to be Isaac's wife?" he asked them. Rebekah's father and brother spoke for her. "Plainly God has planned all this," they said. "We cannot go against His leading." Then the servant took out the presents he had brought with him, presents of gold and silver jewelry and beautiful clothing for Rebekah, and presents for her family too. At last he and his men had something to eat, and they spent the night with Rebekah's family.

The next morning Eliezer was eager to start back again. Rebekah's family would have liked to delay the parting, but at last they asked Rebekah, "Are you ready to go with this man?" Rebekah knew that God was leading her. She said, "I will go." So she and her handmaids climbed on the camels and rode back to Canaan.

I told you that Isaac was lonely. He was walking alone in the fields when he saw the camels coming. Rebekah got off the camel. She pulled her veil over her face. Isaac took her to his mother Sarah's tent. He loved her very much. He was comforted after his mother's death. He was not lonely any more.

This is the story of a happy marriage. Everyone who had anything to do with this marriage asked God for guidance and followed God's leading — Abraham and Eliezer, Rebekah and Isaac, and Rebekah's father and her mother and her brother. I do not suppose that you are thinking of getting married yet. But God is not interested just in your future husband or wife. He is just as much concerned about your friends. If you are lonely, as Isaac was, you can talk to Him about your loneliness. For He has planned all your life, your friends too, just as surely as He had chosen Isaac's wife long before Isaac himself had ever thought about her. You do not need big words or fancy sentences to talk to God. Just close your eyes. Tell Him what troubles you. Ask Him to direct your life. And then, if you walk in the path He shows you, you can be sure you, too, will find friends, and happiness, and a full and even exciting life.

18
The Plot That Failed

Genesis 27

Sometimes even their mother has trouble telling twin brothers, or twin sisters, apart. They look alike. They dress alike. They act alike. It even seems as if they think alike.

Nobody had this trouble with Jacob and Esau. They were twins all right, but two boys could hardly have been more different. Esau was red-skinned and hairy. Jacob's skin was smooth and fair. Esau was the outdoor type. He loved to wander through the fields and woods, bow and arrow in his hand. He became an expert hunter. Jacob was an indoor, homekeeping boy. He liked to stay with his mother in the tent, his head filled with clever schemes.

The twins did not get along well together, either. They quarreled and fought. There was bitter jealousy and rivalry between them. Esau was the older, and would, in the natural course, have inherited both a double share of his father's property, and also the promises of God. Jacob envied him this. And yet, before the twins were born, God had said that the older should serve the younger. Esau resented this. What was worse, their parents, Isaac and Rebekah, joined in. They played favorites. Isaac loved Esau better, because of the delicious venison he brought home from his hunting. Rebekah preferred Jacob. Isaac and Rebekah had waited and longed and prayed for twenty years before God gave them these twin sons. This should have been a happy home. Instead, it was filled with jealousy and lies.

Can God work through such people as these? Yes, He can. He does. What is more, every one of us started out just like these people. God chose us, as He chose them, when we were in open rebellion against Him. But God does not allow wickedness to continue in His children. Each person in this family had to learn this, and the lesson was hard and painful.

Isaac lived to be a very old man. His eyesight became so poor that he could not see any more. He felt that he did not have much longer to live. He wanted to hand on the blessings given him by his father Abraham to his favorite son, Esau. He knew that God had said the older boy was to serve the younger. But he planned to get around this by blessing Esau before God found out what was happening. He was going to outwit God! He had to outwit Rebekah too, for she loved Jacob the most. So he called Esau secretly. "I am growing old," he said. "I do not know how much longer I will live. Take your bow and arrows and kill a deer for me. I long to taste once more that delicious venison stew you make. And after I have eaten it, I will give you the blessing." Quickly Esau picked up his bow and arrows. In his heart he gloated, "Now I will get the blessing after all!"

What Isaac did not know was that Rebekah was hiding just inside the tent door, spying on her husband. She strained her ears to hear: "I will give you the blessing." This was just what she had expected, but still it made her angry. This was nothing but a trick on Isaac's part to get around God's promise. But Rebekah was more clever than her husband. She, too, had a scheme. *Just you wait and see, my husband, which one of us is smarter when it comes to tricks!* O Rebekah, Rebekah, can you not wait a little while for God Himself to fulfill His promise? Have you forgotten so soon that these very sons of yours were God's answer to your prayers? And Isaac! You were once laid bound hand and foot on the altar as a sacrifice to God, and God Himself, speaking out of heaven, gave you back your life! Would you now try to get around God's plan by a trick?

As soon as Esau was gone, his mother went looking for Jacob. She called him softly, "Where are you?" "Here I am, Mother," he said, as he came running. "Hurry!" Rebekah said, "and bring me two young animals from the goat herd. I am going to make stew for your father just the way he likes it. He has sent Esau to kill a deer, and then he is going to give him the blessing. But you and I will get there first!" Jacob did not mind tricking his blind father. He was only afraid of being caught. "My brother Esau is hairy, and my skin is smooth," he said. "My father cannot see the difference, but he will feel it. I will end up with a curse instead of a blessing!"

"If that happens," Rebekah answered, "I will take the curse on myself. Only hurry! We do not have much time." So Jacob brought his mother two young goats, and she made a stew for Isaac, just the way he liked it. She gave Jacob Esau's best clothes, which, like every-thing Esau owned, smelled of the fields and the woods. She fastened the hairy skin of the young goats on Jacob's hands and on his neck. So Jacob came to his father.

"My father!" he said. "Here I am," Isaac answered. "Who are you?" Jacob said, "I am Esau, your oldest son. See, I have brought the meat you asked for. Come and eat it, and then bless me." Isaac was suspicious. "How did you find it so quickly?" he asked. And Jacob lied, "God helped me to find it!" "Come here and let me feel you," the blind Isaac insisted. So Jacob came near, and Isaac felt his hands and neck. "The voice is Jacob's," Isaac said, "but the hands are Esau's." So Isaac ate the stew Jacob had brought, and then he blessed him. "God give you plenty of food," he said, "even the fatness of the earth. Let nations serve you, and your brothers bow down before you. Everyone that blesses you shall be blessed."

Jacob did not linger. He was in a hurry to leave. And he did not get away a minute too soon. For he had just left the tent when Esau arrived with the venison stew he had made. "Come and eat the venison I have prepared for you," he said to his father, "and then give me the blessing." Isaac asked, "Who are you?" Esau was surprised his father should ask. "I am Esau, your oldest son!" he said.

Then Isaac shook and trembled with fear. For in a flash he saw that this was the doing of God Himself. No man can trick God. No man can prevent the fulfillment of God's promises. Esau might be Isaac's favorite son, but it was for God, not Isaac, to choose who should inherit the promises. "Your brother came and stole away your blessing with trickery," he said sadly to Esau. "But it is God who has chosen him, and God will surely bless him."

"Do you not have a blessing left for me also?" Esau cried out bitterly. "I have made you your brother's servant," Isaac said, "but you shall not serve him forever. In the end you shall break free."

What did Esau say to this? Did he say, "God has the right to decide. Let Him put me wherever He thinks best"? No, he did not. He forgot that no man can be happy unless he is in God's way. He was very angry. He thought, "I will get even with my brother! My father cannot live much longer. As soon as he is dead, I will kill Jacob!"

And Jacob and Rebekah, those two who could not wait for God to fulfill His own promises, what happened to them? Their trick did not bring them joy either. It brought them sorrow instead. But that is another story.

19
The Gate of Heaven

Genesis 28

Jacob had been walking for three days already, and yet he had covered only a little bit of the way. He was all alone with no servant to talk to, not even a camel or a donkey to share his journey. He was used to being alone with his sheep in the field — after all, he was a shepherd, or at least he had been — but he had never felt so alone as now. For this was a permanent loneliness. He could not go back home again. His brother Esau was waiting to kill him.

Has it ever happened to you that, in a careless moment, you did something you later wanted to undo, but you could not? You said something mean, and wished you could bite the words back? You told a lie, and found no way to untell it? You did something wrong, and regretted it bitterly? That is just where Jacob found himself now.

Behind him lay all the pleasant scenes of home, all the happy memories of his carefree youth. Behind him lay his mother whom he loved so dearly. Behind him — this was the bitterest thought of all — was his father whom he had treated so badly. Isaac was feeble and blind, and not expected to live long. It was not likely Jacob would ever see him again. Not likely he would ever get a chance to throw himself at his father's feet and cry, "Forgive me!"

Ahead of him — he did not know what there was ahead of him. It was a strange country he was going to, and strange people whom he had never seen, though they were kinsfolk of his mother's. He had no gifts with which to win their friendship, no cattle with which to start a herd of his own. And the way was long, and weary, and dangerous for a man traveling all alone.

The sun set as he climbed the steep, rocky path to the top of another of the seemingly endless hills. There was no town here, no inn where he could spend the night, not even a lonely shepherd's tent. He ate a little of the bread he carried in his bag, and then lay down on the rough ground and rested his head on a stone for a pillow. At last he fell asleep, lying there alone on the mountain, worn out as much by his bitter thoughts as by his journey.

Yet he was not alone. God's children are never alone, no matter where they find themselves. God does not forsake those who trust in Him, even though they sin against Him. God is willing to forgive, and He does not limit His love to those who deserve it. If He did, not one of us would ever see the heavenly home.

Jacob dreamed a dream as he slept there on the rocky ground. He saw a staircase before him, running from the earth all the way up to heaven itself, and up and down that staircase walked the beautiful angels of God. What were the angels doing there in that lonely spot? They were caring for God's child, even for Jacob himself. They were carrying up to God messages about the troubles and the needs of Jacob, and bringing back down to Jacob the forgiving love, the ever-watchful care of God Himself.

At the top of the staircase stood God, the God who had appeared so often to his grandfather Abraham, and to his father Isaac, but who

Jacob had never dared to hope would speak to him too. But now God was speaking even to Jacob. "I am the God of Abraham and Isaac," God said. "I am going to give to you and your children this very place where you are sleeping. You will have as many children as the dust of the earth, and all the people of the world will be blessed in your descendants. I will take care of you wherever you go, and I will bring you back safely to your home again; for I will not leave you until I have done all these things which I have promised."

Then Jacob woke up, and everything around him seemed different from the way it had looked when he lay down to sleep. This was not a lonely, desolate mountaintop. "Surely," he exclaimed, "God is in this place, and I did not realize it! This place is nothing else than the house of God. This is the very gate of heaven." He lifted up the stone he had used for a pillow and set it up on end as a monument to mark the place where God had spoken to him, and he poured out oil from his bottle as an offering to God. He called the place Bethel, which means *the house of God*. And there Jacob made a solemn promise to God.

"If God will be with me," he said, "and take care of me, and give me food to eat and clothing to wear, and bring me back at last to my father's house in peace, then God shall be my God, and this stone that I have set up shall be His house, and I will give back to God in thanks one-tenth of everything He gives me."

You and I have never dreamed a dream like this one. But God has written this story down in His Word so that you and I, too, can learn what Jacob learned that night. God is speaking to you even now as you read this story, just as He spoke to Jacob long ago. It does not matter what you have done that is wrong. The death of Jesus is enough to pay for all your sins. If you trust in Jesus, God will never leave you. He will go with you wherever you go. Though you cannot see them with your eyes, God's angels are watching you, are caring for you even now. He is calling you to turn away from your sins, to put all your trust in Him, and to seek His help to live a new life, a life that is pleasing to the God who has done so much for you.

20
Bitter Lessons

Genesis 29, 30

One day, when I was even younger than you are, I discovered that the door to the cupboard where the Christmas presents were hidden had been left unlocked. Though I knew that this was wrong, I opened that door. And there on the shelf I saw a toy piano — the very thing I had been hoping and begging for, for weeks, but had not really expected to get. My triumph did not last long. For my mother discovered what I had done. On Christmas day she gave that piano not to me but to my next older brother. It was a bitter lesson.

This is not the way it happened when Jacob tried to snatch beforehand the gift of the promise. God did not change His mind and give the gift instead to Jacob's brother. God never changes His mind. Indeed, God knew before He chose Jacob that Jacob did not deserve this gift. If you and I had to wait for God's blessings until we deserved them, we would go unblessed to our graves. No, God did not change His mind. He changed Jacob instead. And that, too, was a bitter lesson. It was a whole series of bitter lessons.

The first lesson came almost at once after that shameful moment when Jacob kneeled before his blind father and lied, "I am Esau, your oldest son. It was God who helped me shoot a deer so quickly!" When Esau found out what had happened, he said, "I will kill him!" And so now Jacob was running for his life. Yes, Jacob, the one of the twins who always liked to stay at home, was now hurrying, footsore and frightened, along the road to the north. Can you guess what must have gone through Jacob's mind on this lonely, dangerous journey? The Holy Spirit was working in his sinful heart, and there is no better time for the Holy Spirit to awaken us to our sin than when we are alone and in danger. Surely the Holy Spirit whispered to Jacob's heart, "You did wrong! You should have trusted God, and waited for His time." But Jacob did not listen. Even after God had spoken wonderful, undeserved promises to him in his dream, still he did not admit his sin. He thrust the thought of sin far behind him. The lesson was bitter, but Jacob had not learned it yet.

At last he came to Haran, where Laban, his mother's brother, lived. Like Eliezer before him, he stopped at the well outside the city. But unlike Eliezer, he never thought of asking God to help and guide him. His head was still full of schemes. He was planning his own life, and did not feel he needed God. The shepherds came to the well to water their flocks. "Do you know a man called Laban?" Jacob asked them. "O yes, we know him well," the shepherds answered. "Look, there comes his daughter Rachel to water her father's sheep." Rachel, like her aunt Rebekah, was very beautiful. Jacob looked at her, and he fell head over heels in love with her at first sight. He did not ask, as Eliezer had, "Is this the woman God has chosen to be my wife?" No, by hook or by crook, he was going to marry Rachel.

Jacob had no dowry to give for Rachel, as was the custom in that land. He had none of the rich gifts of fine jewelry and costly clothing Abraham had sent to Rebekah. After Jacob had been at his uncle's house a month, Laban said to him, "Just because you are my nephew, you must not work for me for nothing. What shall I pay you for your work?" And Jacob, the schemer, answered, "I will work for you seven years for your daughter Rachel." Laban was a greedy man, and this arrangement pleased him. "It is better for me to give her to you as your wife than to give her to a stranger," he said. "Stay here and work for me."

So Jacob worked seven years, caring for his uncle's sheep. He loved Rachel so much that the seven years seemed to him no longer than a few days. At the end of the seven years he said to his uncle, "Give me my wife." Laban made a great wedding feast, and when night came he brought Jacob's bride, heavily veiled, as the custom was then, to the darkened tent. The next morning, when it grew light, Jacob discovered that he had married not Rachel, but her older sister Leah. Yes, that was the second bitter lesson. That day Jacob discovered what it is like to be tricked by someone else.

Jacob went angrily to Laban. "You have tricked me," he said. (You should be ashamed even to speak that word *tricked,* Jacob. Remember what you did to your father?) Laban had an answer. "It is not our custom to marry the younger sister before the older. You shall have Rachel also, if you will work for me another seven years for her."

So Jacob served another seven years, and now he had two wives. But the marriage he had been so sure would make him happy turned into another bitter lesson. For his two wives did not get along together.

His house was filled with envy, quarreling, bitterness, anger. God saw that Jacob loved Rachel, and hated Leah. He sent four sons to Leah, one after the other, to comfort her. He did not give any children to Rachel. Rachel complained to Jacob, "Give me children, or I will die of jealousy!" Jacob answered angrily, "Am I God to give you children?" Neither one of them thought to pray to God for children, as Isaac and Rebekah had, when they had no children.

Slowly, painfully, but with sure purpose God was teaching Jacob that the man who receives God's promises must change his life. He must be made over. He must admit his sin, and yield his life entirely to God's direction. That is the only way God can use us in His kingdom, and it is the only road to happiness.

21
Holding Onto God

Genesis 32

Jacob had come this way before. It was a long time ago, but he had not forgotten. "Go and visit my brother Laban in Haran," his mother had said to him, "until your brother forgets what you have done to him. In a few days, when Esau's anger has cooled, I will send for you to come home again." The few days had lengthened into twenty years, and still no message from Rebekah that it was safe to come home. Twenty long years, and yet Jacob still felt the old clutch of fear at his heart when he saw the familiar wooded hillsides that told him he was almost home.

That other time when he had been so afraid, he had been alone. A man who travels by himself can run if he has to. But now he had his two wives with him, and his eleven little sons. The oldest of them was not more than twelve, and the youngest was still a baby. Besides that there were all the animals, hundreds of sheep and goats and cows and camels, and all the servants who looked after them. It would be easy for Esau to spot such a caravan, and impossible for them to escape, once they had been discovered.

Still, it was twenty years ago. Perhaps by this time Esau had forgotten how badly Jacob had treated him. He was never one to hold a grudge, once his hot temper had cooled. *I will send him a friendly message,* Jacob decided. *I will admit Esau is older than I am. Most likely he is more powerful, too. I will ask his permission to come home. Perhaps Esau will forgive me after all.*

He called two of his servants. "Go on ahead," he said to them. "When you meet Esau, give him this message: 'Your servant Jacob says, "I have been at our Uncle Laban's all these years. I have flocks of animals, and servants too. I send you this message in order to find favor in your sight." ' " The servants went on ahead. A day or two later they were back. "We gave your message to Esau," they told Jacob, "but he did not send you any answer. He is coming to meet you, though, and he has four hundred men with him."

Now Jacob was more afraid than ever. He remembered all too well that Esau had sworn to kill him. He divided all the people with him, and all the animals, into two groups. "If Esau attacks one," he thought, "perhaps the other will escape." Jacob was so afraid that he turned to God for help. There is nothing like great danger to drive a person to God. You and I ought not to wait until we are in bad trouble before we ask God's help. But most of us are all too much like Jacob. When things go well, we like to plan our own lives. It is not until we are in deep danger that we cry out frantically to God for help.

"O God of my grandfather Abraham," Jacob prayed, "and of my father Isaac, I have not deserved any of the blessings You have shown me. For I was all alone when I came this way before, and now I have two companies. Save me, I pray You, from the hand of my brother, for I am afraid of Esau, afraid that he will kill me, and my children, and their mothers." God heard Jacob's prayer. God had not forgotten the promise He had made to Jacob that night so long ago when Jacob dreamed of the angels on the steps climbing up to heaven, the promise that He would bring Jacob back to his home in safety. But there was something that Jacob *had* forgotten. He had forgotten that when he tricked his brother Esau, and lied to his father Isaac, he was sinning against God. Jacob was dreadfully afraid of Esau, but he was not enough afraid of sinning against God.

There was a little brook where Jacob was camped. That night he sent all the servants and the animals across the brook. He sent his wives and children across too. He himself stayed behind alone. He was dreadfully troubled, and dreadfully afraid. He did not know whether he would live to see another night. As Jacob sat there all alone in the darkness, something very strange happened. A man appeared. No, it was not a man. God Himself appeared, in the form of a man. God wrestled with Jacob. He wrestled with Jacob all night long. He wanted to teach Jacob, so that he would never forget again, that God was displeased with his sin. As the night wore on, and Jacob wrestled with God, he realized more and more that God could not bless a man who was not sorry for his sin. Now Jacob fought desperately to win God's forgiveness, fought so desperately that he actually began to win the match. Not that he was stronger than God. But when a man is truly sorry for his sins, and begs for God's forgiveness, he can always win God's blessing.

But there was still something else Jacob must learn. He must learn that he was not strong in himself, that he could be strong only if he depended on God. God reached out and touched Jacob's leg with his hand, and instantly Jacob's leg was sprained. He could hardly wrestle any more. Still he would not give up. "Let Me go," God said; "it is almost morning." But Jacob answered, "I will not let You go unless You bless me." "What is your name?" God asked. And he answered, "Jacob." "You shall not be called Jacob any more," God said, "but Israel, because you have wrestled with God, and have won His forgiveness."

Suddenly it was morning, and God was gone. Jacob said in amazement, "I have seen God face to face, and my life has been saved!" After that night Jacob limped when he walked. Whenever he walked on his lame leg, he remembered that God's blessing is only for those who are sorry for their sin, and that no man is strong in himself, but only if he trusts in God.

Jacob crossed over the brook, and he saw Esau coming with four hundred men behind him. Jacob went on ahead of his wives and children, and as he came near to his brother, he bowed himself humbly before him seven times. But Esau ran to meet Jacob, threw his arms around him, and kissed him. Both of them burst into tears. After all, they were twin brothers, and they had not seen each other for twenty years.

22

The Two-Way Promise

Genesis 35

Did Jacob change after he saw God face to face, after God wrestled him to his knees? The answer is yes — and no! Certainly that night he learned something he never forgot. He learned that God demands that those who call themselves His people show this by their changed lives. He learned how helpless you and I are except in the strength given us by God. Every limping step he took on his lame leg the rest of his life reminded him of these things.

And yet, the old, scheming, deceitful Jacob was still there. It kept cropping up at the most unexpected moments. You do not find all your problems solved, all your battles won, the day you kneel at Jesus' feet, and yield your life to Him. You might even say, in one sense, that this is the day the real struggle in your life begins. For learning to be the kind of person God expects us to be is a hard, lifelong, painful struggle. It was that for Jacob too.

The wonder of it is that our God does not leave us alone to face this struggle. For that night when God stopped Jacob beside the brook, and wrestled with his guilty heart the whole night through, that night was not the first time God had appeared to Jacob. Twenty years before that, when Jacob had been a frightened man running for his life, God had spoken directly to his great need. He had come to the homesick fugitive with promises, promises so gracious, so totally undeserved, that Jacob had been quite overcome. "I am going to give this place where you are sleeping to you and to your children," God had said. "I will go with you to this strange land where you must now find refuge. I will care for you, and I will surely bring you back again to your home."

As soon as it grew light that morning so long ago, Jacob got up. He set on end the stone he had used for a pillow. He poured a little oil over it — for this was all he had to offer God. He called the place Bethel, for, he said, "This is the very house of God. This is the gate of heaven. God is in this place, and I never knew it."

But he wanted to do more. The promise of God, so undeserved and so unexpected, awoke an answer in his heart. He would make a promise in return. He knelt down. "O God of my fathers," he said, "if truly You are willing to be my God too, to care for me in the strange place to which I am going, and to bring me back at last to my father's house in peace, then You *shall* be my God. This stone which I have set up shall be Your house, and of all that You give me I will surely give one-tenth back to You."

This had all happened long years ago. Had God kept His promises? Sometimes you and I make promises we cannot keep. Sometimes we even — I admit it with shame — make promises we do not really mean to keep. But God's promises stand sure. You can stake your life on them and never see them fail. God *had* gone with Jacob to the distant land. He *had* provided him with all he needed, yes, and with far more: food, clothing, and even great flocks of sheep and cattle and camels. He had given him two wives to comfort his homesickness, and eleven sons and one daughter. And God had brought him back in peace to his own land. God had even softened the angry heart of Esau, so that this reunion, at the very thought of which Jacob trembled even after twenty years, had been a reunion not of anger and threats, but of love, of arms thrown around each other's shoulders, and even of tears of joy. Yes, God had kept his promises.

And Jacob? How well had he kept his part of the two-way promise? He had gone on with his old, deceitful, scheming tricks. Even after that night beside the brook, even with his lame leg to remind him, he still was quite sure he could look out for himself.

It was already ten years since he had come back to Canaan, but he had not gone back to Bethel, where God had given him so wonderful a promise. He had not renewed his part of the two-way promise. He had not offered thanks to God for His matchless mercies. At last God had to stoop down from heaven to remind Jacob of his promise. "Go back to Bethel," God said to him. "Make an altar there, and worship the God who helped you there when you were in great trouble."

Jacob's heart was smitten. How could he have delayed so long, forgotten so easily? And now that he must face God again, he looked at his own life. He was ashamed of what he saw. His servants, yes, and even his beloved wife Rachel, carried idols about with them, and worshiped them. Almost everyone in his household wore magic ear-rings to ward off evil spirits. Jacob collected all the idols. He collected all the magic earrings, too. He dug a deep hole beneath an oak tree, and buried them out of sight. "Put on clean clothes, every one of you," he said to his family and his servants. "It will help us to remember we cannot come before God unless we have cleansed our hearts."

So they came at last to Bethel, where God had spoken to Jacob thirty years before. They built an altar there, and offered sacrifices to their faithful God. God had reached down His mighty arm from heaven. And Jacob, sinful, unworthy, had tremblingly reached up his arm to God. And God took Jacob's hand in His, never to let him go.

So it is with you. God reaches down to you too. He comes with amazing, undeserved promises. But He always expects an answer. Perhaps you first heard those promises when you were so small you could hardly understand them, much less answer them. Now you are older. You can understand now, and you can speak. You know how faithfully God has cared for you, how many blessings He has showered down upon your head. Have you answered Him yet? Have you knelt down, as Jacob did at Bethel, and promised, in answer to God's promises, "If You will care for me, and go with me wherever I go, then surely You *shall* be my God!"?

23
God's Mystery Plan

Genesis 37

In the school where my husband teaches — and probably also in the school you attend — there is what is called a Long Range Planning Committee. This committee tries to discover how many children will enter kindergarten, or high school, or college, five years, and ten years, from now. This is so that there will be enough classrooms and teachers and desks and books to go around. After the committee has studied this carefully, they send out a sheet full of numbers, and call a meeting of the people who support the school, to decide whether they need to build an addition. Sometimes all their careful figuring and planning turns out wrong. There are so many things about the future we do not know, so many things that can change in five or ten years.

God also has a long-range plan, much longer than any of ours. His plan reaches all the way from the day He picked up a handful of dust and formed it into a man to the day when our Saviour comes again on the clouds of heaven. God's plan never turns out wrong, because God knows everything that will happen. Indeed, He is the very one who makes it happen. God does not send out papers filled with numbers, or call a meeting to decide what to do next. God's plan is secret; it is a mystery. There is a special reason for this secrecy. God wants us, His children, to walk by faith, not by sight. He wants us to place our hand in His, and then go forward, seeing just one step at a time.

Sometimes the part of the plan that arranges your life, or mine, calls for difficult tasks. Sometimes it takes us places we do not really want to go. Sometimes we find we are disappointed, or sick, or lonely. These things are not accidents either. They are part of God's plan for us. They teach us lessons we could not learn otherwise. They make us strong, and patient, and brave. So that we can know this for sure when trouble does come, God has written down for us the story of one part of His great plan. It is the story of one man for whom God had planned a dazzling future, but who first of all had to learn patience and strength and trust by walking a hard path.

It was a much harder path than any of us has yet walked for God. The man was Joseph. Perhaps I should say he was a boy, for he was only seventeen when God led him down this dark, mysterious road. Joseph was the youngest of Jacob's twelve sons, except for little Benjamin, who was only a baby. He was his father's favorite. But he was not a favorite with his brothers. They were jealous because their father liked Joseph the best.

All of the boys were shepherds. For God's people still lived in tents. They still did not own any of the land God had promised to their great-grandfather, Abraham. They were still looking for that better city where God Himself lives among His people. Jacob's sons spent most of their time in the fields, caring for their father's sheep. Several of the older boys were rather wild. Joseph carried tales of their wrongdoing back home to his father. This made his brothers hate him even more. One night Joseph dreamed a dream. "Listen to what I dreamed!" he boasted to his brothers. "We were all binding grain in the field. And all of your bundles came and bowed low before my bundle." His brothers answered scornfully, "Do you think you are going to rule over us?" And they hated him more and more.

A few days later Joseph came to them again. "I had another dream," he said. "This time the sun and the moon and the eleven stars came to me and bowed low." Now even Joseph's father was angry. "Do you suppose," he said, "that I and your mother and all your brothers are going to bow down before you?" Still, his father thought about the dream. He wondered what it could mean.

One day the older boys had taken the sheep to Shechem, about fifty miles from where their father had his tents set up. Jacob called Joseph. "Go and see how your brothers are getting along," he said, "and bring me news of them." So Joseph set out, wearing his beautiful, many-colored coat, the coat his father had made especially for him, and for which all his brothers envied him. His brothers saw him coming a long way off. "There comes the master dreamer!" they said to each other. "Let's kill him, and throw his body in one of the water holes. We can say some wild beast has eaten him. We will see then what becomes of his dreams." But Reuben, the oldest brother, was troubled by his conscience. "Do not kill him," he said. "Just throw him into the hole alive." So his brothers tore off the beautiful coat, and threw Joseph into the deep hole.

As the brothers sat comfortably around the fire eating their dinner, laughing at the faint screams they heard from the hole, they saw a caravan of merchants approaching, carrying spices to Egypt. One of the boys had an idea. "Why should we stain our hands with our brother's blood," they said. "Let us sell him as a slave to these merchants instead!" So they pulled Joseph out of the hole, and sold him to the merchants. The merchants paid the brothers twenty pieces of silver for their new slave. They took Joseph along with them to Egypt.

Then the brothers took Joseph's many-colored coat. They dipped it in the blood of a goat. They brought the blood-stained coat to their father. "Look!" they said. "We found this. Can it be your son's coat?" Poor Jacob recognized the coat. "It *is* Joseph's!" he cried. "A wild animal has surely torn him to pieces!" Jacob mourned many days for his favorite son. Though the other boys tried to comfort him, they were secretly glad they had gotten rid of Joseph.

But God had other plans. Joseph's trip to Egypt was part of God's wonderful plan to bring a Saviour into the world; and the path Joseph walked was part of God's wonderful mercy to you and to me.

24

Sold Into Slavery

Genesis 39

When he woke up, Joseph lay still a moment, shivering as he remembered his dream. Then, as the slanting rays of the rising sun hit the roof of the tent, he sat up and shook himself slightly, to rid his mind of the dark memory. Any minute now his father would call him to breakfast, and they would smile together at the bad dream.

The tent flap lifted, but it was not the familiar, loved face of his father that looked in. This was the greedy, evil face of the merchant he had seen in his dream. The man spoke roughly, "Up, you lazy good-for-nothing! Do you imagine you are the chief's son, that you lie so long in bed? Water the camels at once, or we will see whether this stick can make you move faster!" Cursing angrily, he kicked at the boy lying on the tent floor. As Joseph shot out of the tent door, there was a burst of mocking laughter from the men sitting around the campfire. "The new slave is not too smart," one of them said. "I doubt that he is worth the twenty pieces of silver we paid for him."

In a flash it all come back to Joseph. It was not a dream at all. It had really happened. He remembered the black looks of his brothers when he had found them yesterday. He remembered their grim silence as they tore off his beautiful coat. He remembered the darkness of the hole they had thrown him into, his desperate efforts to claw his way back up the steep sides, only to fall back again and again. He remembered his cries for pity, and the hard laughter of his brothers up above him. He remembered his quickly rising hopes when they at last threw down a rope for him to catch hold of, and the greedy faces of the merchants as they bargained with his brothers. How indifferently his brothers had turned away as the merchants carried him off! How longingly he had looked back until he could no longer see the tents and the sheep and his brothers sitting around the fire!

This was the time when at home he and his father usually prayed together. He could not stop to kneel down now, but as he carried the water to the camels, he breathed a prayer in his heart. He did not know what was going to happen to him, but God knew. God was here in this strange place just as surely as in his father's tent at home. He prayed for help, for strength, for a stronger trust. He prayed that God would go with him wherever he went, would care for him, would be his God. After he had prayed, he felt better.

After many days' travel, each day taking Joseph farther from his home, they came at last to Egypt. Joseph had heard stories of the wonders of Egypt. His great-grandfather Abraham had once lived here for a while during a famine. But Joseph was not to see these wonders. Not yet. He was stood on a platform, and auctioned off to the highest bidder. The man who bought him, so it happened, was Potiphar, the king's chief of police. I say "happened," but this was not chance. It was all part of God's mysterious plan. There was a reason why Joseph became a slave in the police chief's home.

The work of a slave was hard and degrading. He had no rights. His master could beat him for the smallest offense, or even for no fault at all, just to give vent to his anger. He could beat him to death if he wished, and no one would call him to account. What could be worse than to be a slave in a strange country?

When the future seems hopelessly dark, you can do one of two things. You can curse your God and die. Or you can turn to Him in desperate prayer. Many a person has found that God is nearest to those whom all human help has failed. In fact, God has a special, tender care for those who cry to Him from the very depths. And God has special lessons, too, which He teaches to His children when they are in bad trouble. Lessons they could never learn in any easier way. Joseph was learning to be patient. He was learning to trust God. He was learning to pray as he had never prayed before.

And though Joseph never imagined such a thing, God was even now preparing for him a dazzling future. He was teaching Joseph the very things he needed to know for that future. And God was answering his prayers too, though the answer certainly was not what Joseph had hoped for. God did not rescue him from slavery, and send him back home to his father. But God did move Potiphar's heart — for the police chief's heart, like the king's, is in God's hand, to turn it wheresoever He wishes. Potiphar found he liked Joseph. He saw that whatever Joseph did turned out well. He did not guess that it was God who made it turn out well. But he gave Joseph more and more to do. Before long Joseph was in charge of all the household. He learned how to deal with important officials, how to handle money wisely, how to speak Egyptian well. It was important that he know these things, though Joseph never guessed why.

What could be worse than being a slave? So Joseph thought at first. But now an even harder lesson was given him to learn. Joseph was young and handsome. Potiphar's wife fell in love with him. She wanted Joseph to love her too. "How can I betray my master's trust, and sin against God?" Joseph said. This made the woman very angry. Her love turned to hate. She determined to get even.

When Potiphar came home that night, she said, "See, that Hebrew slave you brought here wants me to run away with him!" Potiphar rose up in fury. He had trusted Joseph with all that he had, and now, he thought, Joseph was trying to steal his wife. Before Joseph knew what had happened, he found himself bound hand and foot in the dungeon.

And was the prison, too, part of God's plan, part of Joseph's education? Yes, that is exactly what it was.

25

The Hole

Genesis 40, 41

The house belonging to the chief of police has several stories. The rooms where Potiphar and his family live are at the top. Beneath them are the workrooms — kitchens, storerooms, slave quarters. And at the very bottom, dug deep into the rock, is the dungeon. In this dismal prison, which they call "The Hole," Joseph now sits, chained to the stone floor with heavy iron chains. The Hole is dark and wet. The air is heavy with despair. Can the hand of God reach down even into this dark place? Past the heavy, barred gate? Past the guards? Past the clanking chains on Joseph's legs? There is no place, however far, however dark, that God's hand cannot reach.

God did not send an angel to bring Joseph out of prison. For prison was part of God's plan. But He did soften the heart of the jailer towards Joseph. The jailer — for who can resist the power of God? — removed the chains from Joseph's legs. He gave his prisoner simple tasks to do in the dungeon. He allowed him to clean the cells, to wait on the other prisoners. And everything Joseph did turned out well. Not because Joseph was so smart. It turned out well because God planned it that way. Soon Joseph was running the prison, just as he had run the police chief's household. And all the while Joseph was learning new lessons — lessons of patience, lessons of trust. He was finding out more and more about the marvelous faithfulness of our God.

One day there was a great commotion in the prison. Two new prisoners arrived. These men were not slaves, like Joseph. They were great nobles from the king's court. One, the chief butler, was in charge of the king's wine cellars. The second was Pharaoh's chief baker, in charge of all the cooks and the ovens. No one knew what they had done, or why they were put in prison. The jailer assigned Joseph to wait on them.

One night both the chief butler and the chief baker dreamed, each of them, a dream. They had never heard of the true God, but it was God who sent the dreams. For the dreams, too, were part of God's plan. When Joseph came into their cell the next morning, the prisoners were sad. "What is the matter?" he asked them. And they answered, "We have each of us dreamed a dream, and no one can tell us what it means." Joseph answered, "Only God knows the meaning of things. Tell me your dreams." The chief butler said, "I dreamed I saw a vine with three branches. I squeezed the grapes on the vine into Pharaoh's cup, and gave it to him to drink." And Joseph (the Holy Spirit helping him to understand the dream) answered, "The three branches are three days. In three days Pharaoh will restore you to your position, and you will again hand him his cup as you used to do. I beg of you, when this happens, do not forget me, but mention my name to Pharaoh, and bring me out of this Hole. For I was stolen away from the land of the Hebrews, and here in Egypt I have not done anything for which they should put me into this dungeon."

When the chief baker heard this, he also told his dream: "I dreamed I had three baskets of bread on my head, filled with all kinds of baked foods for Pharaoh. But the birds flew down and ate them out of my basket." And Joseph said, "The three baskets are three days. In three days Pharaoh will cut off your head, and hang you on a tree."·

Three days later was Pharaoh's birthday. He called the chief butler out of prison back to his post in the palace, but he hanged the chief baker. Yet the chief butler did not remember Joseph. He forgot him.

Two years passed. Joseph still waited in prison, waited for God to answer his prayers. Then one night God sent a dream to the Egyptian king himself. Pharaoh dreamed that he stood beside a river. Seven fat cows came up out of the water. They were followed by seven thin cows, all skin and bones. The thin cows ate up the fat cows. Pharaoh woke up, but before he could think what such a dream meant, he fell asleep again. This time he dreamed he saw seven fat, full ears of corn. After this he saw seven thin ears, blasted by the east wind. The thin ears swallowed the fat ears.

Early the next morning Pharaoh called for all his wise men and his magicians, but no one of them could tell him what the double dream meant. Then the chief butler said, "Now I remember my fault. When I and the chief baker were in prison, there was a Hebrew slave there who explained our dreams. And everything really happened just as he said it would." So Pharaoh sent for Joseph.

"I have heard you can explain dreams," Pharaoh said. "Not I," Joseph answered. "Only God can explain dreams. God will give Pharaoh an answer of peace." So Pharaoh told him the dream. Joseph said, "The two dreams are one in their meaning. God has told Pharaoh beforehand what He is going to do. The seven fat cows and the seven good ears of grain are seven years of great and abundant harvests in the land of Egypt. The seven thin cows and the seven blasted ears of corn are seven years of terrible famine which will follow the years of abundance. Now let Pharaoh look for a wise and careful man, and let him gather up a fifth part of the harvest in each of the seven years of plenty. Let him store it carefully in storehouses, so that when the seven years of famine come, there will be food in the land of Egypt, and the people will not die of hunger."

Pharaoh turned to his advisers, who stood beside his throne. "Where," he said, "could we find another man like this, a man with the spirit of God in him?" Then he said to Joseph, "See, I have set you over all the land of Egypt. No man shall dare to lift up his foot or his hand without your consent. Only in the throne itself will I be greater than you are." Pharaoh took off his royal ring and put it on Joseph's hand, and put a golden chain around his neck, and had his servants dress him in fine linen clothes such as kings wear. He called for his own chariot to drive Joseph through the city streets. And as the chariot passed, heralds ran before it, commanding everyone, "Bow the knee! Bow the knee!"

26
As We Forgive

Genesis 42-45

It was nearly two years now since it had rained. There had been no harvest this year. The grain had withered and blackened soon after it sprouted. Every day the ten brothers took the sheep out to the fields, searching for a low spot where there might still be some grass. When they came back, they kept their eyes on the ground. They could not bear to see the terrible questions in the eyes of their wives. They could not bear to hear the hungry cries of their children.

One day a train of camels stopped nearby. "Where are you going?" the father, Jacob, asked the men. "What is there to trade for in this terrible famine? Who will buy fine linen or perfumes when he is starving?"

"We are going to Egypt," the traders answered. "We have heard that there is grain in Egypt. We will sell whatever we have to bring home food to our families." That night Jacob called all his sons to his tent. "Why do you look at each other with despairing looks?" he said to them. "Go down to Egypt, and buy for us too, so that we may live, and not die of hunger." Early the next morning the ten brothers set out. Jacob kept the youngest boy, Benjamin, at home. He had not forgotten that terrible day twenty years ago when Joseph had disappeared, and all that was ever found of him was a torn, bloody coat. Ever since that day Jacob had been reluctant to let Benjamin out of his sight.

Joseph was now governor in Egypt, charged with all the buying and selling of grain. When the brothers arrived, they were taken directly to his office. He himself interviewed all foreigners who came to buy grain.

When he saw his brothers, the governor gave a start of recognition. But the brothers did not notice. They bowed low before him, their faces humbly touching the ground. Perhaps the governor had been hoping to see his brothers. Perhaps he had even expected they would come. He longed to reach out his arms to them. But he did not reveal himself yet. He wanted to test them first, to see if they had changed since they sold him as a slave.

"You are spies!" he said to them harshly. "Oh, no, my lord," they answered desperately. "We are twelve sons of one man. Our youngest brother is at home with our father, and one of us is dead. We have only come to buy food for our families."

"We shall see whether your story is true," Joseph answered. "You may take grain home to your families. But one of you must remain here in prison as a hostage. And you need not come back for more grain unless you bring along that youngest brother you talk about." Joseph longed especially to see his youngest brother Benjamin, who had been only a baby when Joseph left home. For Benjamin was his full brother, the only other son of his mother Rachel. The other boys were half brothers.

The brothers said to one another, "This is our punishment from God. It is because we heard our brother Joseph cry to us for mercy, and we would not listen." They did not realize that the governor could understand them when they spoke to each other in their native language. But when Joseph heard these words, he had to escape quickly into the next room. He could not keep the tears from his eyes.

When Joseph came back he had Simeon bound and put in prison. He sent the other nine home with grain for their families. Now there was food again for Jacob's family. But all too soon it was gone!

"Go back to Egypt," Jacob said to his sons. "Buy more grain." They answered, "The governor solemnly warned us that we should not see his face again unless we brought Benjamin with us. If you will let us take him along, we will go. Otherwise it will be useless." Jacob said, "Why did you ever tell the man you had another brother?" And they answered, "The man asked us all about our family. How could we have guessed he would say, 'Bring your youngest brother along!'?" Judah, one of the boys, said, "Trust the boy to me, and if I do not bring him back safely, let me bear the blame forever. If we had not delayed, we could have been gone and back by this time." Then their father said,

"If it must be so, take the boy, and go. And God Almighty give you mercy before the man!"

When the brothers arrived in Egypt, they were surprised to hear they were to eat dinner with the governor. Simeon was brought out from prison, and they were royally feasted and entertained. Afterwards they were given grain, and sent on their way. They did not understand at first why the governor was so friendly, but they soon found out. Joseph had one last test for them, to discover whether they really loved and cared for Benjamin. Joseph had his servants hide his own silver cup in Benjamin's bag. The brothers were scarcely out of the city, when they were overtaken by Joseph's servant. "We treated you well," he said, "and in return you have stolen my lord's silver cup."

"Certainly not!" they answered indignantly. "Look through our bags. If you find the cup, the one who has stolen it shall die. And all of us will become the governor's slaves." "No," the servant said, "only the one who is guilty shall become my lord's slave. The rest of you may go home in peace." The servant searched all their bags, and, sure enough, he found the cup in Benjamin's bag. The brothers were overcome with confusion. They all returned to the city with Benjamin. When they came to Joseph's house, they fell on their faces before him.

"My lord," Judah said, "our father is an aged man. And this boy is his favorite, because he is the only one left of his mother. His brother is dead. If we return home without him, it will kill his father. I beg of you, let me stay and be my lord's slave, instead of the boy."

Joseph could not stand it any longer. He cried out, "I am your brother Joseph! Is my father yet alive?" His brothers could not answer. Perhaps they thought, "Now we shall pay for our wickedness!" But Joseph did not want to get even with them. "Come nearer," he said. "I am Joseph your brother, whom you sold into Egypt. Do not be angry with yourselves for what you did. It was not you that sent me here, but God. He sent me ahead of you, to save your lives. Hurry home, and bring my father, and your wives and children. There are still five years of dreadful famine coming." Then Joseph threw his arms around his brothers, and wept with joy to see them again.

Was it easy for Joseph to forgive his brothers? No, it was not easy. And, what is more, they did not deserve to be forgiven. How many years Joseph had spent, first as a slave, and then in prison, because of his brothers' cruel deed! But in one sense you and I are even more guilty than they were. For we sent our beloved Saviour to the cross, and even to the pangs of hell. And He has forgiven us freely, gladly, all our guilt. This is why, out of grateful hearts, we, like Joseph, must each one of us forgive our brothers whatever wrong they have done us.

27
Where He Leads Me

Genesis 45, 46

The old man sat at the tent door, his eyes fixed on the distant horizon. That is where they would first appear when they came back — *if* they came back at all. It seemed to him they had been gone overlong already.

God had given him twelve sons, and then He had taken one of them back again, and all Jacob had ever seen of him was his torn, blood-stained coat. Now the other eleven were gone too. Simeon had never returned from the first trip to Egypt. He had been thrown into prison there. Perhaps all his sons were in prison, even the youngest, Benjamin, who had been all he had left of his beloved dead wife, Rachel.

He felt very alone, and yet he was not really alone. All the family tents were pitched near his. Sometimes one of his sons' wives came to stand beside him, to speak to him, to stare with him at that distant horizon. They shared his trouble, these ten daughters-in-law of his.

Sometimes the grandchildren gathered in a little circle about his feet. He looked sadly at their thin, white faces. He told them stories to help them forget the gnawing pain in their empty stomachs. He was very careful to tell these stories exactly as they had happened. For these were not made-up fairy tales. They were true stories, the precious stories about how God had spoken to his family. The children had no story-books, no schoolbooks either, not even that most important book of all, the Word of God. What God had said and done, what He had promised and how wonderfully He had fulfilled each promise, what He had commanded — all this had to be carefully treasured up in their memories,

and told by fathers to sons. And then by sons, in turn, to their sons.

He told them about his grandfather, Abraham, and his long journey; about how God had faithfully kept His promise to give Abraham a son, long after it had become impossible. He told them about his father Isaac, and his mother Rebekah, who had left her own family in Haran to become Isaac's bride.

He told them about his twin brother Esau, and how they had quarreled when they were both boys at home. He told them just what happened, even though he was ashamed of many of the things he had done. He told them how Esau had sold his birthright, and how he himself had shamefully deceived his blind father to steal the blessing. He told them about his lonely, frightened escape to Haran, about his dream of a ladder with angels walking up and down it, about how God Himself had spoken to him, and had promised: "I will take care of you wherever you go. I will not leave you. I am going to give this very land where you lie sleeping to your children." He stopped in his story, thinking back, remembering, as old people love to do. How marvelously God

had already fulfilled this promise! God would surely take care of his boys in Egypt!

Suddenly there was a shout from the camp. The women and children came running. For there, in the distance, a long train of men and donkeys and wagons came into sight. Even so far away the figures seemed familiar. But whose were all those wagons? Jacob tried to quiet the wild, hopeful beating of his heart. Slowly the men came nearer. At last they stopped beside his tent. Jacob looked eagerly from one to the other, scanning their faces. All his sons were home safe, even Simeon who had been in prison in Egypt!

The oldest boy, Reuben, stepped forward. "Joseph," he said, "is still alive. He is governor of all Egypt!" His father stared at him as if he did not understand his words. He felt dizzy, as if he were going to faint. Reuben's wife put her arms around his shoulders. "You will scare him to death," she said, "telling him news like that so suddenly. You should have told him gradually." Jacob took hold of her hand to steady himself. "It is all right," he said. "Tell me just what happened." And so they told him all about Joseph, his fine palace in Egypt, and everything he had said to them. And when their father saw the wagons Joseph had sent to carry him to Egypt, he said, "It is enough. Joseph, my son, is still alive! I will go and see him before I die."

What an excitement there was that night in the camp, as they sat up late around the fire, telling over and over again everything that had happened in Egypt! And what a bustle of preparation the next day, as they began to pack for the journey! There were seventy sons and grand-sons, and one or two great-grandsons, even. And that did not count their wives. Then there were the great herds of cattle, and the many servants. Joseph had sent a great many wagons for the old people and the little children, and many donkeys loaded with provisions for the trip.

At last all was ready, and they set out. They traveled south until they reached Beersheba, at the southern edge of Canaan. Here Jacob offered a sacrifice to God. One thing he had learned in his long, troubled life, and that was not to rush ahead without waiting for God's guidance. He wanted to be very sure that God approved of their leaving the Promised Land. That night God appeared to him in a vision. "Jacob! Jacob!" God called. And Jacob answered, "Here I am!" God said, "I am God, the God of your father. Do not be afraid to go to Egypt. I will go with you. I will make a great nation out of your children there. You shall see Joseph again. And I will surely bring your children back to this land which I have promised them."

The next day they packed up again and went on, secure in the wonderful knowledge that God went with them. And so they came at last to Egypt. As soon as Joseph heard that they were near, he got into his chariot and drove out to meet them. He and his father threw their arms around each other's necks, and both of them burst into tears of joy. Jacob said to Joseph, "Now I am ready to die, since I have seen your face again, and you are still alive!"

28

The Wanderers

Genesis 48

Tere's a new girl in my class," Susie said at the supper table, "and is she ever queer!"

"What do you mean, queer?" Mother asked. "Well," Susie said, "she is so dark, and her clothes are awful, and she talks funny too. When she answers a question, all the kids laugh." "You should be ashamed of yourself, young lady," said big brother Ben. "That poor little Cuban kid trying to learn English, and you laughing at her!"

Susie turned red. "I didn't mean it that way," she said. Mother shook her head at Ben. "I know you didn't mean it, Susie," she said. "You just didn't think. But maybe a Christian little girl ought to think. When Grandma is here Sunday, you ask her what it feels like to be a little girl in a strange country." Susie's eyes opened wide. "You mean people laughed at my Grandma?" she said. "Yes," Mother said, "people laughed at Grandma. People who don't think often laugh at strangers." Susie looked very sober.

Every single one of you has someone in his family who was once a stranger far from home. Perhaps even your father or mother, or a grandmother, like Susie's, or a great-grandfather or great-grandmother. Someone who left a comfortable life and people they knew well, to come to a strange country where people spoke a language that was hard to learn. Many of them came because they could not worship God as they wished at home. Some came so that their children and grandchildren would have a better chance in life. And some, like our Hungarian and Cuban friends, ran terrible risks, climbing through barbed wire, or floating days on the pitiless ocean waves in a rowboat, barely escaping with their lives, to find a land where they could be free.

It is great fun to take a vacation trip to visit a different state, or even a different country. But it is not fun if you know you cannot go home again, that you will probably never see again the house where you grew up, the children you played with, the street you know so well. But at least those of our family who came to America — and, we hope at last our friends from Hungary and Cuba too — could start a new home in this country. They suffered terribly. They never really got over being homesick. But after a while the new house, the strange streets, even the different language became familiar, and at last they called this new country their home.

But what if there is no end to the journey? No new house in a new town? No home? What if you had to go on wandering all your life long? Yes, there is someone in your family to whom this happened. His name is Abraham, and you are truly his child if you are a Christian. And if you are a Christian, it was partly for your sake that he did this. Abraham, and his son Isaac, and still later his grandson Jacob lived for two hundred years in a tent. Not because they were too poor to build a house. They could have gone back to Ur if they had wished. Or they could have built themselves a city of their own in Canaan, that country flowing with milk and honey which God had promised to them and to their children. Instead they chose to live in a tent. For they were not staying in Canaan. They were just stopping there on their way to somewhere else. Nothing would satisfy them but that city with the sure foundations, the city whose builder and maker is God Himself.

And then a terrible famine drove them to Egypt. Now they set up their tents and pastured their flocks in Goshen, on the banks of the Nile River. Were they happier in Goshen than they had been in Canaan? No, Egypt was for them just one more waystation on their lifelong journey back to God.

Jacob lived seventeen years in Egypt. One day, when the aged man had grown quite feeble, a messenger came to Joseph. "Your father is sick," he said. So Joseph took his two sons, Ephraim and Manasseh, now teen-age boys, and went to visit his father. His father said to him, "Once I thought I would never see your face again, and now God has let me see your children also! Bring them near, so that I can bless them." Joseph brought the boys close to his father's bed, and Jacob laid his hands on their heads, and said, "The God before whom my fathers Abraham and Isaac did walk, the God who has fed me all my life long until this day, the God who has redeemed me from all evil, bless the boys, and let them grow into a multitude in the earth." Then he added to Joseph, "Soon I am going to die. But God will still be with you. He will surely bring you back again to the land He promised to your fathers. And I have given you one extra portion of my property, more than to your brothers."

Jacob had once been a schemer, a deceiver. By the grace of God he became a giant of faith, who strides across the pages of our Bible. And you and I, trying with our short legs to walk in his footsteps, remember that he said almost at the end of his long wanderings, "God fed me all my life long, and redeemed me from all evil." And in our mind's eye we see the tent he chose to live in, and for one short moment we seem to catch a glimpse of him sitting even now where he most wanted to be, at the marriage feast of the Lamb, in the city God prepared for him, because the great God of heaven and earth was not ashamed to be called his God. May God create in the heart of each one of us a homesick longing for that city!

29
Standing on the Promises

Genesis 49, 50

The old man rested on the side of his bed, leaning on his staff. He was very feeble, and almost blind. His twelve sons stood around him. They leaned forward to catch his last words. He could no longer tell one of his sons from the other by their faces — only by their voices. And yet, at this moment, when the eyes of his body were so dim, the eyes of his spirit shone brighter than ever. Or should we say, it was God's Holy Spirit that shone through his eyes? This was the man who had once wrestled with God. And God had wrestled with him, not just that one night by the brook Jabbok, but all his life long. Until now at last, as he rested on his deathbed, he was so completely conquered by the love of God that he became, as it were, a transparent glass through which the beauty of God shone.

He became a prophetic voice through which the Spirit of God spoke, telling of amazing and glorious things that would happen in the far distant future. Yes, Jacob became a prophet. He spoke to each of his twelve sons in turn. He reminded them of their past sins, not in anger, but in loving warning. He foretold the place their children would take in history. He spoke to Reuben, to Simeon, to Levi, and then to Judah. "Kings will be born of you," he said to Judah. "There will always be a king among your children, until the great Peacemaker comes. All people will bring willing obedience to Him." He spoke to Zebulun and Issachar, to Dan and Gad, to Asher and Naphtali. He spoke to Joseph. "The God of your fathers shall help you," he promised. "Great blessings shall come to the one who was separated from his brothers." He spoke to Benjamin, the youngest of his sons.

"I die," he said to his sons. "Do not bury me in Egypt. Bury me with my fathers in the cave of Machpelah. Abraham and Sarah are buried there, my father Isaac and my mother Rebekah, and there I buried my wife Leah." And when he had said this, he lay down again on his bed. Peacefully he yielded up his spirit to the God he loved. Joseph burst into tears. He threw himself on his father and kissed him. It was gain for his father to die; for it was certainly very far better to depart and be with Christ. But the separation was hard for Joseph.

Because Jacob was the prime minister's father, a great state funeral was given him. The Egyptians mourned for him for seventy days. And while they mourned, the doctors skillfully embalmed his body, so that it could be taken back to Canaan, to be buried with his fathers, as he had wished. And then there was a great procession. All his children and grandchildren and great-grandchildren went along; only the very little ones were left in Egypt. The important officials of the Egyptian court went too, and a great company of chariots and men on horseback. And so they brought his body back to Canaan, and buried it beside his parents and grandparents; there to wait until that great Peacemaker (who he had prophesied would be born in Judah's family), our Saviour Jesus Himself, comes again on the clouds with a great shout of the trumpet. For then the bodies of all those who trusted in Him will be caught up to meet Him in the air.

When they had all come back to Egypt, Joseph's brothers were afraid. "Perhaps," they said to each other, "Joseph has just been waiting until our father is dead to pay us back for what we did to him. Perhaps he really hates us." They sent a messenger to Joseph. "While our father was still alive," they said, "he commanded us to ask you for forgiveness. Now, we beg of you, forgive our wicked deeds. We, too, are servants of the God of our father, Jacob." Close behind the messenger came the brothers themselves. They fell on their faces before Joseph. "Behold," they said, "we will be your servants."

Tears came to Joseph's eyes. He loved his brothers. Nothing had been further from his mind than to seek revenge. "Do not be afraid," he said to them. "Am I in the place of God? As for you, you meant evil against me, but God meant it for good, to save the lives of many people. I will surely take care of you and your little ones." With words like these he comforted them.

So Joseph and his brothers lived together in Egypt in peace. Joseph saw his grandchildren and his great-grandchildren growing up around him. He was not a wanderer, as his father had been, but he was a stranger just the same — as every Christian must be in this world. For we must all look for that better country, where we, too, shall see His face.

For every man there is a time to die. Joseph's time came when he was one hundred and ten years old. Like his father Jacob, he was ready and glad to go. But he thought less of himself than of his brothers whom he was leaving behind. "I die," Joseph said to them, "but God will surely remember you, and bring you from this land back to the land He promised to Abraham and Isaac and Jacob. You must not bury me here in Egypt. When God brings you back to the Promised Land, you must carry my bones back with you." And so he died, and his body also was embalmed, and was placed in a coffin, as was the custom in Egypt, to wait for the fulfillment of God's promise.

And was that promise fulfilled? Yes, you can be as sure as Joseph was, that God will fulfill His promises. Our fathers, our mothers, our teachers, our friends — one by one they all end their wanderings, and return to God, their Maker. Some day you and I too will pass through that gate which leads to heaven. But our God remains the same, yesterday, today, and forever. There is no end to His faithfulness. Three hundred and fifty years after Joseph died, God brought His people out of Egypt with a mighty deliverance, and an outstretched arm. And his descendants did not forget the promise made to Joseph. They carried his body back with them to Canaan.

30

The Trailblazer

Last summer we visited the Cumberland Gap. We stood high up in the narrow mountain pass where Daniel Boone stood when he first saw what no white man had ever seen before — the rolling plains of Kentucky reaching as far west as the eye could see. Today a good road runs through this pass. But when Boone discovered this way through the mountains, there was only a faint trace in the darkness of the forest — here a crushed leaf, there a bent twig, to show that moccasined feet had once passed this way. Daniel Boone suffered great danger, he suffered hardship, he was even a slave among the Indians for some years, in order to find the path to Kentucky. And after he had found it, he came back to Virginia to lead the first pioneer families through the mountains. He was a trailblazer — a man who maps out the way, no matter how much it costs him, who maps it out not for himself, but for others who are to follow.

Joseph was a trailblazer too, though he did not understand this till afterwards. "God sent me ahead," he said to his brothers, "to save your lives." And he himself was as much amazed at the wonderful planning of God as his brothers were. Every man's life is precious, but the lives of those twelve sons of Jacob were doubly precious. From one of them was to come the Saviour who would save you and me from our sins. Joseph was sent ahead not only to save the lives of his brothers, but also to save for all the children of God the precious, life-giving promises. When Joseph suffered all those years as a slave, and later in the dungeon, he was blazing a trail where you and I could follow in joy and comfort, a path we could follow that would lead to life itself.

You and I are not hemmed in by mountains, as were those pioneers Daniel Boone led to Kentucky. Or are we? Do we have mountains we cannot climb over by ourselves? Mountains that shut us off from our true home? You and I are not going hungry to bed, as did Joseph's brothers. Or are we? Are we, too, starving for the true bread, the bread which, when a man eats it, he is never hungry again? Do we need a trailblazer who can lead us out of the wilderness where we are lost?

Perhaps you remember that when Adam and Eve left the garden, God set a cherubim with a flaming sword to close the way back to the place where God and man had walked together. And yet that place was our home. It was the only place where we could ever really be happy. Is there no way back to the garden? Is there no one who can find the lost trail? Open the locked gate? Turn aside that flaming sword that bars our way? Is there no trailblazer for you and me?

You know the answer as well as I do. There is only one Person in all the world who can find the way back to that beautiful garden for us. That person is our Saviour, Jesus. That is why He was born as a baby on Christmas Day. That is why He, like Abraham and Isaac and Jacob, was a homeless wanderer while here on earth. "For," He said, "the foxes have holes, and the birds of the air have nests, but I have not even a place to lay my head at night." (Do you remember how Jacob once laid his head on a stone for a pillow?) That is why, like Joseph, He who had done no wrong, suffered for the sake of those who mocked and hated Him. That is why, like Joseph, He asked God to forgive those who had wronged Him.

I do not mean that Jesus walked in the footsteps of Abraham, and Jacob, and Joseph. It is the other way around. Abraham, and Isaac, and Jacob, and Joseph were faint figures, seen beforehand by God's Old Testament people, of our Saviour. They were signposts pointing to the Son of God, who was going to die on Good Friday, and rise from the dead on that happiest day of all the year that we celebrate as Easter. "I am the Way," He said, and never were truer words spoken. For He gave His very life to blaze a new trail from this lost world back to the friendship of God Himself. A way back for Abraham and Jacob and Joseph. A way back for you and me, and for all who put their trust in Him.

In a sense you might say that Jesus' work was finished on that first Easter morning. He had opened the way, and now you and I must walk in it. But in another, truer sense, this is not the way it is at all. For Jesus never leaves us to walk in this path alone. Even now He is sitting at the right hand of His Father, ruling the whole world. The lives, the hearts, the decisions of all men lie in His mighty, controlling hands. He is weaving, as it were, a great tapestry, and He is working all men, good and bad, into the pattern — just as, so long ago, He wove Joseph and his brothers into His tapestry. The picture He is weaving is the glory of our God.

But he is not so busy with these great plans that He forgets about you and me. He watches over each of His children day and night. "And lo, I am with you always," He has promised. He knows us better than we know ourselves. He knows even the secret, sinful thoughts and wishes we would be ashamed to speak aloud. He plans our lives day by day. And when we sin, He wrestles with us, as He wrestled with Jacob. He prays for us too, and His prayers are always answered. And He is expecting us to join Him there in that blessed world. Some day He is coming again to lead us over the mountains, along the path He has blazed, back to that wonderful garden, where we shall be like Him, for we shall see Him as He is.

III
THE TENT OF GOD

I have not dwelt in a house since the day that I brought up the children of Israel out of Egypt, even to this day, but have walked in a tent (II Samuel 7:6).

31

In the Hands of God

Exodus 2

*T*hat morning I was baby-sitting. My little brother was only three, and if he was not watched he ran into the street. I was trying to make myself a doll. I had an onion for a head, and a few bits of sheep's wool for hair. I made a body out of wheat stalks and wrapped a piece of cloth around her for a dress. I was rocking my baby in my arms when Mother came back, carrying the water she had brought from the well.

She smiled when she saw the doll, and came and sat down beside me. "Can you keep a secret, Miriam?" she asked. "Of course, Mother. I am a big girl now. I am almost twelve." "Something wonderful is going to happen," Mother said. "God is going to send us another baby."

"A real live baby? Oh, Mother!" And then an awful thought came to me. My little brother Aaron was the youngest boy in all our village. Since he had been born, the Egyptian king had made a law that all our baby boys must be drowned. My father said it was because God had blessed His people with so many sons that the Egyptians were afraid of us. For they saw that soon there would be more of us than there were of them. I remembered the cries of other mothers on our street when their babies were torn from their arms. My throat grew dry. I couldn't seem to speak.

"What if it is a boy?" I whispered. "We are all in God's hands, Miriam," Mother said. "Never forget that God is stronger than the

107

Egyptians. Tonight, when you say your prayers, pray to God for the new baby too."

That was a busy time. There were little dresses to sew, and a cradle to be woven out of the wide strong grass which grows by the riverside. Every night after supper Father and Mother would kneel down to pray. Once I woke up in the middle of the night, and Mother was still kneeling in the corner. "Why do you pray so long, Mother?" I asked her the next morning. "I am praying for the baby," she said. "Did you pray for me, too, before I was born?" I asked. "Of course, Miriam. You were my first baby. And I still pray for you every night."

One morning I woke up, and Father was getting the breakfast. Mother was still lying on the bed. "Come here, Miriam," she said softly. "I have something to show you." And there was a tiny real live baby boy, with a funny wrinkled nose, and a tuft of black hair on the top of his head. "Oh, Mother," I said, "he is beautiful."

Mother let me help care for the baby. It was especially my job to watch by the door. If an Egyptian soldier came down the street, and baby brother was awake, I would play one of my singing, jumping games. As the baby grew bigger and stronger, it was harder and harder to sing loud enough to drown out his cries. One day we had a narrow escape. An Egyptian officer passed the house just as the baby started to cry. I sang as loud as I could, but he stopped and seemed to listen. "Mother!" I whispered under my breath, without stopping my game. Mother picked up little Aaron, and spanked him hard. He ran out of the door howling. The Egyptian put his hands over his ears and went on.

"This cannot go on," Mother said. "Something will have to be done!" That afternoon, while the baby was asleep, she went to the river and brought home an armful of reeds. She started to weave a new, bigger cradle. But when she took down the jar of tar and smeared the bottom, I began to cry. "Mother! What are you doing? He is my brother!" "He was God's baby before he was ours," Mother said. Her eyes were crying, but her voice was quiet. "God loves him even more than we do. We must not be afraid to trust him to God's care."

That night my mother and my father knelt a long time praying. The next morning, while it was still dark, Father took the baby in his arms and kissed him. "God take care of you, my little son!" he said. Then he was gone. Mother bathed the baby, and dressed him in his best dress. Then she fed him, and laid him in the new basket cradle. "You and Aaron come along," she said, picking up the basket. She carefully set the basket in the water at the river's edge. "You stay here and watch, Miriam," she told me. Then she took little Aaron's hand and went home, not looking back.

At first I shivered as I sat there. Then the sun came up and warmed me. Soon I heard voices. It was the princess coming with her women to bathe. She often came here. I hid in the weeds. The princess saw the basket floating in the water. "Fetch me that," she said to one of her women. The girl waded into the river and lifted out the basket. When they opened the top, the sun woke my baby brother up, and he began to cry. I held my breath. But when she saw his little wrinkled nose, and the funny tuft of hair on the top of his head, the princess laughed. "It is one of the Hebrew children," she said. "I will adopt him. He shall be my son."

I came a little closer. "Shall I call someone to take care of him for you?" I asked. "Yes, go and do that," the princess said. So I ran as fast as I could and called my mother. When my mother came, the princess said, "Take care of this baby for me, and I will pay you for it." So we took my baby brother home again. That night I am sure there was not a happier family anywhere in the whole world. After supper we all knelt together to thank God for His love and care. And now I understood what my mother had said: "We are all of us in God's hands."

32

A Letter from a Mother

Exodus 2

I *My dear friends,* hope you do not mind that I call you my friends. For though we live almost halfway round the world from one another, and though we are separated by more than three thousand years, yet we *are* friends. For we love and serve the same God. He is the only God there is. And He is altogether worthy of your trust. This is really what I want to speak to you about.

I suppose there are times in everybody's life when the future seems dark and threatening; when you begin to wonder whether God does hear your prayers, or whether He has perhaps forgotten you. The story I want to tell you is about such a time in our family.

The days in which God set our lives were not easy days. The very blessings God had showered upon us made us hated and feared by the Egyptians. Please do not think that I am complaining about this. Though we were slaves of the Egyptian king, though my husband had to work long hours at back-breaking work, and was often severely beaten, though our lives even were in danger — yet through all these troubles God had been good to us. In our poor home there was love aplenty. We had two fine children — a daughter Miriam nearly twelve years old, and a son Aaron almost two. Best of all we had the precious promises of God to keep up our courage whatever happened. And it is easier to remember the promises of God when you are in bad trouble than when everything goes smoothly. This is one of the things we learned.

And then God sent us another son, and this is what frightened us. How, you ask, can a beautiful baby boy frighten his parents? Let me explain it to you. By this time there were so many of us Israelites in Egypt that the Egyptian king, whom they call Pharaoh, was alarmed. "Soon," he said, "there will be more of them than there are of us. Then they will take over our country." Pharaoh called his soldiers. "Every baby boy born to the Israelites," he said, "must be thrown into the river to drown. Only the baby girls can be allowed to grow up."

You can see why we were troubled. I held my precious new son close in my arms. He was a gift from God. Surely God did not want us to let him be drowned! This was the one thing we could be sure of. All of the rest we must trust to God. And so we hid our baby. He was a good child, healthy and easily contented. At first it was not hard to keep him quiet. Miriam, and even little Aaron, helped. Can you imagine, my friends, how many anguished prayers went up to God that He would help us? That He would show us what He wanted us to do? If you have ever been in bad trouble yourself, perhaps you can imagine.

As the baby grew bigger and stronger, it grew harder to keep him hidden. We had several close escapes. And then I had an idea. Though I did not know it then, I understand now that it was God Himself, answering our prayers, who gave me this idea. I went to the river's edge and gathered an armful of papyrus reeds. I wove them into a little basket. I daubed the basket with pitch so that it would not leak. I bathed the baby, and fed him, and dressed him in clean clothes. Then I laid him in the basket. He quickly fell asleep. I carried the basket to the river's edge and set it in the water among the reeds along the shore. I left Miriam there to watch it. I took little Aaron's hand and went home to pray. I did not dare to look behind me for fear I should lose my courage.

Miriam stayed a little while, hiding in the reeds. The baby slept quietly, floating in the basket. Suddenly there was a commotion. The princess, Pharaoh's daughter, had come to bathe in the river. She saw the little basket, and said to her servants, "Whatever is that in the river? Go and get it for me!" A servant girl brought the basket, and just then the baby woke up. He began to cry. When Pharaoh's daughter saw our beautiful baby boy, she pitied him. She said, "This must be one of the Israelite babies." Just then Miriam came out of the reeds. "Shall I run and find a nurse to take care of the baby for you?" she asked. The princess said, "Go!" So Miriam ran home and called me. The princess said to me, "Take this child and look after him for me. I will pay you wages. When he is old enough to leave home, bring him to me at the palace. I am going to adopt him."

What a happy family ours was that night! How we all of us together thanked God for answering our prayers, and promised always to remember His faithful love!

The princess called the baby *Moses,* because she had found him in the river. For more than three years we were allowed to care for our precious little son. We taught him everything we could about the only true God. And then we took him to the palace to live with the princess. It was hard to leave him there, but we were not afraid. For we had seen with our own eyes how wonderfully God cares for those who put their trust in Him.

It was not till much later that we found out *why* God wanted our baby to grow up in Pharaoh's palace, where he could learn all the wisdom of the Egyptians. There was a reason, but we did not understand that then. We just had to trust in God.

What I wanted to tell you, my friends, is that God is all-powerful. No king, however mighty, can prevent His plan. And God is absolutely trustworthy. No matter how dark your future may seem, God is caring for you. You can trust yourself, and all your loved ones, to His marvelous care.

Your friend, Jochebed
Mother of Moses

33
More Than All the Treasures of Egypt

Exodus 2

have you ever wondered what it would be like to grow up as a prince, or princess, in a king's palace? Moses had fine linen clothes to wear, and toys to play with such as ordinary children only dream of. He had golden necklaces and rings, and slaves without number to wait on him. Not that his life was all pleasure. He had to study hard and long — for kings' sons must know more than ordinary folk. Egypt in those days was a great center of learning. Moses studied history and geography, astronomy and mathematics, and law. He took his turn at military service also, and learned how to be an effective army officer. It was important that he know how to lead and command an expedition. It was important that he know history and geography and law. It was important that he be well read, and a skillful writer. Not that he ever, in his wildest imagination, guessed why he needed all this learning, all these skills. His future, like yours and mine, was hidden in the secret counsel of God.

And when his education was completed, he had his own suite of beautifully furnished rooms in the palace, and his own servants to wait on him. He had his own horse and chariot, to go wherever he wished. He ate at Pharaoh's table, and if there was any food he longed for, he had only to speak, and no expense was spared to get it for him. What more could any young prince possibly ask for?

And yet there was something more that Prince Moses wanted, something his mother, the princess who had adopted him, could not buy for him. Moses was homesick. When he lay on his silk-cushioned bed at night, he remembered the dark, cramped hut where his real father and mother and brother and sister still lived. When he sat down to Pharaoh's banquet, with the soft-spoken slaves stepping all around him, and the sweet music sounding in his ears, he remembered what his mother had told him about the God of his fathers, about His never-failing promises, about the Saviour who was to come some day. Yes, there was something Moses wanted more than all the treasures of Egypt. Moses, strange to say, would rather have been a slave among his own people, God's people, than a prince in Pharaoh's palace.

One day, as he was wandering unhappily about the city, he came upon one of Pharaoh's many building projects. A long line of ragged slaves, Hebrew slaves, Moses' own kinfolk, were at work on the building, stooped beneath their heavy loads of bricks. As the young prince came around the corner of the building, he heard the whistle of the Egyptian overseer's whip, and one of the slaves stumbled and fell bleeding to the ground. A great surge of righteous anger swelled up in Moses' heart. He looked hastily up and down the street. There was no one coming. With one blow of his bare fists he killed the overseer. Hastily he hid the body beneath a pile of sand.

The next day he came back to the same spot. Two of the Hebrew slaves were quarreling together. "Perhaps," Moses thought to himself, "this is why I was adopted by Pharaoh's daughter, so that now I can be of help to my people." And he said to the quarreling slaves, "Why do you fight each other? We are all brothers, and must stick together." The men looked scornfully at his fine clothes. "Brothers?" they said.

"What a joke that is! Who asked you to interfere, anyway? Are you going to kill us, as you killed the Egyptian?"

Then Moses was afraid. Someone *had* seen him the day before! He hurried back to the palace. He collected together a few clothes. He did not dare to light a lamp in his room for fear someone would notice he was at home. He sat alone in the dark till very late, till all the guests at Pharaoh's banquet had gone home, and the palace was at last asleep. Then, hesitating at every sound, he crept through the deserted corridors and out of the little secret side gate he had used as a boy. By morning, when Pharaoh heard about the murdered Egyptian guard, Moses was already far away.

He traveled eastward towards the desert. As evening came on he found a well, and sat down wearily by its side. He felt deeply discouraged. He had wanted to do something to help his own people. But he had been a failure, and now he was running away himself. After a while he saw a large flock of sheep being driven to the well by seven girls, all sisters, daughters of one man, Jethro. The shepherdesses drew up bucket after bucket of water for their sheep until the watering troughs were full. Just then another flock of sheep arrived. The young men who herded them whooped with laughter when they saw the watering troughs filled with water. "How nice of you girls to draw water for *our* sheep!" one of them said. And then they drove away the young girls and their sheep, and led their own sheep to the watering troughs. Moses got up angrily. He drove away the boys. He helped the girls to water their sheep.

When the girls came home that night their father, Jethro, said, "How does it happen you are home so early today?" And one of them said, "There was an Egyptian at the well. He protected us from the shepherds, and helped us draw water for the sheep." "Where is he?" Jethro asked. "Why didn't you bring him along with you, so that he can have supper with us? Go and get him right away."

That night Moses had supper with Jethro and his family. Jethro liked Moses, and Moses liked Jethro. He stayed on, learning to care for the sheep. After a while he married one of Jethro's daughters. A little son was born to them. Many years passed. Though he never guessed it, Moses' education was continuing here in the lonely pasture lands. He learned to look out for himself, to sleep beneath the stars with only a stone for a pillow. He learned to be content with simple food, and to work hard till his soft hands grew strong and calloused. But most of all, as he wandered alone about the hillsides with his father-in-law's sheep, he thought about the God of his fathers, about the promises He had made to Abraham and Isaac and Jacob. And he thought about his own people who were slaves in Egypt. Often, late at night, he prayed to God for their deliverance.

God heard his prayers. He saw the sufferings of His people in Egypt. He remembered what He had promised to Abraham and Isaac and Jacob.

34
The Reluctant Messenger

Exodus 3, 4

The valley was narrow at this point, and the rocky walls rose steeply on either side. But the shepherd did not notice the wild beauty of the scene. He had eyes only for the safety of his flock. As he walked ahead of them, he looked to the right and to the left, watching for any telltale signs of bears, or perhaps even of lions. He was especially concerned for the newborn lambs and their mothers, who often lagged behind the other sheep. He had come through this pass many times during the nearly forty years he had looked after his father-in-law's sheep. He knew every spring of water, every place where there was pasture, every cave where outlaws or wild animals might be hidden.

Suddenly the rock walls fell away, and the valley broadened out into the plain. The sheep spread out around him to feed. The shepherd sat down. He said a little prayer of thanks to the God of his fathers for one more safe journey, and then he took out his lunch of bread and cheese. The air shimmered in the heat. On the further side of the rock-strewn ground, where the red Sinai mountains stood up abruptly from the flat land, a thin wisp of smoke rose into the air. A dry bush, no doubt, which had burst into flame from the glare of the sun. He had seen such things before.

As he sat there, his thoughts drifted back to the time so long ago when he had lived in Egypt. He was not sorry to have left the luxury of the palace behind. He was happy here. God had given him a wife and two fine sons. But it was his brothers left behind in slavery that troubled him. He remembered their bent backs, their hopeless groans, the sharp crack of the overseer's whip. He put his hand over his eyes and prayed again. "O God," he prayed, "remember Your promise to Abraham and Isaac and Jacob. Have mercy on Your suffering people, and rescue them." He made one last check of the sheep, and then he lay down to rest in the shade of a little clump of bushes. He had been up that morning at dawn, and had walked many miles since. He was very tired. In a moment he was asleep.

He awoke suddenly a little later. It was almost as if someone had called his name, though there was no sound except the buzzing of the bees in the bushes. The sheep were feeding quietly. He stood there a moment, slightly puzzled, and then he noticed the smoke in the distance. There was a thick column now, and he could see bright flames even at this distance. "If it was just a bush, it would have burned up long ago," he said to himself. "I will go and see what it is."

He fastened his sandals, tightened his belt, and set out across the shimmering fields. The sheep raised their heads to watch him as he went, but he did not call them, and they did not try to follow. The flames grew brighter as he came nearer. Suddenly a voice spoke to him from the middle of the flames. "Moses! Moses!" the voice said. He stopped dead in his tracks. "Here I am," he faltered. "Do not come any nearer," the voice said. "Take off your shoes. You are standing on holy ground." Hastily Moses took off his shoes.

"I am the God of your fathers," the voice said, "the God of Abraham, of Isaac, and of Jacob." Moses hid his face in his hands. He was afraid to look at God. "I have surely seen the trouble of My people," God said. "I have heard their groans, and I know all about their sorrow. I have come down to rescue them from the Egyptians, to bring them to a land flowing with milk and honey. Come now, I am going to send you to Pharaoh, to bring My people out of Egypt."

It was what Moses had prayed for all these forty years since he had left Egypt. God was answering his prayer. Did he bow his head in thankfulness? No, no! Instead he said, "Not me, Lord! Send someone else! I could never do it!"

Lord, save the people in Africa, but don't send me! Be kind to the friendless boy or girl in my class at school, but don't expect me to invite him over. The other boys and girls would laugh at me. Comfort the boy who has lost his father, the girl whose mother has died, but don't ask me to visit them! I wouldn't know what to say. Thy will be done on earth by someone else, or maybe by a miracle from heaven. But I am not ready, not qualified, not willing to be a part of Your plan, I am not content to accept the part You have chosen for me to do.

Does God answer such prayers? Yes, He answers them. But he does not accept our excuses and conditions. He brushes all these to one side. He sends us where He wants us to go, and then He supplies whatever it is we need to do His work.

"Who am I," Moses said, "that I should go to Pharaoh, and should bring the children of Israel out of Egypt?" Then God answered, "I will certainly go with you. And I give you this sign: when you have rescued them, you shall all of you together worship God in this very mountain here."

Moses said, "When I come to the Israelites, and say 'God has sent me to you,' they will say, 'What is His name? How can we know what god you are talking about?' What shall I tell them?" God said, "Tell them this: 'The Lord God of your fathers, the God of Abraham, Isaac, and Jacob, has sent me.' For this is My name forever. I know that the king of Egypt will not let you go. But I will stretch forth My hands, and perform wonders. And after Pharaoh has seen that, then he will let you go."

"O Lord," Moses said, "I am not eloquent, not up till now, nor even since You have spoken to me. I am slow of speech and slow of tongue." But God answered, "Who made man's mouth? Who makes a man dumb, or deaf, or seeing, or blind? Is it not I, the Lord? Now, therefore, go, and I will be with your mouth, and teach you what you should say." But Moses still objected, "Oh, Lord, I beg You, send someone else."

God was angry with Moses' excuses. But though He was angry, and though Moses thought of one excuse after another, God did not release him. "Your brother Aaron," God said, "is even now on his way to meet you. He can speak for you, since you say you cannot speak. Go now, and carry My message to Pharaoh!"

And Moses went. He took the sheep back home. He picked up his wife and his two sons. He set out for Egypt. Along the way he met Aaron. Aaron ran to his brother and kissed him. Together they set out to do God's work — in their own weakness, but in God's strength.

35
Who Is God?

Exodus 5, 7-11

Who is God? And why should I listen to Him? I don't know your God. And I won't do what He says!" These scornful words were Pharaoh's answer when Moses appeared before him to ask that he free the Israelites.

I don't know if you have ever in your secret heart asked this question: "Who is God? Why should I do what He asks?" But if you have — if you don't know who God is and if you are not yet ready to answer when He calls — then it will be worth a few minutes of your time to find out how God answered these questions. For God did answer Pharaoh. Not in words, but in actions which speak louder than words. For the language Pharaoh understood best — perhaps the only language he understood — was the language of power. And so God spoke to him in this language. But Pharaoh would not listen. And in the end this cost him his life.

And if, instead, you have known about God as far back as you can remember, then you, too, ought to listen. For God's words, God's acts, had a double meaning. They said one thing to Pharaoh, and another quite different thing to God's people.

There were two men working together in the corner of the building. When the Egyptian overseer was near, they tended strictly to business. When he was at the other end of the project, they could talk if they wanted to. Mostly they were too tired, too sunk in despair, to bother.

But today there was an undercurrent of excitement on the whole construction project. "They say," Shimei said, "that Moses spoke right up to Pharaoh, that he told him he *must* let us go." His companion laughed bitterly. "And who would do the dirty work of Egypt if Pharaoh let the slaves go free?" he asked. "This Moses of yours is a dreamer. His head has been touched by the desert sun."

"They say," Shimei insisted, "that the God of our father Abraham appeared to him out of a bush that was on fire, and that God promised to *make* Pharaoh let us go." "You are a fool, Shimei," his companion said. "It is four hundred years since the God of Abraham has spoken to anyone. For all we know He may be dead." Shimei turned pale at these mocking words. "Don't say such things!" he begged. "Remember the promises He gave to our fathers. We must believe, and we must pray." "The men to whom those promises were given are long since dead," his companion said. "On my way home tonight I will offer a sacrifice to one of the Egyptian gods. Perhaps *he* can make Pharaoh treat us better."

Just then the voice of the court crier sounded in the street: "Bow the knee! Bow the knee!" The men dropped their tools and fell on their faces. It was Pharaoh on his way to bathe in the River Nile. The little procession wound through the city streets and stopped among the reeds at the river's bank. Suddenly a tall, bearded man stepped out of the reeds and spoke sternly to Pharaoh:

"The Lord God commands, 'Let my people go!' You say you do not know God. You shall know who He is by this sign." The tall man stretched out his rod, and at that very moment the water of the sacred river, the Nile, which the Egyptians worshiped as the source of life and fruitfulness, turned to stinking blood, and the whole river was filled with dying fish. There was no refreshing bath for Pharaoh that morning. Pharaoh was grateful to have just a little clean water for a drink. It was seven days before the river flowed fresh and clear again. But Pharaoh would not listen; he would not let the people go.

The next week Moses appeared to Pharaoh again, this time in the king's palace. "Thus says the Lord, 'If you do not let My people go, I will fill your land with frogs.' " Then Moses stretched out his arm, and a great, endless stream of slimy frogs crawled croaking out of the river and spread over the whole land. Early the next morning Pharaoh sent for Moses. "Pray to your God," he said, "to take away these frogs, and I will let the people go." Moses said, "Name the time when you want the frogs to leave your houses and return to the river." Pharaoh said, "Tomorrow!" "As you say," Moses replied. "For by this sign you will know there is no god like the Lord God." So Moses prayed, and God took away the frogs. But when Pharaoh saw that the frogs were gone, he refused to listen.

God spoke to Pharaoh again. He turned the dust of the ground into lice, so that every man, and even every animal, in all the country of Egypt crawled with tiny, biting, itching lice. The magicians who lived in Pharaoh's court said to him, "This is done by the very finger of God!" *They* heard the God of heaven and earth speaking, but Pharaoh would not listen. Once more Moses met Pharaoh on the river bank. "Thus says the Lord, 'Let My people go, or I will fill your land with swarms of flies, but there will be no flies where My people live, so that you may know and understand that I am the Lord of all the earth.'" And the whole land of Egypt swarmed with flies. Hurriedly Pharaoh sent for Moses. "Pray your God to take away the flies," he said. "I will pray to God," Moses said, "but you must not try to trick us again." So Moses prayed, and God took away the flies. But when the flies were gone, Pharaoh would not let the people go.

What more could God say to Pharaoh to awaken him from his blindness and his deafness? God sent sickness to the Egyptian cattle, such terrible sickness that they died. Pharaoh would not listen. God sent boils to the Egyptian people, great, painful, throbbing sores. He sent hail, and terrible lightning, and thunder, such as no man had ever seen before. He sent locusts that ate every green leaf and filled the houses of the Egyptians. He sent thick darkness, darkness so thick that no man could leave his house for three days and three nights. "All these," God said to Pharaoh in actions that could not be mistaken, "are in My almighty power. I have only to speak, and the forces of nature, the animals, the weather, even sickness and health, respond to My word."

The Egyptian magicians trembled as they watched the power of God. "If you do not listen," they said to Pharaoh, "all Egypt will be destroyed." But Pharaoh would not listen. He stopped up his ears. He hardened his heart. "Get out of my sight," he said to Moses. "If you dare to appear here again, you shall die for it!" And Moses said, "You are quite right. You will not see me again."

And God's people — where were they all this time? They, too, had heard God speaking, but they had not heard what Pharaoh heard. There had been no flies, no sickness, no hail, no thick darkness in the Israelite homes. They had heard the voice of a loving God, one who uses His mighty power to protect His children, a God who cares for all who trust in Him, as a Father cares for his little ones.

You and I, too, are slaves, just as surely as the Israelites in Egypt. We are slaves to our own sinful hearts; we are bent down beneath the burden of our own wicked desires. Only God can free us. He alone can break the chains that bind us. Only Jesus our Saviour can pay the terrible, hopeless debt we owe. But if we trust ourselves to Him, then He Himself will bind up our broken hearts, will open the prison gates and set us free. Then we, too, shall know, as those Israelites so long ago, who the God of heaven and earth is.

36
God Accepts a Substitute

Exodus 12

Did God have something more to say to Pharaoh? Yes, He had a last message, but it was a message of judgment, such as comes at last to all men who refuse to listen to God. And in a sense you might say it was a message to us too. There is a time when God invites, when He calls, when He freely offers us salvation. But if you will not listen, if you turn your back on God, if you shout loudly to drown out His voice, then there surely comes a day when you find your ears have grown deaf, so that you no longer hear His blessed voice; when your eyes have been darkened, so that you no longer see those arms extended in invitation.

But first, before the terrible judgment which Pharaoh had brought on himself, God spoke to His people. Moses called all the Israelites together. "Every family must sacrifice a lamb," he said. "After you have sacrificed the lamb, take some twigs, and paint the blood on the outside of your doors. Then roast the lamb, and eat it that same night. Eat it standing up, all dressed for a journey. For tonight God Himself is going to pass all through the land of Egypt. When He sees the blood on your doorway, He will not allow the destroyer to come in.

"From now on every year is to start with this day. This is to be your New Year's Day celebration. You shall celebrate it as a feast to God, you and your children forever. This is the Lord's Passover. For on this day the Lord will bring you out of Egypt with a mighty arm and an outstretched hand."

The children of Israel did not understand what Moses was talking about. They were still slaves. Nothing seemed less likely than that Pharaoh would let them go. And what good would the blood of a sacrificed lamb painted on their doors do them? And who was this destroyer Moses talked about? And what a strange name for a holiday — the Lord's Passover!

But though they did not understand, they listened, they obeyed. They had seen the wonders God had done, and they had recognized His voice speaking to them. Each family sacrificed a lamb. They brushed the blood on the fronts of their houses. Then they roasted the lamb, and the whole family ate it, standing up around the table, dressed as if ready to set out on a journey. While the Israelites ate the lamb they had sacrificed, and the Egyptians slept, undreaming, in their beds, God Himself went up and down the streets of Egypt. And as He passed, the destroying angel entered into every house, and in every house he entered, the oldest child died, from the son of Pharaoh who sat on the throne to the son of the prisoner who lay chained in the dungeon. Pharaoh got up in the middle of the night. Everybody in Egypt got up. A great cry of anguish echoed from one end of the country to the other, for in every house there was one dead person. Every house except those where the doorway was marked with blood. Those blood-stained houses God had passed over.

Pharaoh sent for Moses. "Get out from among my people!" he cried, "you and all your people! Take your cattle, and all your possessions, and be gone, before we are all dead men!" And the Egyptian people streamed out of their houses, offering the Israelites gold and silver jewelry and fine clothing — anything to hurry them on their way. And so the people left Egypt. They left in such a hurry that the bread dough the women had mixed did not have time to rise. They had to carry it with them in pans, to bake along the way. Ever after this they ate bread without yeast in it when they celebrated their New Year's feast, God's Passover, to remember how they had had to leave Egypt in the middle of the night.

They had lived in Egypt more than four hundred years. Now again they resumed their pilgrim journey, as their father Abraham had so long ago. But they did not travel alone. God Himself went with them. He led them with a fiery pillar at night, and with a pillar of cloud in the day. Day or night the Israelites had only to raise their eyes, and they could see the visible sign that the living God journeyed with them. If you have ever set up your tent in the woods, where there is no electric power to light the campground, you know what darkness really is. You light a lantern and set it on the table, and it spreads a tiny circle of light around your tent. But if you leave that circle, to go to the shelter house or the beach, it is so dark that you cannot see one step ahead of yourself, you cannot even see your hand in front of your face. It was never dark like that in the Israelite camp. For God, who traveled with them, lighted up the entire camp with the brightness of His presence.

Do you wonder why God passed over the houses where He saw the blood painted on the doorway? Was it because the people who lived in those houses were better people than the Egyptians who died? No, that was not it. The Israelites, like the Egyptians, were sinners. And the person that sins must die. There is only one exception. And that is if someone else dies in the sinner's place. What God was telling the Israelites that night, what He is even now telling you and me, is that God is willing to accept a substitute. God passed over the houses with the blood on the doorway because a lamb had died in those houses instead of a sinful man. Not any lamb, but a special lamb, the Lamb of God. That little lamb sacrificed by each family so long ago on that dark night in Egypt was a sign that pointed forward to our Saviour, Jesus, who was going to die long afterwards for the sins of the Israelites, for my sins and yours, for the sins of everyone who trusts in Him. Pharaoh heard the voice of God, but he refused to listen and to believe. God's people heard God's voice, and they believed, and obeyed. For there is no other way given under heaven by which a man may be saved from that death we all so richly deserve.

37

Through the Deep Waters

Exodus 14, 15

Freedom often has a disappointing taste. The man in prison pins all his hopes on the day of his release. But when the prison gate clangs shut behind him, and he is once again free, does he find his life suddenly pleasant, easy, filled with joy? Nations that have longed for independence experience, too, that freedom only brings new problems. They find they now have less to eat, not more; they have riots, instead of order; a native dictator takes the place of a foreign master. Perhaps you yourself have discovered something like this. The first few days of your vacation are sheer delight. But soon the long, empty days grow dull, instead of exciting. By the end of summer you are quite ready to go back to school.

For the Israelites, too, freedom had a bitter taste. They had been slaves for longer than any one of them could remember. They had hardly dared to hope for freedom. And now, wonder of wonders, God had stretched out His mighty arm. He had forced Pharaoh to let God's people go. The Egyptian people had loaded them with gifts. The whole world lay before them. Their troubles were over. So they supposed.

But they were wrong, dead wrong. And if you think your life will become simple and easy if you just become a Christian, then you are dead wrong too. God has never promised an easy life to any of His children. He has promised to watch over us and take care of us. But there is no such thing as a vacation for a Christian — not this side of heaven. Your education goes on as long as you live. God teaches you, and then He tests to see if you have learned. And if you fail this examination, you get a second chance. Patiently God teaches again, and tests again. And a third chance, and even a fourth chance. But not, of course, forever. There is an end to the patience even of God. There comes a time when He says at last, "It is enough. They refuse to learn." And then the day of opportunity is gone forever, and the dreadful day of judgment has arrived.

Each of us has to learn this by experience — just as the Israelites did. The shortest road to the land God had promised His people ran north and east along the seacoast. This was the road Jacob and his sons had taken when they came to Egypt so long before. But now there lived along this road a fierce, warlike people, the Philistines. So God led the people south instead. After two days' travel, they camped on the shore of the Red Sea. There was wild desert and high mountains to the south of them, and in front of them the breaking waves.

Back in Egypt Pharaoh and his people had begun to recover from the terror of the Passover night. At first they had been so overcome with grief because of the dead children, that they had no thought but to get rid of the Israelites at once. But now they looked around them. They saw all the back-breaking work to be done, and no slaves left to do it. "What have we done?" Pharaoh said to his noblemen. "We have let our slaves escape!" Pharaoh took six hundred chariots, his best horsemen, and all his army, and he hurried after the fleeing Israelites. Late at night he found them camped on the shores of the Red Sea.

The Israelites were trapped between the mountains and the sea and the Egyptian army. God had deliberately led them into this trap, to test whether or not they had learned to trust in Him. They were terrified when they saw the Egyptian army rushing down upon them. "Were there no graves in Egypt," they said to Moses, "that you have brought us out to die here in this desert?" But Moses said to them, "Do not be afraid! This is the last time that you will ever see the cruel Egyptians." Even as he spoke, the pillar of cloud which had been leading the people moved from in front of the camp, and came and stood behind the camp instead, between the Egyptians and the people of God. It gave light to the Israelites, but only thick darkness to the Egyptians. It was God Himself standing between His people and their enemies!

Moses lifted up his arm, and God sent a strong wind which drove the water of the sea back. "Tell the people to go forward," God said. So the Israelites stepped forward into what had been, just a minute before, the wild waves of the sea. Only now the water stood up as a wall on either side of them, and they walked across the sea on dry ground.

It took many hours for so many people to cross to the further side. Towards early morning the Egyptians noticed what had happened. They, too, stepped into the dry path between the walls of water. They drove their chariots right into the middle of the sea. When the last of the Israelites had reached the shore, God said to Moses, "Reach out your arm again." Moses stretched out his arm, and the wild waves swept back into their place. Pharaoh and the whole Egyptian army disappeared beneath the stormy water forever.

As it began to grow light, and the Israelites, now safe on the further side, saw what God had done, they were overcome with wonder, with gratitude, with a new trust in God. They had walked through the very middle of the sea, with the walls of water towering over them on either side! But God, by His mighty power, had saved them from drowning. They sang a beautiful song of praise to God:

I will sing unto the Lord, for He hath triumphed gloriously:
The horse and the rider hath He thrown into the sea.
The waters were gathered together, the floods stood upright as a heap.
The enemy said, I will pursue, I will overtake,
I will draw my sword, my hand shall destroy them.
Thou didst blow with Thy wind, the sea covered them.
Who is like unto Thee, O Lord, doing wonders?
Thou in Thy mercy hast led forth Thy people.

38

Trust and Obey

Exodus 15, 16

It is your birthday. Your best friends have been invited over. Mother has made the things you like best of all to eat. And by your place at the table is a mysterious and fascinating pile of packages.

As you open each present, you are careful to thank the person who gave it to you. But after your big day is over, how often do you think to thank Mother and Dad for the skates, the sled, the bicycle? Do you even stop to *feel* thankful afterwards? An elephant, they say, always remembers. But you and I are better at forgetting. And, to our shame, we have to admit we are especially quick to forget the presents God has given us.

In this we are very much like the Israelites who lived so long ago. They had seen such wonders as dazzled their eyes. Ten times God had spoken. Ten times He had reached out His powerful arm to give His children protection, and freedom, and life itself. And then, at the end, He had led them through the middle of the sea on dry ground, with the water standing up like a wall on their right hand and their left.

That day they had remembered to say "Thank You!" all right. They had sung their thanks to God in a beautiful song of praise. Would they, *could* they ever forget the presents God had given them? Yes, they were weak, sinful men and women, boys and girls, just like you and me. It was *forgetting* they were good at, not remembering. Less than a week later everything was gone from their minds, just as if it had never happened.

They had left Egypt in a great hurry. The women who were making bread could not even stop to run the loaves into the oven. They carried the unbaked dough along. Later, along the road, they built a fire and baked their bread. The men carried water bags made of animal skins slung over their shoulders. A pan of unbaked dough, a skin of fresh water — these were poor supplies for a long journey. But God had promised to bring them to a land so rich that it was flowing with milk and honey. They had already seen His power and His love with their own eyes. Surely He would also care for them along the way!

A land of milk and honey, did you say? It was a desert God led them into — a lonely, trackless wilderness, with no food anywhere, and scarcely any water. After they left the shore of the Red Sea they marched for three days. Three hot, dusty days, beneath the blazing sun. The last of the precious water in the water bags was gone. Their throats were dry and parched. Their voices cracked when they tried to speak.

God was testing them once again, to see whether they remembered His blessings and His care. That is why He led them through the desert. Would they trust Him only when everything went well? Or would they remember, and trust Him even when there was no water anywhere?

Sometimes God leads you and me through the desert places of life also, and for the very same reason. He is testing us to see if we remember how He helped us in the past. He is asking us to trust Him even when everything looks hopeless, when it seems impossible that God's promises can come true.

At last, on the late afternoon of the third day, they saw trees against the sky — and where trees are there must be water. Their hearts lifted; their dragging footsteps quickened. Eagerly they lowered their jugs into the well. Hands reached out for the precious water. They drank deeply. And then they spit it out again, their faces twisted with disappointment and anger. This water was so bitter no one could drink it!

An angry murmur ran through the crowd. They turned on Moses. "What are we to drink?" they asked. Moses knew where to go for help in time of trouble. He brought the problem to God in prayer. God showed Moses a tree, and when Moses had thrown the tree into the water, the water became sweet. There was plenty for everyone to drink, and to fill their waterskins as well. It was another blessing to remember — or to forget.

After a time the Israelites moved on again. Now they were no longer thirsty. They were hungry instead. The bread they had brought along was gone. There were no stores in the desert where they could buy more, no farms. "We would rather have all died the night God killed the Egyptian children," they protested. "At least in Egypt we had enough to eat."

God showed amazing patience with His wayward people. "Tonight," He said, "I will send you plenty of meat, and tomorrow you shall be filled with bread." That night God sent quails, delicious small birds, to the camp. They settled on the ground in great flocks, and God's people had only to reach out their hands to get more meat than they could eat. The next morning the ground was covered with small, round flakes. "What is it?" the people asked. And Moses answered, "It is bread sent to you by God. Each morning each one of you must gather enough for his own family. On the sixth day gather twice as much. For the seventh day is the Sabbath, God's day of rest. God will send no bread on the Sabbath."

As long as His people traveled through the desert, God sent them this miracle bread from heaven. The Israelites called the bread *manna.* It tasted like a sweet, spicy cracker. There was always enough for everyone, and twice as much on the day before the Sabbath.

Yes, God cared wonderfully for His children. And He shows the same loving care to us today. He gives us food and water, clothing, and houses to shelter us from the weather, and so many other blessings that if you should try to count them all, you would never be done. What can we return to Him for all that He has done for us? We can *remember,* instead of forgetting. We can say "Thank You!" not just once, but with all our lives. Above all, we can always trust in Him no matter where He leads us.

39
God Is My Banner

Exodus 17

We built an altar on the hillside there, and we called the place God-Is-My-Banner. A strange name for a place, you say. An even stranger way to speak about our God. Is God a flag? My friend, if you could have been there with us that day, if you could have seen the battle, you would not think it strange at all. Perhaps I can explain it to you so that you, too, will understand.

We were slaves, all of us. The cruel sun beating down on our heads hour after hour, the stinging lash of the overseer's whip, the mocking laughter of the soldiers as they tore the newborn babies from their mothers' arms, the hopeless sobbing of the mothers — these were the things we remembered best.

It is true, our fathers had once been free men. We had heard stories about their riches and their power, about how kings had honored them, how God Himself had talked with them, and eaten with them, and given them special promises. But that was all so long ago. It was hundreds of years since God had spoken to any of us. Some of us still clung to those promises given so long ago. But many others among our people thought that this was foolish. It was the Egyptian gods they worshiped.

And then suddenly everything was changed. We might have forgotten the promises, but God had not forgotten. He appeared again to one of us. He appointed him our leader. He freed us from our cruel masters. He led us out of Egypt with such signs and wonders as no man had ever seen.

Everything was changed, it seemed, except our own sinful hearts. It was a new way of living we had to learn, the way of trusting in God for everything we needed, even such simple things as a drink of water and a bite of food for an empty stomach. And how hard this lesson was for us to learn! How much — I am ashamed to write it down, and yet I must, because it is the truth — how much we grumbled and complained and trembled about the future! How patiently God bore with our wickedness! How generously He supplied everything we needed!

But it was the battle I wanted to tell you about. We had traveled some weeks already across the desert. Food and water had been scarce, but God had marvelously supplied all our needs, and everything was going well. And then one morning on the distant horizon there appeared a line of galloping men, coming swiftly towards our camp. They were not friends; that was very plain. There were no women and children among them. They were armed and mounted. Their banners, coming on before them, gleamed in the sunlight. We had no horses, scarcely any weapons, no banners to lead our men, no training in the arts of war. The Egyptians did not teach their slaves to fight, you can be sure of that. And yet, strangely, no man among us panicked.

Our aged leader, Moses, appointed young Joshua as our captain. And then Moses climbed the hill, taking Aaron and Hur along. There on the quiet mountainside, far above the noise of battle, he raised his arms in prayer to God.

Joshua quickly selected the men he wanted. He formed us into companies, and we marched out to meet the enemy, to fight with our bare hands if necessary. Those who had been the quickest to complain when water or food was scarce spoke no word now. In this hour of desperate danger we one and all threw ourselves on the mercy and the promises of God. And then the strangest thing occurred. We, unarmed and untrained, fought better than the enemy. And yet it was not we, but God, who was fighting for us. It was God who heard the prayer of Moses, who came to our help in that hour of dreadful danger.

The day wore on. The enemy was on the run. Victory seemed certain. But Moses had grown tired. He could not hold his arms up any more. He dropped them to his side. At that very moment the tide of battle turned, and we were once again in danger. Aaron and Hur brought a stone for Moses to sit down on. And then, one of them on each side, they held up his arms of prayer. At once the mighty power of God again sustained our weakness. That day was a mighty victory. But it was God, not we, who won it.

So now you see why we built the altar, and why we called that place God-Is-My-Banner. That day God truly was our banner. He went before us into battle. He won the victory. He defeated our worst enemies.

But there was something more we learned that day, something more precious even than a mighty victory. And it is this especially that I would like to share with you. For God meant you to have a share in it. He commanded us to write it down on purpose so that you could know it too.

You and I may look strong, we may feel strong, but we are really very weak. We could not lift a finger or draw a breath without God's help. And what is worse, far worse, we are wicked. We are selfish, ungrateful, proud, complaining. We could never save ourselves. But if you turn to God in prayer, He will listen. He will answer. He will save you from your worst enemies, from your greatest dangers. His mighty strength will work through your helpless weakness. His holy goodness will replace the filthy wickedness in your heart. You do not need to climb a mountain, as our Moses did. You can speak to Him right now, in your secret heart of hearts. You can say, "I am no good. I have made a mess of everything. Help me! Save me! For the sake of Your precious Son who died for all who trust in Him."

And He will surely answer. I know He will. I saw it with my own eyes.

40

The Mountain of God

We had traveled many weeks through the desert, and had come at last to the very mountain where our leader, Moses, had been called by God to lead us out of Egypt. A broad plain spread before us, and here we set up our tents. Beyond, the sheer, red rocks rose steeply up, towering, it almost seemed, to heaven itself. Moses went up into the mountain to speak with God. And the rest of us — well, there were always plenty of things that needed doing after we had been traveling for days. There was food to be cooked, the animals to be watered and pastured, the children to be watched so that they did not stray too far away. The older folk lay down in the shade of the tents to rest. Travel was especially hard for them.

When Moses came down again, he called us all together. We could see by his face that he had something more important than usual to tell us. "You have two days to get ready," he said. "Then God Himself is going to come down upon the mountain to speak to you. You must prepare yourselves so that you are more fit to meet the mighty God of heaven and earth. Wash all your clothes, and clean your hearts too." Never had such a thing been heard of before! God had appeared, our fathers told us, to our ancestor Abraham, and his children, Isaac and Jacob. And God had appeared to our leader Moses. But that God should speak to a whole nation, delivering His own message, by His own voice! We were overcome with amazement.

What a flurry of washing there was that day and the next in the camp! The women stood in line at the water springs, to beat the clothes clean, and they spread them on the rocks to dry. That was the easy part. But clean your hearts? How does a man clean his heart? However hard we tried to put away the old thoughts of selfishness, of discontent, of anger, of pride, and to fix our minds entirely on our God, the old sins always came flooding back again. It was too hard for us. We could not do it. Somehow we knew that God Himself would have to help us clean our hearts.

"Remember our father Abraham," one of the elders said. "He was too old to have a son, but still he trusted in God. We, too, will have to trust in God to help us do what we cannot do ourselves."

Moses spent that day building a fence around the bottom of the mountain. The children stood and watched him with round, wide eyes. "Why do we need a fence?" they asked. "If anyone touches the mountain," Moses said, "he will die. I put up the fence to protect you from the terrible power of God."

That last night I doubt that anyone in the camp slept very much. Early on the third day there was a fearful noise of thunder sounding from the mountain, and such dazzling flashes of lightning as no one of us could bear to watch. And then a trumpet sounded, first far away, and then louder, and louder, and still louder. It was God calling us to the mountain. There were plenty of brave men in the camp, but even the bravest of us shook and trembled. Not one of us wanted to go out to meet with God; but when God calls, a man must answer — whether he is afraid, or not.

Slowly, with trembling feet, we came to the bottom of the mountain. The whole mountain was on fire, and the smoke went up to heaven like the smoke of a giant furnace. And then, as God approached, even the ground beneath our feet began to shake and tremble. Then Moses spoke, and God answered him out of the thick cloud upon the mountain. Yes, my friend, we all of us heard the very voice of God Himself speaking to us. Never in my whole life have I been so afraid. Even now, long afterwards, when I remember that meeting, my heart stands still and my hands shake.

Do not look at me with scorn or pity. Courage, my friend, starts with the truth. It begins with daring to take a good look at yourself, with finding out how big — or, perhaps, how little — you really are. And it includes knowing your opponent, and how big or small he is, as well. That is why I count this terrifying experience as one of the great blessings of God in my life. I see that you are smiling. God, you say, is not our opponent. He is our Father, our Guide, our Protector. And you are right, of course. Our God is all of these. But there is a sense in which He is our opponent also. Or perhaps it would be better to say He is our Judge.

And just because He is our Judge, it is so dreadfully important to know how great God is, and how very, very small you and I, His children, are. And even more, to know how righteous and holy and pure God is, and how stained with sin the hearts within our breasts. That is just what I and my friends learned that dreadful day when we met with God beneath the mountain. That is what I would like to help you see as well. Because you see, my friends, truth is not only the beginning of courage. Even more important, it is the beginning of salvation, God's salvation. It is not until you have really seen for yourself the desperate, the absolutely hopeless condition you are in, that you will turn to God for help. Then — when you know at last that you yourself are helpless — you will throw yourself entirely on the mercy and the forgiveness of our God. And God will hear your cry. He will help you to clean your own sinful heart by His almighty power.

41
The Broken Promise

Exodus 32, 33

If some time soon your parents should pack up everything that can be moved, and you and your family — your uncles and your aunts, too, and all your cousins, and even your grandparents — should move to a new country, where no one could speak English, and no one had ever heard of God or Jesus, and if you should settle down there to stay, not knowing whether you could ever come back — how long do you think you would remember America? Oh, you would speak English at home, of course. And you would pray and praise God together in your little circle. But just suppose you had no Bible to remind you about God. You had to listen to what your parents and your grandparents tell you God has said, and what they can remember about what God told their parents and grandparents before them.

Presently the old folk die off, one by one. Now you are one of the parents, and you try hard to remember exactly what your father and your mother told you about God, and about America. You tell your children, and after a while your grandchildren. The young ones have never seen America. They have never heard about the true God either, except for what they hear at home. All around them are hundreds of heathen idols, some of them statues, others live animals, bulls and cats, still others the dazzling lights in the sky, the sun and the moon. "The true God," you tell the little ones clustered around your chair, "cannot be seen with eyes. He it is who rules the whole earth, even this distant, strange land that has never heard of Him." Eventually you die too, and your children, and their children. The memory of America grows dim. Memory of the true God grows dim too. Some still pray to the unseen God of their fathers. But others take to praying to the idols they see around them.

That is the way it was with the Israelites in Egypt. They had lived there four hundred years. And now God brought them out with great marvels and wonders. He gathered them together at the foot of the mountain of Sinai, off in the wilderness, where there would be no one to interrupt. And there He told them about Himself, about how He wanted them to live, and how they were to worship Him. "I am your God," He said, "who rescued you from Egypt and from slavery there." And then He gave them His law, which you and I know as the Ten Commandments.

When the people of Israel heard the voice of God Himself actually speaking to them out of the thunder and smoke of Mt. Sinai, they were not able to bear the sound. "You speak to us," they said to Moses, "and we will listen. But do not let God speak to us, or we will die!" So Moses went up alone into the mountain to God, and when he came back, he told the people all the words of God. And the people made a solemn promise to God. "All the words which the Lord has spoken," they said, "we will do!"

There were so many things the people had to learn! So many things they had forgotten! So many things they had never known! Three times Moses climbed, trembling and hesitant, up the shaking mountain slopes, through the thick darkness, to listen to God. The third time he stayed forty days, writing down what God told him. He left his brother Aaron in charge of the Israelites.

The people down below got tired of waiting. They could not see God at all, and now they could not see Moses either. They grumbled together, and soon an angry mob collected. They came to Aaron. "Make us some gods to lead us out of this desert," they said. "We do not know what has become of Moses." So quickly they had forgotten what God had done for them! So soon they had broken their solemn promise to keep the law of God, "Thou shalt have no other gods before Me"!

Aaron was afraid of the angry people. "Break off your golden earrings," he said, "and bring them to me." So all the people took off their earrings, and gave them to Aaron. Aaron melted the gold in the fire, and with it he made a golden calf for the Israelites to worship. The Israelites bowed low before the golden calf. "This is your god, O Israel," they said to each other. "It is this golden calf that brought you out of the land of Egypt!" Aaron was troubled when he heard these wicked, lying words. "Tomorrow," he said, "we will celebrate a feast to the Lord." Did Aaron suppose that the Lord of Hosts would share a feast with a golden calf? The next day they had a great celebration. The Israelites offered sacrifices to their new idol, and then they had a great banquet. They danced around the golden calf Aaron had made.

High up on the mountain God saw what was happening. He saw the people dancing around their new idol, singing, "This is the god who brought us safely out of Egypt!" God was very angry. He said to Moses, "I will destroy these ungrateful people. I will make a nation out of your children instead." Moses pleaded with God to forgive the people. "Remember Your solemn promise," he said to God, "that You made to Abraham, and Isaac, and Jacob, that their children should be as many as the stars of the heaven, and that You would surely give them the land of Canaan."

Then Moses went down the mountain. In his hands he carried the two stone tablets on which God had written the Ten Commandments with His own finger. He met Joshua as he came down. Joshua said to Moses, "There is a noise like the noise of fighting in the camp." "I do not hear the shouting of war," Moses answered. "It is singing that I hear." Then Moses saw the golden calf, and the people dancing and singing before it. He was filled with anger. He took the two tablets of the law in his hand, and threw them violently on the ground. The tablets on which God had written broke into thousands of pieces.

Moses took the golden calf and ground it into fine powder. He mixed the powder with water, and made the Israelites drink it. The next day Moses went back up the mountain to God. "This people," he said to God, "have sinned a terrible sin. Is there any hope for them? Can You forgive them?" And God answered, "I promised Abraham and Isaac and Jacob to give the land of Canaan to their children. I will send an angel to lead you. But I Myself will not go with you. For these people are so sinful that it would be dangerous for them if I were to live among them, for fear that along the way I should utterly destroy them."

"Do not say that!" Moses begged. "How can we ever make the journey unless You go with us? Be merciful, and remember these are Your people." God listened to Moses' prayer. "I *am* a God of mercy," He said, "slow to get angry, a God who forgives sinners, though I will also punish those who do not trust in Me. My presence shall go with you, and I will give you rest." And Moses bowed his head to the ground and worshiped God for His forgiving mercy.

Yes, the Israelites broke the solemn promise they had made to God. But you and I — we have made solemn promises to God also. How often we sing, "O Jesus, I have promised to serve Thee to the end." How long does it take us to break that promise? Forty days? You know the answer. We cannot keep our promise forty minutes. If God should add up our sins, there would be no hope for us, no hope at all.

God forgave the Israelites their terrible sin. He forgives us, too, if we are truly sorry. He forgave them, and He forgives us because His Son, our Saviour Jesus, has paid the price of our sins. You and I cannot keep God's law because of our sinful hearts. But Jesus kept it for us. If we trust in Jesus, God will give us a new heart, and He Himself will travel with us, and teach us how to keep His law.

42

The Tent of God

Exodus 32, 33, 40

We are an excitable, emotional people — I admit it. We are quick to laugh and dance, and equally quick to weep. Today it was despair we felt, a despair born of our burden of guilt. Our leader,

Moses, had gone back up the mountain to God. "You have sinned a great sin," he told us. "I will try to find out if God can forgive such a sin."

None of us had the heart to go on with his usual work while we waited. Could God forgive us? The memory of the golden calf we had worshiped rose to mock us. How could we have forgotten so soon the wonders God had done before our very eyes? And His command to worship no other gods? And the solemn promise *we* had made to Him? All around us lay the threatening desert. It frightened us. The country we hoped to reach — that country flowing with milk and honey which God had promised to our fathers — was far away. No one of us had ever seen it. No one of us knew how to get there. Ever since we left Egypt God Himself had led us. He had gone before us in a pillar of cloud during the day, a fiery pillar when it got dark. Would He take away His guiding pillar? This was what we deserved. We knew it was. Would He leave us to die here, our bones whitening in the desert sands? Could God forgive such a sin as ours?

When at last Moses came back, we gathered silently around him, eager to hear what God had said, and yet afraid. "I confessed your sins," he told us. "I begged God to forgive you. And He said, 'I will send an angel to show you the way, but I Myself will not go with you.'" Our hearts sank at this news. It was as we had feared. We had brought judgment on ourselves by our sin. "I pleaded with Him," Moses went on. "If You do not go with us Yourself," I said, "then do not send us into the desert."

He paused, and we listened with heavy hearts. After a moment he said, "I hardly know how to tell you about what happened next. I dared to say, 'Show me Your glory.' He answered, 'You cannot see My face and live. But see, here is a crack in the rock. Hide in this crack while I pass by. I Myself will cover you with My hand, so that My glory does not blind you.' So I hid in the crack, and God passed by before me. And then I heard His voice saying, 'I am Jehovah, a God of mercy, slow to get angry, and overflowing with love and kindness and grace, a God who *forgives* sinners. Yet those who will not trust in Me shall surely die at last. As for your prayer, I have granted it. My presence *shall* go with you, and at last I Myself will bring you to a place where you can find rest.'"

There was not a sound in the camp as Moses told us these things

— not even a child who cried, or a dog that barked. How wonderful our God was! How good to us who did not deserve His mercy! It was amazing, beyond belief!

"There is something more," Moses went on. "You feel you can hardly believe God's free forgiveness? This is not the half of it. We are to build a house for Him, where He may live among us. Every one of you who wishes to may bring presents for God's house. Bring whatever you would like to give — gold, or silver, or precious jewels, or fine linen, or rare woods, or oil, or spices. If you do not have any of these to give, you may help to spin and weave the curtains, to carve the wood, to cut the stones, to mold the metal."

A house for God? Where He would live among us? Who had ever dared to imagine such a thing? And the kind of house He wanted us to make! For God's house was not to be a temple built of giant stones, taking tens of years to erect, such a temple as we had been forced to build for the Egyptian idols. No, God's house was to be a tent! Like ours, only, you understand, more beautiful. Yes, the great God of heaven and earth, whom the heaven of heavens cannot contain, declared He would live among His people in a tent!

And even that did not exhaust His goodness. The stately Egyptian temples — indeed every temple man had ever heard of — stayed in one place. If you wished to meet with the idol, you made a pilgrimage to where his temple stood. But that was not Jehovah's way. He came to us; He did not wait for us to come to Him. His house was to be a movable house, which could travel with His people as they wandered from place to place in the desert. As He Himself said later, He walked among His people in a tent. When we wandered forty years in the wilderness, He wandered too. He shared our trials, our hardships. He shared — do I dare to say it? — even the judgment of sin which we brought on ourselves. He identified Himself with us.

I wonder if you can imagine, my friends, how our hearts overflowed with love and gratitude when we heard all this? We brought gifts for His house, so many gifts that at last the boxes overflowed, and Moses had to say, "It is enough. Do not bring any more gifts." And how we worked to build that house, following ever so carefully the plan which God Himself had drawn! At last all was ready. We set up the beautiful tent of God. In the inner room we placed the golden ark, covered by the two cherubim whose wings overshadowed the mercy seat. This was the very heart of God's tent — the tabernacle, as we called it in our

language. For it was only because of the mercy of God that it was possible for a holy God to live among a sinful people like us. And when everything had been set up, according to the plan God Himself had given Moses, then the glory of God came down upon His tent, and His majesty filled the holy place. From then on the tent of God always stood in the very center of our camp. We had only to lift our eyes, and we could see the glorious cloud hovering above it, the visible sign that God Himself was right here among us. When it was time for us to move, the cloud lifted up. Then we carefully took down God's tent, covering the holy ark with a veil to protect it from careless eyes, and carrying it on the shoulders of the consecrated priests. When we came to a new camping place, the cloud once again came down upon the tent. Through all our journeys, in plain sight of all of us, God showed Himself in a cloud by day, and a fire by night, above His tent.

43
"The Pattern I Showed You"

Exodus 25-27

It is always interesting to visit another church. I do not mean to attend the services on Sunday, but to look at the building some time during the week. If you take a trip for your vacation, this is one thing you should be sure to do.

In California and New Mexico and Texas you can go to see the white adobe missions built by the Indians, when the only Christians in these places were the missionary priests and their copper-skinned converts. Some of these churches are still being used. Others were leveled by earthquakes, and the crumbling walls have been left in ruins in memory of the missionary and the Indian Christians who were buried together in the disaster. In Plymouth, Massachusetts, you can walk to a log church with people dressed like the early Pilgrims, the men carrying their guns, and the women in their long, somber robes leading little children by the hand. This is not the actual first church built by the Pilgrims, but a reconstruction, and the Pilgrim worshipers are the great-great-grandchildren of the people who prayed in that first church.

In Boston you can visit the church where the lanterns were hung during the Revolutionary War to warn the settlers of the coming of the British — you remember Paul Revere's ride? In this church each pew is surrounded by a six-foot-high white wooden wall, so that the worshipers could concentrate all their attention on God, and not be distracted by those who sat nearby. In the city of Quebec there is a fishermen's church, and all along the walls are hung small, scale models of fishing boats that God saved from shipwreck in answer to the prayers of the fishermen and their families. In Jamestown, Virginia, you can sit down on the rough benches of the little log chapel in the fort, and try to imagine how those first white men felt, three hundred and fifty years ago, surrounded by the unknown horrors of the wilderness and the fierce Indian tribes, and what the worship of God must have meant in strength and comfort and peace to people in so desperate a situation.

But you do not need to travel to visit different churches. Right where you live there is a lot to see. Ask your father and your mother to go with you some time to look at some of the church buildings nearby. There is one thing you ought to remember, though. Whatever Christian church you visit, never forget that it is the house of God. You do not need to look glum, or talk in whispers, but you should go in with reverence, for God has been here among His people.

The very first house of God you cannot visit, for it has been destroyed long since. The people who worshiped there had never heard the name of Jesus, though there were signs all around them pointing to the Saviour God had promised.

When your congregation decides to build a new church, you hire a Christian architect, and he draws a plan for a church that will help you to worship God as He tells us He wants to be worshiped. The Israelites could not draw such a plan. They had no Bible, and they did not yet know how God wished to be worshiped. So God Himself was their architect. He drew their plan.

"Build it," God said to Moses over and over, "according to the pattern I showed you on the mountain."

This first house of God was not built of brick, or of stone, or even of wood. It was made of cloth and skins, with a wooden framework for support. Yes, you are right. The very first house of God was a tent. The people of God were traveling. They were on their way to the Promised Land. And so they needed a place to worship that could travel too, that could be taken down and carried with them when they moved, and set up again when they stayed somewhere for a little while.

But there was still another reason, I think, why this first house of God was a tent. The Israelites were living in tents. And so God, in His amazing understanding of their needs, planned a house for Himself that would be like the houses of His people. Yes, the great God of heaven and earth, whom the heaven of heavens cannot contain, declared He would live among His people in a tent!

The worshipers themselves did not ever go into that part which was the house of God, or tabernacle, as they called it in their language. They stayed outside in a large courtyard. There was a high fence around the courtyard, and linen curtains hanging on the fence, so that they were not distracted by the sights and sounds of the camp around them. God's sky itself was their roof, and there were no pews or benches. They did not sit down; they stood up instead.

There was a basin in the courtyard where the priests could wash themselves before they went into the house of God. They washed their hands and feet, to show that they were sinful, and needed to be cleansed before they could come near to God. There was an altar in the courtyard too, where sacrifices were offered to God, to remind the people that their sins could only be paid for by the shedding of blood.

The tent itself, which was God's house, stood at one end of the large courtyard. It was divided into two rooms, with a curtain, or a veil, as it is sometimes called, hanging down between them. In the outer room, the holy place, there was a seven-branched golden candlestick which burned day and night, to show that the worship of God never stopped. Opposite the candlestick was a golden table, and on it twelve loaves of fine bread, as a sign that it is God who provides us with our daily bread. In the center of this room was the golden altar of incense. The sweet smell of the incense stood for the prayers of God's people, always being offered to Him.

The inside room was called the holy of holies, because it was here that God Himself dwelt. Here was the ark, a box made of fine wood, and covered inside and outside with gold. Inside the ark were the stone tablets on which God had written the Ten Commandments.

The cover of the ark was the most important thing in the whole tabernacle. It was made of pure gold, and on it two golden cherubim stood facing each other, their wings outstretched to cover the center of the lid. This center was the mercy seat, the place where the merciful God of heaven and earth met with His people. The presence of God, here in His house, was shown by a dazzling and glorious light just above the mercy seat.

The high priest was the only person allowed to go into this holiest part of the tent where God was present. He could go in just once a year, and then only if he brought with him the blood of the sacrifice that had been offered in the courtyard.

This first house of God was very different from the church you go to on Sunday. And yet, perhaps, not so different after all. The sins of the people, their need of a Saviour, and the mercy of God — all these were there in that very first place of worship. And it is these very things that are important in your own church. You know a lot more about God and His plan of salvation than the ancient Israelite did. You have seen the reality of the Saviour whom they knew only in a shadow. But you and I must still be saved just exactly as they were, by trusting in God's promises, and by the blood of our Saviour, Jesus Christ.

44

Slow to Believe

Numbers 11

*t*here is a famous story about the starving peasants just before the French Revolution. When the queen, who lived in such extravagant luxury that she could not even imagine what it was like to be hungry, heard that the poor were crying for bread, she said, "If they don't have bread, why don't they eat cake?"

The situation of the Israelites was just the opposite. They had plenty of bread, but they wanted cake too. They cried out — if I may dare to translate it into terms of our own lives — for Danish pastry, fresh strawberries, and steak, to go with their bread.

For over a year now God had rained bread from heaven down upon His people. "Can God prepare a table in the wilderness?" they had asked unbelievingly. The answer was that God could, and God did. Day after day the manna came. It never failed. There was always enough for all that great host of people — almost two million of them, there were.

But God's very faithfulness led to further complaints. Because they had bread enough to eat every day, they grew tired of bread. They forgot what it is like to be hungry. They said, "We are sick to death of this bread. We remember the fish we ate in Egypt, and the cucumbers, and the melons, and the leeks, and the onions, and the garlic. Here there is nothing to look at but this manna! Our soul is dried up from eating manna every day!" And every one of them, grown men though they were, stood at the door of his tent, and wept bitter tears because they had only manna to eat.

God knows better than you and I do, what we need. He plans our lives carefully, and He sends us exactly what it is best for us to have. But if we do not really trust in His care — if we are not willing to be satisfied with what God sends — if we complain over and over, bitterly, rebelliously — then sometimes God sends us the very thing we have been clamoring for, and He makes this answering of our prayers a lesson. It is a lesson that shows us how much better God knows our real needs than we do. It is a bitter lesson to learn, but just because of its bitter taste, it is one we do not quickly forget.

That day in the wilderness God was angry with His complaining people. He said to Moses, "Tell the people to get ready. For tomorrow I will send them so much meat that they will eat it not for one day, or two days, or five days, or ten days, or even twenty days, but for a whole month. You will eat it till it comes back out of your nose!" Even Moses found this hard to believe. "If we should slaughter all our flocks and herds," he said to God, "we would not have enough meat for all these people. Or are You going to send us all the fish there are in the sea?" "Has My arm become short," God answered, "so that I cannot do what I promise? Now you will see whether what I have said will happen, or not!"

Have you, too, Moses, forgotten the wonders God did in Egypt? And how He rolled back the sea and brought His people through the middle on dry ground? How He gave you water in the desert out of a rock, and bread out of heaven? Yes, even Moses had forgotten. Even Moses doubted the power of God. But do not point your finger at him until you have first looked into your own heart. God has done many wonderful things for you too. Do you never doubt His power and His love? Are you never afraid?

The next day God sent quails. Great flocks of them flew over the camp and fell to the ground. On every side of the camp, as far as a man could walk in a day, the ground was covered with quails. In some places they were piled as deep as three feet. The greedy people rushed out to pick them up. They ate quail until they could not swallow another mouthful. They spread the rest out to dry in the hot sun, as they had learned to dry fish in Egypt. The next day they ate quail, and the next, and the next. They stuffed themselves until the quail came out of their noses, until they could no longer look at a piece of quail, or smell the smell of it roasting on the coals, without feeling sick. Until they wished never in all their lives to see a quail again.

And even as they ate, while the meat was still between their teeth, God sent sickness to those people who had complained, who had not been willing to trust that God knew, and would provide, everything they needed. It was a terrible sickness. Many of the people died. And so what had started out as a hilarious feast, ended up as a funeral. There in the desert they buried those people who had refused over and over again to learn God's lesson, who would not trust Him even after all He had done for them. And the rest of them, sobered and saddened, went on. It was a hard, bitter-tasting lesson God had taught them.

And even you and I find this story, which ends in a mass grave in the wilderness, an unhappy story. We would much rather listen to more cheerful things. But God has set this tragic story down in our Bible because He wants us to know about it. Can you guess why? It is because God does not like to teach His children such painful, hard lessons. He wishes us to learn in easier ways. He hopes that when we hear how those who refused to trust came to a bitter end, that we will learn from their experience.

But if we will not learn — if blessings do not make us trust — then God will have to teach us, too, in the hard way. To us, too, He will send sickness and pain and trouble and loss, that we may learn in our very trouble to cry to the only one who can help us.

45

"I Wish That I Were Dead!"

Numbers 13, 14

I wish that I were dead!" Have you ever spoken those bitter, rebellious words? If you have, it may be you did not really mean them. People who say this are usually trying to show how very angry they are. They do not expect God to act upon their wish. But, whether you mean the words, or whether you just hope to impress others, it is a dreadful thing to throw the precious gift of life back in the face of God.

This is exactly what the Israelites did when at last they reached the Promised Land. They had been on the way for more than a year. Most of this time they had spent at Mt. Sinai, where they had learned God's law and how God wanted them to worship Him. After God had taught them all these things, they started out again on their journey to Canaan. God kept His promise to go with them. He led them all the way to the very edge of the Promised Land.

Now that they were so near their new home, God commanded Moses to send out spies, to discover who lived in the land, and how to go about taking it. Moses chose twelve men to be spies, one from each of the tribes. "Go and spy out the land," Moses told them. "Find out whether the people that live there are strong or weak; whether there are few of them, or many; whether they are farmers living in the country, or live in cities with walls around them. See whether the land is fruitful, whether there are forests, and bring us back some of the fruits of the land."

So the spies set out. They traveled from the south of the country all the way to the north, and back again. As they came back, they cut down a branch of grapes, to show the children of Israel. The branch was so heavy that it took two men to carry the wooden pole from which it hung. They also brought some other fruits with them, figs and pomegranates. After forty days they came back.

"The land is a beautiful country," they said. "It is very fruitful, truly flowing with milk and honey. These grapes that we brought back will give you some idea of the fruits of Canaan. It is a lovely land, but we will never be able to conquer it. The people who live there are very strong. They have cities which are fortified, and they themselves are giants. They are so big that when we saw them, we felt like little grasshoppers."

When the people heard this, they lifted up their voices and wept bitter tears. "We wish that we had died in Egypt, or here in this desert!" they said. "Why did God bring us so far only to be killed? Our women and our children will all be sold as slaves. Come! Let us turn around, and go back to Egypt!"

The Israelites were forgetting something. They were forgetting the most important thing of all. They were forgetting that God had promised to go with them, that even now He was present among them in the beautiful tent of meeting.

Two of the spies, Joshua and Caleb, did not agree with this report. They were shocked that the Israelites had no faith in God who had brought them all this way, performing so many wonders. "If God is with us," they said, "we do not have to be afraid. He has promised to bring us into the land. He will defend us against the people who live there." The Israelites refused to listen. They picked up stones, to kill Caleb and Joshua. Then suddenly they stopped in their tracks. For the glory of God appeared above the tent of God. All the people saw it.

"How long will it be," God said, "before these people learn to trust Me? After all the wonders I have done among them, still they do not believe. They shall not be My people any longer. I will make a nation of your children instead, Moses!" Moses pleaded with God, as he had done before when the people made the golden calf. He said, "Then the Egyptians will say that You were not able to bring Your people into Canaan. They have heard that You live among this people, that the cloud of Your glory stands above the tent of God, that You Yourself lead the people as they journey. Forgive the sin of Your people, according to the greatness of Your loving-kindness!"

"I will forgive them," God said. "But not one of these people who have seen all My wonders and still do not trust Me, not one of them shall ever see the country I promised to their fathers. Instead they shall wander in the desert here for forty years. They wished they had died in the wilderness. I will give them their wish. They shall all die here! Only their little children, who they said would be slaves, only these little children shall ever see the Promised Land. But Joshua and Caleb, who trusted in Me, shall enter Canaan."

So the Israelites had to turn their back on the beautiful Promised Land they had come so far to see. They had to wander forty years in the wilderness. Not one of them ever set his foot in Canaan. They were not able to enter in because they did not trust in God. Only Caleb and Joshua and the little children ever saw the country flowing with milk and honey.

God has done great things for you and me too. He has filled our lives with blessings. He has led us all the way. He has sent His own Son to earth to be our Saviour. Have you ever thought what your answer should be to all this? The answer God wants from you is the answer of trust. He wants you to believe in Jesus. He wants you to put your trust in His promises. He wants you to go forward confidently with your hand in His, saying, "God is my strength. Of whom should I be afraid?"

46
The Choice Belongs to God

Numbers 17

When I was a child, my father carried a cane whenever he took a walk. The only canes I see today are those carried by people who are blind or are crippled. Their canes are strong and useful, but hardly ornamental. But long ago, when I was a child, a man carried a cane to show that he was a gentleman. It showed that he was a teacher, or a minister, or a doctor. My father had a collection of canes. They were made of many different sorts of rare woods. Some were intricately carved; others had silver heads or handles. When he met a lady on the street, my father would touch his hat with his cane. And sometimes, if the weather was fine, and his spirits were high, he would even twirl his cane in a little sort of flourish, almost like our majorettes twirl their batons.

This is a story about canes. Only in those days they did not call them canes. They called them rods. But, like my father's canes, their rods were not something to lean on. They were instead the symbol of the authority of the man who carried them. Perhaps you remember that God told Moses to stretch out his rod over the Nile River, and the water turned to blood.

Moses was not the only one among the Israelites who had a rod. Each of the tribes had a prince, and each prince carried a rod to show his authority. Even God, the Bible tells us, has a rod: *I will fear no evil; thy rod and thy staff they comfort me.* The rod God carries reminds us that He rules our lives in power, so that we do not have to be afraid of anything that happens.

The monotony of their food was not the only thing the Israelites complained about. They complained about their leaders, Moses and Aaron, too. "They are no better than we are!" they said. "Why should they put on such airs? After all, we are all of us God's people. We are all holy, aren't we?"

In a sense, they were right about this, of course. All God's people are holy. But the person who belongs to God (the *really* holy person) is not the man who demands that he get his rights. He does not wish to lord it over others. If you are really God's child, then you have given yourself to Him completely, in trust. You trust Him for your daily needs. You are content with what He sends you, for you understand God knows what you really need better than you yourself do. And you are willing to serve Him wherever He places you.

The Israelites were quite ready to accept God's blessings. They were not yet ready to yield their lives to God, to let Him choose where each one of them should serve. And so, as He so often does, God stooped down from heaven to show whom He had chosen as leaders in a sign which even the dull eyes of the Israelites could see.

"Tell the children of Israel," God said to Moses, "to bring you their rods, one rod for the prince of each tribe. Write the name of the owner on each rod. Since Aaron is the prince of the tribe of Levi, put his name on the rod of Levi. Put all the rods in My tent, before the ark where I meet with My people. I will show these people whom I have chosen to serve as priest in My house." So Moses collected twelve rods, one for each of the princes of the tribes of Israel. He laid them all in the holy place, in front of the ark where God dwelt among His people.

The next morning all Israel assembled outside the tabernacle, to find out whom God had chosen as priest. Moses went into God's tent, and brought out the rods. Eleven of the rods were exactly as they had been the evening before, dead, and dry, and lifeless. But the rod with Aaron's name on it had come alive. Though it was months, perhaps years, since it had felt the life-giving sap of the tree from which it had been cut, this morning, by the almighty power of God, Aaron's rod had leaves on it, and almond flowers, and even ripe nuts. The other princes picked up their rods. Without a word they turned away and went back to their tents.

God said to Moses, "Put Aaron's flowering rod in the ark, in My tent, so that children not yet born can see this proof that I am the one who chooses. For unless they learn to trust their lives to My direction, they will surely die!" So Moses put Aaron's rod in the ark, together with those two other precious treasures of the Israelites, the tablets on which God had written the Ten Commandments with His own finger, and the jar of manna which reminded the people of how God had fed them with bread from heaven all those long, weary years in the desert.

Yes, the right to choose belongs to God. He chose when and where you would be born. He chose your parents. He chose how tall you would be, and the color of your hair, your skin, your eyes. He chose what talents He would give you. And He chose all this in love, because He wanted someone like you to serve Him in His kingdom. He also chose where you are to work for Him. If we truly trust Him, we will pray:

> *I'll go where You want me to go, dear Lord,*
> *Over mountain, or plain, or sea.*
> *I'll do what You want me to do, dear Lord.*
> *I'll be what You want me to be.*

47

Goð Will Provide a Lamb

Numbers 21

It was a hot, dry afternoon. The wind, blowing across the drifting sand dunes, whipped the tiny, sharp grains into the people's ears and eyes and noses. Little knots of men stood in the open spaces between the tents. A murmur of discontent rose from their mingled voices, and hung like a dark cloud over the camp. "Why did we ever leave Egypt?" they said. "God, and Moses here, have brought us to a place where there is neither grain nor water! And how we loathe this horrible, light, tasteless manna!"

Suddenly there was a shout from the middle of the camp. "Snakes! Poison snakes!" The people scattered frantically in every direction. But there was no escaping. A moment later the cry echoed from the left, and then from the right, from the front, and from the back of the camp. "Snakes! Poison snakes!" In a flash the whole camp was in an uproar. What had been a murmur of discontented unbelief, became a shriek of pain and terror. Many of the people were bitten, and where the deadly fangs sank into arm or leg, there followed the fire of fever, and at last death itself.

Was it an accident that the snakes invaded the camp at that moment? The Israelites knew that it was not. They had sinned. And they knew that the sinner deserves to die. Is there no hope, then, for the man who rebels against God? Yes, there is hope, but only in the mercy of God. This was one thing the Israelites had learned in those forty long years of wandering in the desert. The men — those who could still walk — came to Moses. "We have sinned," they said, "in speaking against God. Pray to God to forgive us, and take away the snakes." Moses loved these weak, faltering, doubting people he had led so long and so far. He begged God to forgive them, and to remove the punishment the people so richly deserved.

God answered Moses' prayer. "Make a fiery snake out of brass," God said, "and set it up on a pole. I will give life to everyone who looks at the brass snake trusting in My promise." So Moses made a brass snake, which burned red and hot in the sun when he set it up on a pole, even as the victims of the snake bite also burned red and hot with fever. And those who were sick with the raging fever — those men who deserved to die because of their sin — had only to look at the brass snake in trust, and they were well again.

And so God, in His great mercy, forgave and healed the rebels. But at the same time, as He so often does, God was teaching His people a lesson. Those ancient Israelites had no Bible. They did not know, as you and I can, about *how* God was going to save His people. They never in their wildest dreams imagined that God would send His own Son to take the punishment of their sins upon Himself, so that they could be forgiven.

Slowly, one step at a time, as you teach a little child, God was teaching them. He had already taught them that He was willing to accept a substitute to pay for their sin. Every time they brought a little, innocent lamb in sacrifice, they were reminded of this wonderful fact. God accepted the little lamb, which had done no wrong, in the place of the sinner. And the sinner was forgiven. Now God was teaching them another lesson. Can you guess what it was? Can you figure out what the Israelites learned from that snake made of brass?

The red, fiery snake was like the victims of the snake bite. For they, too, burned red and hot with fever. The brass snake was like them, and yet it was different. For there was no poisonous venom in the brass snake's body. So this is one thing the Israelites learned that day. The promised Saviour would be like themselves. He, too, would be a man. He would even suffer as they did. But there would be one tremendous difference. The dreadful poison of sin would not be found in the Saviour, as it was found in every one of us.

And then I think there was a second, very important thing they learned. And this is the very heart of the Christian good news. It is this: *salvation is a free gift!* The people had sinned. They all deserved to die. Heathen idols demanded that their worshipers cut themselves, beat themselves, starve themselves. But God gives forgiveness away free. All that those dying snake-bite victims had to do was simply to look at that brass snake on the pole, and trust in God to heal them.

There is one more thing the brass snake tells us, but I do not think the Israelites understood this. We understand it, because Jesus Himself has explained it to us. Why was the brass snake raised up on a pole? *That's easy,* you say. *It was so all the people could see it.* Of course, you are right. But there was another reason, too. The brass

snake was lifted up on the pole because our Saviour, the one to whom
the brass snake pointed, was going to be raised up on a cross. Jesus
tells us that He *had to be* lifted up on that cross. Do you know why
there was this *had to be?* It was because every one of us has this
deadly venom of sin in our very lifeblood. And it *had to be* because of
the marvelous love Jesus had for us, poor, miserable, rebellious sinners
that we are. He chose of His own free will to die in our place. He was
the Lamb whom God provided to be our substitute. And from that
dreadful cross, He calls to you, calls now, calls in love and in forgiveness: "Look unto me, and be saved. For there is no one else who can
save you!"

48
An Angel in the Road

Numbers 22

This is a story about a fortune-teller and a donkey. The
fortune-teller was called Balaam, and if you greased his palm with
silver or gold, he would tell you what was going to happen. If you
could pay a large enough fee, Balaam would even try to change the
future to suit your wishes. He would curse your enemies, and bless
your friends — always supposing you could pay. And many people
supposed that even the gods had to follow Balaam's forecasts.

Balaam, like all fortune-tellers, was a heathen. But he had heard
of the amazing wonders performed by one special God, the God of
the Israelites. Balaam had heard how this God brought plagues on the
cruel masters who enslaved His people in Egypt, and how He had
dried up the Red Sea so that His people could cross over on dry ground.
Clearly a God who could perform such wonders was no ordinary God.
And so Balaam, being a practical man of business first of all, thought
it might be worth his while to seek a connection with such a God.

Not, you understand, that he had any intention of loving and trusting the one true God. It was only that he hoped to make use of His extraordinary power.

And then the very chance he had been looking for arrived. It dropped, as it were, like a ripe plum on his doorstep. For one day there arrived at Balaam's house a group of messengers. Not ordinary men who could pay with a sheep or an ox for a favorable fortune. These men were princes, and they had been sent by Balak, the king of Moab. And in their hands they carried rich rewards of silver and of gold. "Come with us at once," they said to Balaam. "There are people camped on our borders who have come from Egypt, so many of them that they cover the face of the earth. Come and curse them for us, for they are too strong for us to fight."

Balaam knew well enough who those people come from Egypt were. These were the very people whose God he hoped to claim as his God. If he had been a true prophet of God, he would have sent the messengers home at once. For how could he curse God's chosen people? But Balaam's eyes gloated covetously over those rich rewards of silver and gold. "Stay here overnight," he said to the messengers. "I will see what God allows me to do." That night God met Balaam. "Who are these men with you?" God asked him. "You are not to go with them, nor are you to curse this people, for I have blessed them!"

Reluctantly, the next morning Balaam sent the messengers, and the silver and the gold, back to Balak, the king of Moab. "God," he said sadly, "refuses to allow me to go with you." Balak thought this was just a trick. He thought Balaam was simply waiting for him to offer more money and richer rewards. He sent other messengers, with this message, "If only you come, I will give you whatever you ask." "I cannot come unless God allows it," Balaam said, "not even if Balak should give me his house full of silver and gold. But stay overnight. I will try again to get God's permission." That night God said to Balaam, "I will allow you to go with the men, but you must speak only the words which I tell you."

And so the next morning Balaam saddled his donkey, and set out. What was he thinking about as he rode that donkey? Was he reminding himself that he must faithfully report exactly what God told him? I do not think so. I think he was dreaming about that house full of silver and gold. He was hoping that somehow or other he could manage things in such a way as would please Balak. He was not worried about how to please God.

And God, who reads the thoughts of every man, was angry at Balaam. He sent His angel to stand with a drawn sword in the road where Balaam would pass. Balaam did not see the angel; his head was too full of visions of silver and gold. But the donkey saw the angel. She left the road and turned into the field. Balaam took his stick and beat the donkey.

Then the angel stood further on, in a narrow path, with vineyard walls on either side. The terrified donkey crashed into the wall, and crushed Balaam's foot against it. Balaam beat the donkey again. The angel of God went further on, and stood in a narrow pass, where there was no room to turn to the right hand or to the left. When the donkey saw the angel this third time, she refused to go any further. She lay down under Balaam.

Balaam was furious. He laid his stick on the donkey over and over. Then God opened the donkey's mouth, and she said, "What have

I done that you have beaten me these three times?" Balaam's thoughts were so taken up with greed, and now with anger too, that he never even noticed that his donkey was talking as men talk. He said, "If I had a sword in my hand, I would kill you!" The donkey answered, "Am I not your own donkey, on which you have ridden all your life? Have I ever done this before?" And Balaam said, "No!"

Then God opened Balaam's eyes, and he, too, saw the angel standing in the road with the drawn sword in his hand. The angel said to Balaam, "Why have you beaten your donkey these three times? If she had not turned aside, I would surely have killed you, and saved her alive!"

Now even greedy Balaam was terrified. Quickly he climbed off the donkey's back, and fell on his face on the ground. "I have sinned," he said. "I did not know that you were standing in the road. If you wish, I will turn around, and go home again."

But the angel said, "No, go with the men. But remember! You must say the words which God tells you!" So Balaam went on with the princes of Balak. He had had a terrible scare, but perhaps, after all, it would turn out as he wished. For did not God tell him to go with the men?

49
What's in It for Me?

Numbers 23, 24

What's in it for me? Have you ever asked yourself this question? Does it pay to be a Christian? Will I get something out of it, in return for what I have to put into it? If I do what God asks, will He do what I ask? What's in it for me?

This is the question Balaam asked himself when he first heard about the power of the true God. Is there some way I can latch onto this power? Can I strike some sort of a bargain with God? If I offer Him something He wants, will He give me what I want? What's in it for me?

It was not a good question. It was a bad question. God is not a man to be bribed to change His mind. You must never ask, "How can God serve me?" The question is instead, "How can I serve God?"

You and I ought to know this. But Balaam had no Bible. He had never even heard of the law of God. Perhaps that is part of the reason why God performed two separate miracles to stop Balaam in his head-long rush towards destruction. He sent an angel with a drawn sword to bar Balaam's path; and He opened a donkey's mouth. And He set down the story of what happened so that you and I, too, could learn from Balaam's experience. The question is not, Balaam, whether it will pay you to do what God wishes. You are going to do what God wishes whether you want to or not. In the end it is always God's plan that rules our world. Every one of us must serve Him. The only question is: Will we serve willingly, gladly? Or will we strike out in angry rebellion even while we do His will? Which did Balaam do? I shall let you decide that for yourself.

After he had been stopped by the angel, and by the donkey that talked, Balaam went on. He was badly frightened by what had happened. But was his heart changed? Had he stopped longing for Balak's silver and gold? I wonder. As soon as Balak heard that Balaam was coming, he went out to meet him. "Why did I have to send for you twice?" he asked Balaam. "Don't you know I can promote you to a position of great honor?" And Balaam, remembering all too well the angel, the sword, and the open mouth of his donkey, answered, "Well, I am here now. But I can't say anything to help you except what God tells me."

King Balak brought Balaam to a mountaintop from which he could see the camp of the Israelites. Balaam said, "Build seven altars here, and sacrifice a young bull and a ram on each altar." So Balak built seven altars, and sacrificed seven young bulls and seven rams, hoping perhaps that such a fine display of sacrifices might persuade God to take their side.

Then Balaam said, "You, King Balak, stand beside the sacrifices we have offered. I will go a little way off, and see if I can discover what God has to say to you." As he went out, God met him. Balaam said to God, "See! I have built seven altars, and offered You a ram and a young bull on each altar." God put a word in Balaam's mouth, and he returned to Balak, who was standing with all the princes of Moab beside the fourteen sacrifices. Balaam spoke the word which God had given him: *Balak has sent for me to curse Israel. How can I curse whom God has not cursed? Who can count the dust of Jacob? Let me die the death of the righteous. Let my last end be like his.*

Balak was angry at these words. "I sent for you," he said, "to curse them, but you have blessed them instead!" And Balaam answered, "I have to say what God puts in my mouth." For Balaam remembered the angel, the sword, and the talking donkey.

Then Balak took him to another place. "From here," he said, "you cannot see all of them, only the edges of their camp. Curse them for me from here." Again Balaam said, "Build seven altars, and sacrifice seven young bulls and seven rams, and I will go out and meet God." And he went out, and came back. Balak asked, "What did God say?" And Balaam answered: *God is not a man to change His mind. He has said it, and He will do it. I have been commanded to bless His people; He Himself has blessed them, and I cannot change it.*

Then Balak said, "Don't speak at all! Neither bless them nor curse them!" Balaam answered, "I told you I have to do what He says!" So Balak took him to another place. "Perhaps," he said hopefully, "it will please God to curse them from here." There they built another seven altars, and offered still another seven young bulls and seven rams. And the Spirit of God came on Balaam, and he said, *How goodly are thy tents, O Jacob. Blessed is everyone that blesseth thee, and cursed everyone that curseth thee.*

Balak slapped his hands together in anger. "I called you to curse my enemies," he said, "and you have blessed them these three times. I was going to promote you to great honor. Now then, get back to your home. God has kept you back from honor!" Then Balaam answered, seeing in a trance what God would bring to pass in the distant future: *I see him, but not now. I behold him, but not nearby. A star shall rise out of Jacob, and a king out of Israel.*

The marvels of our God are very wonderful indeed. For, by the power of God's Spirit, Balaam saw *why* it was that Israel was blessed; why both Balak and Balaam ought to have treated them kindly, not looked for ways to curse them. It was not because the Israelites deserved God's blessings. Ever since God had brought them out of Egypt, the Israelites had grumbled, and complained, and doubted God.

But God was faithful; He blessed them because one day, in the far distant future, a Star and a King were going to come from this people. A Star who would light up the whole world, and a King who would rule in love and justice. And that Star and that King are our Lord and Saviour, Jesus.

What happened to Balaam? He had said, "Let me die the death of the righteous." But he was speaking God's words, not his own wishes. He did not go home to his own country. Instead he stayed with the Moabites. He said to them, "Invite the Israelites to the temple feasts of your idols. Then God will be angry with them, and will truly curse them." The Moabites took his advice. The Israelites came to their feasts, and worshiped Baal-Peor, the Moabite idol. And God *was* angry. He commanded Moses to attack Moab. In that battle the Moabite army was destroyed. And the magician Balaam was one of those who were killed.

50
Moses Is Satisfied

Deuteronomy 34

He was an old man now, and his work was nearly finished. He had written down carefully all that God had told him, and had given it to the priests, to be stored with the other great treasures of the nation, beside the ark in the holy place of the tent of God.

He had led the people through the desert, past hostile heathen nations, till they were now camped on the shore of the Jordan River. For forty years he had taught them, and been patient with them, and begged God to forgive them. For they were not an easy people to lead. How quick they were to complain! How easily discouraged! How slow to learn to trust in God!

And yet he loved them. They had tried his patience almost past enduring. They had rebelled. They had blamed him for all their troubles. But they *were* his people. And they were God's people. And he loved them.

He loved them so much he was willing to pay for their wickedness with his own most precious possession — his hope of heaven and God Himself. After that dreadful day when he came down the mountain, and found God's people dancing around a golden calf, he had said to God, "Oh, this people have sinned a great sin! Yet now if You will forgive their sin . . . ; and if not, I pray You, blot me out of the book which You have written!" But God had forgiven them. Again and again God had forgiven His sinning people at Moses' prayer.

He sat now in front of his tent, and his eyes wandered from the people he loved to the river and the mountains and fields which lay beyond it. There was the land which God had promised to Abraham and Isaac and Jacob. A fair land, the spies had said, a land flowing with milk and honey. How he longed to see it! Even more, how he longed to lead the people he loved into it! For all these forty years that he had wandered with the people through the desert, it had been the promise of this land that had sustained him.

But he was not to cross the river. He was not to see the land of milk and honey. Another man had been chosen by God to lead the people there. For it was not only the people who had sinned; not only the people who had doubted God. He, Moses, had sinned too. He had failed as leader, and God had taken his office away from him and given it to Joshua.

There was no bitterness or rebellion in his heart as he remembered that day — though he had been angry and rebellious and bitter when it happened. It was in the desert, and the people had cried once again for water. And God, as He always had done so wonderfully, had heard their cry. "Take your rod," God said to him, "and speak to the rock, and it will bring forth water for the people and their cattle to drink." But he was angry. He was quite out of patience with this headstrong, complaining people. He lifted his rod and struck the rock violently, instead of speaking to it as God had commanded. He struck it twice! "Hear now, you rebels," he had said in great anger, "must I and my brother Aaron bring water out of this rock for you?" In his anger he quite forgot that he was the leader. He forgot that it was his task to show the people the power of God, never his own power; to teach them to trust, not to set them an example of distrust and disobedience.

"Because you did not believe in Me," God had said to him, "you shall not lead this people into the land I have given them!" It was a bitter disappointment, even though he knew that he had deserved it. He begged God to let him cross the river and see the longed-for Promised Land. So often he had prayed God to forgive the people, and God had granted his prayer. Now he prayed for himself, but God did not give him what he asked for. "Be satisfied with what I have decided," God said. "Do not speak about this any more. Climb this mountain here, and look to the east and the west and the north and the south, and see what the land is like with your own eyes. For you are *not* to cross this river."

He knew that it must be right, for it was God's will. Much as he loved the people, he loved God even more. His one great longing was to do what God wanted him to do. He had had a taste of the friendship of God when he spent those long days on the mountaintop. There God had spoken to him face to face, as a man speaks to his friend. There was nothing this life could offer him that did not seem pale and tasteless by comparison with the joy of that friendship.

And so he did not tremble when God said to him, "Get you up into this mountain, and look at the land, and then die here in this mountain." He said a last good-by to the people he loved, and to Joshua, on whose shoulders now fell the responsibility of leading God's people. "The eternal God is your dwelling place," he reminded them, "and underneath you are the everlasting arms." And in that assurance he climbed the mountain. And God, his God, whom he so loved, met him there. God Himself showed him the land, from the north to the south, and from the east to the west. "This is the land," God said to him, "that I promised to Abraham and Isaac and Jacob."

Then Moses lay down on that lonely mountaintop and died. And yet, how can I call it lonely? For God stood beside him. And God Himself buried his body there. God had not granted his prayer to cross the river. But God had something far better to give him than the land of Canaan. God Himself had prepared a city for him, a city where there was no sin, or sorrow, or parting, or death. When Moses awoke he was indeed satisfied. For he was forever with the God whom he had loved and served. For Moses the journey was over.

IV
THE HEART OF THE TENT

Hereby ye shall know that the living God is among you (Joshua 3:10).

51

Two Spies on a Rooftop

Joshua 2

We were not cowards, but neither were we fools. It was an honor to have been chosen by our leader as spies, but we knew well enough what happens to spies who are caught. And so we set out on our mission with sober thoughts, and with a prayer to God that He would prosper our journey, and bring us back to our families in safety.

We slipped away from the camp. The river had overflowed its banks with the spring rains. It was not easy to find the fording place, and even after we were sure where it was, crossing over was difficult. Once safely on the further side, we rested a while to dry our clothes, so that no one we met would suspect we had come from across the river. Then we joined the farmers on their way into the city to sell their crops. The gates were wide open, and we walked boldly through them, laughing and talking with our new companions as if we had visited Jericho many times before. I say boldly, but inside, our hearts were trembling. We dared not look around us too curiously, or behind us, to see if we were being followed.

The pattern of the city streets was strange to us, but somehow, with God's help, we found our way to a back alley where a friendly woman smiled at us from the door of her house. "Can we lodge with you tonight?" we asked her, and she replied, "Come in, and welcome!" We thought no one had noticed us, but scarcely had we got inside the door when we heard a commotion in the distance. "Where are they, those strangers?" someone shouted. And another, "Surely they are spies!"

"Hurry!" the woman said to us. And she led us up to the rooftop. There was a great pile of flax stalks laid out there to dry. We lay down, and she covered us deep beneath the stalks. We tried to lie perfectly still, and again we committed ourselves to the protection of God Almighty. For we knew that He ruled here in this heathen city just as surely as in our camp where His tent stood among His people.

We could hear the police coming down the street, going from house to house. And then they knocked on that very door which we had entered only a few minutes before — or was it the pounding of our hearts we heard? The door hinges squeaked, and we heard the woman's calm voice, "Yes? What is it?" The rough voices of the police answered, "The king says, 'Bring out the men that came to your house tonight, for surely they are spies!'" We held our breath. But the woman answered at once, "O yes, they were here. I didn't know who they were. Anyway, they didn't stay. They wanted to get out of the city before the gates shut at dusk. I am not sure which way they went, but if you hurry, you will catch them yet."

There was a moment's confused arguing in the street below us. Some were all for searching the house. But the woman said again, "If you want to catch them, you will have to hurry!" Then the voices went away, and we could hear the woman barring the door. Later — for the house was built right on the city wall — we heard a troop of horsemen leaving the city. And after the horsemen had left, the city gate clanged shut. Now we were prisoners in this enemy city, and did not know how we could ever escape. There was but one thought in our minds: "May the God of our fathers protect us!" And He did! In a way we could never have dreamed of!

Soon the woman came to the rooftop. She pushed aside the flax stalks, and we stood up stiffly, shaking the dust from our clothes. She said to us, "I know that God has given this land to you. The fear of you has fallen on all the people of the land, so that they melt away before you. For we have heard how God dried up the Red Sea when you came out of Egypt, and how you utterly destroyed the kings on the further side of the river. Now, therefore, swear to me by God that, just as I have treated you kindly, you will treat me and my family kindly, and will save us alive when God gives you the land."

And we said, "Our life for yours, if you do not betray us to the king." Then she took us to the window of the house, cut into the city wall. She let a scarlet rope down the wall, so that we could climb down it. And she said to us, "Escape to the mountains, and hide there three days, till the men sent to catch you have come back. And after that you can go on your way safely." And we said, "When we attack the city, bind this same scarlet rope in the window of your house. And fetch your father and your mother and all your family into this house, and see that none of them goes out into the street." The last sight of the city we had was of Rahab binding the scarlet rope in the window of her house on the wall. And so, under cover of darkness, we escaped to the mountains and hid there in a cave three days.

After that we crossed the river again, and reported to our leader, Joshua. We said to him, "Truly God has delivered all the land into our hands, for the people of the land melt away before us, they are so afraid." And we told Joshua about the woman who had saved our lives, and about the promise we had made to her. He said, "When we capture the city, you two go to Rahab's house, and bring her and her father and her mother and all her family safely out of the city before it is destroyed."

And this is just how it went. For Rahab and her family were saved alive, alone out of all that great city of Jericho, because she had trusted in the one true God, and because she hid the messengers. She was born and grew up in a strange and heathen nation, but, by God's grace, she became as one of us, and her children and grandchildren lived, and played, and grew up, and married, with ours.

52

Crossing the River

Joshua 3

For forty years the Israelites had wandered in the wilderness. Day after weary day, week after lagging week, endless year after year, they had moved their tents from one place to another, and then back again. Though they had doubted God, yet God did not forsake them. In all those forty years God walked among them in His tent. He remembered His promises to Abraham, and Isaac, and Jacob. Their clothes did not grow old, and their shoes did not wear out. How many hundreds and hundreds of miles they had walked across the burning desert sands! And yet their feet never gave out. God fed them with manna from heaven day by day, and when they could not find water to drink, he opened miracle springs from the rocks for them.

But now the forty years of wandering were over. All those who had doubted God, who had wished to die in the desert, all of them had been given what they wished for. They had died and been buried in the wilderness. Moses, their great leader, had died too. He had climbed the mountain, as God had commanded. He had looked at the Promised Land. And then he had died there on the mountain. God Himself had buried him, and no man has ever discovered where his grave is.

Now God had appointed a new leader, Joshua. Joshua was not young, nor was he inexperienced. It was Joshua, you remember, who led the Israelite armies in the war against Amalek, soon after they left Egypt, while Moses sat on the hillside above and prayed to God for victory. And Joshua had been one of the two spies who had not doubted God's power forty years before. Still, it was not easy for any man to follow in the footsteps of a giant like Moses. God understood this. For God knows how weak we are. He remembers that we are made from the dust of the earth. And so He came to Joshua with special promises.

"Moses, My servant, is dead," God said to Joshua. "Now, therefore, get up, and cross over this river, you and all of these people, to the land which I am going to give them. Every place that your feet walk on I have given to you. And you, Joshua, no man shall be able to stand against you all the days of your life. Just as I was with Moses, so I will be with you. Only be careful to live according to the law which I gave to Moses. Be strong and brave. Do not be afraid. For your God is with you!"

The Israelites were camped on the banks of the Jordan River. They could see the fields and hills of the Promised Land, but they could not reach them. The river lay between. The Jordan was hard to cross even when it was low, in the heat of summer. The current was swift and dangerous. There were steep banks, and foaming rapids. But right now it was spring. The river was flooded. The snows on the mountains above had melted, and the river was swollen to several times its usual size.

There was no bridge by which the Israelites could cross this wild and dangerous water. They had no boats either. If he could find the fording place, a strong swimmer could get across as the two spies had. But what about the women and little children? There were flocks and herds too, and all the Israelites' baggage. And on the further side were the fierce, warlike kings, and the men who were giants!

Still the Israelites were not afraid. They did not see how they could ever cross the Jordan. But they trusted in God. God had cared for them through all these years of wandering. He had brought them into sight of their new home. He had promised to give them the land of Canaan. God's promises were sure. They waited for God.

And in the very center of their camp every man could see the tent of God. All day long God's cloud, and all night long God's fire, hung above that tent to reassure the Israelites that the invisible God was still among them. Inside the tent, in the holy place where only the priests were allowed to go, and even they only once a year, with the blood of the sacrifice with them, stood the golden ark, and above it the mercy seat, where God met with His people.

"Today," Joshua said to the people, "God is going to perform a great wonder in your sight. When you see what God is going to do, you will surely know that the living God is among you." Then he said to the priests, "Take up the ark, and go to the front of all the people. When you come to the edge of the river, stand still in the water." The priests saw the wild, rushing water. But they did not hesitate. They did as Joshua commanded.

Then a most amazing thing happened. When the priests stepped into the water, the river stopped flowing. High up above them the rushing water stopped. It piled up into a high wall. A dry path across the river opened before them. The priests went into the middle of the river. They stood there holding the ark of God. All that great crowd of people crossed the river on dry ground. The men and the women, the children, the cattle, the baggage — all of them went safely across where a moment before the fierce, raging waves had broken. The priests stood quietly in the middle until everyone was on the further side.

Then, at last, when everyone had crossed, the priests who held the ark crossed too. The moment they set their feet on the further bank of the river, that very moment the river flowed again, and the wild, raging waves covered the place where God's people had crossed.

53
What Do These Rocks Mean?

Joshua 4

Supper was late that night, because they stayed in the fields until it was dark, to finish getting in the grain. When at last they sat down to eat, Father first said a prayer of thanks to God for the good harvest. They were all hungry after their long day's work, but even after they had eaten, they lingered till well past the children's bedtime, all of them together enjoying the comfortable feeling of work well done.

The little one's eyes drifted shut at last, and even the ten-year-old twins, Amos and Asaph, were trying to keep from yawning. Father stood up briskly. "Off to bed, all of you, at once!" he said. "You need your sleep. Tomorrow we are going to take a little trip."

Immediately all three children were wide awake. "Where? Where?" chorused the twins. And little Rachel begged, "Can I go too?" Father smiled. He picked up Rachel to carry her to bed. "Yes, little one," he said, "we are all going." "Where? Tell us where," the boys begged.

And Father said, "We are going to Gilgal. There is something there I want you children to see." "What is there to see in Gilgal?" Amos asked. Father looked mysterious. "In Gilgal," he said, "there is a pile of rocks." The children stared at him. "What is so great about a pile of rocks?" Amos asked. "We have plenty of those in our own fields." But Father would not tell them any more. "You will see," he said, "when you get there." And with this they had to be content.

The next morning Mother packed a simple lunch. The boys walked proudly at Father's side, but the little one raced around them in excited circles, until at last Father picked her up and set her on his shoulder. Long before they arrived, they could hear a rushing noise in the distance. "What is that?" Amos asked. And Father answered, "It is the river." The river? There were streams near their own fields which were flooded right now, but none of them made a noise like this.

And then unexpectedly Father said, "Well, here we are." The boys looked around, disappointed. It was exactly as Father had said — just a pile of rocks. But they were near enough to the river now to see the green ribbon of the valley, and the spray which the water flung up from the rapids, and the sound was almost a roar in their ears. "I don't see why we came all this way to see that pile of rocks," Asaph said. "But that river, now, that must be worth looking at."

"That is exactly why we came," Father said. "These rocks come from the bottom of the river." The boys stared in disbelief. "But how?" Asaph said. And Amos, "Perhaps in the dry season a strong swimmer could dive to the bottom?" "It was not a dry season," Father said. "It was just about this time of year. Sit down, and I will tell you about it." They all sat down, and Mother spread out the bread and cheese and fruit she had brought. Father asked a blessing, and then, as they ate, he told them the story.

"It happened before I was born. When I was about your age" — he smiled at the twins — "my father brought me here on just such a day as this, and that is how I know about it. Our people were all camped on the further side, and this noisy, dangerous water was between them and the land God had promised. But it is often just when things seem desperate that our God displays His power most wonderfully. Joshua was our new leader; for Moses, you know, died on the other side of the river. Joshua called the priests. He said, 'Take the ark of God, and go before the people, and step into this river.' The priests lifted God's holy ark to their shoulders. They looked at the wild, rushing water. And then they stepped into it."

"That took nerve," Amos said. Father shook his head. "Not nerve. It took faith in God. For the ark is the place where God lives among His people. And so it was not really the priests who were leading the people. It was God Himself. The priests stepped into the water. At that very instant the water stopped rushing past the camp. It piled up into a high wall above them. A dry path opened ahead of them." The children listened with wide-open eyes. "Even the water obeys God!" Asaph said. "Yes," Father said, "He is the God of all the earth. The priests went to the middle of the river. They stood there holding God's ark. All that great crowd of people hurried across to the other side.

"Then Joshua chose twelve men. 'Go down to the bed of the river,' he said, 'and each of you pick up a rock and carry it to the other side.' And so one man from each of the twelve tribes carried a rock across, and that night Joshua set them up here at Gilgal." The children stared with new wonder at the pile of stones. "Yes, those are the very rocks," Father said. "And then, after everybody had crossed safely, at last the priests carrying the ark of God crossed too. As soon as the ark of God was lifted to this shore, the river returned to its bed, and rushed down as before, just as you hear it now.

"Some day," Father went on, "you will have children of your own." The boys looked proud that Father talked to them almost as grown men, but little Rachel giggled at the thought that she would some day be a mother herself. "When your children are old enough to understand," Father said, "you must bring them here, just as I have brought you, and as my father brought me. And then you must show them

these rocks, and tell them about the power and the loving care of our
God, so that they, too, can learn to trust in the promises of God.

"And now," Father said, "perhaps we ought to start for home."

54
The Walls
Came Tumbling Down

Joshua 5, 6

Jericho was the most powerful city in the Jordan valley. It
was the best fortified too. Built on a high hill, with the ground falling
sharply away on all sides, it had in addition thick double walls to
protect against surprise attack. The surrounding countryside was desert.
There was no food here to feed a besieging army. But Jericho itself
was an oasis within the city walls. There were springs of sweet water
here, palm trees loaded with dates of different kinds, and, deep beneath the fortress, enormous storerooms loaded with grain to with-
stand a long siege. Yes, if a man could be safe anywhere in this
uncertain world, he could be safe in Jericho.

And yet the people of Jericho were afraid. They stood on their
city walls and looked down at the enemy camp. The invaders did
not seem dangerous. They had no horses, no heavy machines to batter
down the city walls, no armor to turn back the arrows of the soldiers
on the wall of Jericho. It seemed laughable for them even to dream
of attacking Jericho. But it was not something the people of Jericho
laughed about. There was almost a smell of fear in the streets of
this great city.

Wild rumors had reached the city long before the invading army
appeared. It was said that these people had a God who marched with
their armies when they went into battle. A God who dried up rivers
and seas before their feet, so that they needed neither boat nor bridge.
A God who could not be seen by anyone, and who yet ruled the

heavens and the earth. The sentries at Jericho shivered as they paced back and forth along the walls.

Far below, outside the city walls, the enemy camp slept peacefully. Tomorrow the battle was to begin. But the Israelites were not afraid. God had brought them thus far, through countless trials and dangers. He had never failed them. Hundreds of years ago He had promised to give this land to His people. They would trust in the power of God. Only their captain, Joshua, was still awake. He walked slowly through the sleeping camp, looking up at the city walls above him, trying to plan tomorrow's battle, and praying to God for wisdom and understanding. Suddenly he saw a man standing before him. At once he challenged him:

"Are you a friend, or an enemy?" he asked. And the stranger answered, "I am the Prince of the armies of God. That is why I have come now." Joshua fell on his knees. His thoughts were in a tumult. "I had hardly finished praying," he thought to himself, "and already He has answered me!"

"What are your orders?" he asked the Prince of God's army. "First take off your shoes," God answered. "You are on holy ground." So Joshua took off his shoes. And there in the dark, outside the sleeping camp, God told Joshua how to capture Jericho. Or, perhaps I should say, God told him how God was going to capture the city. For that was how it happened.

The next morning Joshua lined up the Israelite soldiers. They marched around the city of Jericho. In the middle of the army the priests of God marched. They carried the ark, the holy place where God met with His people. The priests who marched in front of the ark blew their trumpets as they went. But there was no other single sound. No man in all that army spoke as they circled Jericho. That was all. They came back to their camp. They sat comfortably outside their tents, laughing together, enjoying their supper. The people on the walls of Jericho stared at them in astonishment. Was this a joke? Or some kind of a trick? Some laughed scornfully. But others were afraid.

The next day the army lined up again. Once again they marched around the city in dead silence. Only the priests blew their trumpets as they walked before the ark of God. Once again they went back to their tents, to talk, to eat, to rest.

The third day they marched again. And the fourth day. And the fifth. And the sixth. No man in Jericho laughed any longer. There was something eerie about those silent marching men, the strange covered box they carried, and the beautifully robed priests who blew their trumpets as they went. Many guessed that what they carried must be the house of their God. And the people of Jericho had heard of other battles where this same God had given victory to these same people.

The seventh day the Israelites got up early. Once again they marched in silence around the city. But today they circled the city seven times. And as they came around the seventh time, Joshua said to the soldiers: "Shout! For God has given you the city!" A mighty shout of victory rose from every man there, even as the priests going before the ark blew their trumpets. At that very instant, the walls of Jericho — those double walls that no man could climb — fell down flat. The army of Israel rushed into the city. Joshua did not forget Rahab. He brought her and her family safely out of the city.

The Israelites had captured the first city of their Promised Land. No, *God* had captured this first city. It was not the shouting of the soldiers, nor the trumpets of the priests, nor even the ark of God that flattened the walls of Jericho. It was the living, unseen God who was among His people. He was fulfilling His promise made so long ago to Abraham that this should be the land of His chosen people.

This amazing story of what happened to Jericho was written down so that you should read it; so that you, too, should know that the promises of God are always sure; so that you, too, should always remember that the living God is present in your life, even though you cannot see Him; so that you, too, should trust in the Ruler of heaven and earth. He captured the city of Jericho for the Israelites. And He will fight your battles too, those battles which are too hard for you to win. He will give you the victory, as He gives the victory to everyone who trusts in the work of His Son, Jesus.

55
God Assigns a Test

Joshua 7

Just before report cards come out, your teacher has a most unpleasant habit. She gives your class a test. She does not do this just to be mean. The truth is — though I don't suppose you will believe this — your teacher hates to correct test papers almost as much as you hate to write them.

Teaching is a little like bricklaying. It is quite useless to lay a second row of bricks until you are sure the first row is straight and solid. And so your teacher gives the class a test to discover how well you have learned, to find out whether she can now lay a second row of bricks upon the first.

Some day you will graduate. But this does not mean that you are through with tests. Now the tests do not ask you to work a problem in long division or to give the date of a battle in the Civil War. The new tests, the ones that grown-up people have to take, are tests in living. Now God Himself is your teacher. He assigns the lessons, and from time to time He gives the tests, to see whether or not you have really learned.

What sort of a test can this Teacher give to discover whether or not a person has learned to love and trust God? What kind of question would you ask? God might test — and He sometimes does — whether you are learning to control your temper, to be patient when you are disappointed, to work faithfully at the tasks He assigns. But the most difficult test to pass is the test of how much you are willing to give up to God. And, sooner or later, God gives this test to every one of us.

How we answer when God assigns this test tells a lot about us. Because, you see, it is quite impossible to love anyone without wanting to give him something. The very inside heart of love is giving. We know this for sure because God took this very way to show us how much He loved us. He gave us Himself, His only Son. And when He wants to know whether or not we love Him in return — not *say* we love Him, but *really* love Him — He asks us to give back to Him something He has given us.

God gave this same test to His people who lived so long ago, those very people who walked thirteen times around the city of Jericho. God had done great wonders before their eyes, to teach them the lessons of love and trust. He had taken them across the Jordan River on dry ground, just as their parents long before had crossed the Red Sea. And then He had given them the first city of their new home as a free gift. Not one of them had had to lift a bow or shoot an arrow to capture the city of Jericho.

And now God paused a moment in their lessons, and He assigned a test. "The whole city of Jericho," God said to Joshua, "this first city which I have given you, I want you to give back to Me. The other cities which I will give you later will be yours to keep. But Jericho is to be returned to me. The gold and the silver are to be placed in My treasury, and everything else is to be burned. You are not to keep any of it for yourselves."

Joshua spoke to all the Israelites. "We are going to dedicate the whole city to God," he said. "Be careful that you do not take anything. It would be a terrible sin to steal something that belongs to God." The Israelites really loved and trusted God. They did not look with longing at the golden dishes, the soft, gaily colored clothes, the sparkling jewelry. They were glad to give back to God a little bit of the many, many things He had given them.

But there was one man — Achan was his name — who did not love God. Achan was greedy. He looked behind him. He looked in front. No one was watching. He put out his hand and snatched a beautiful embroidered coat. Then he picked up a piece of gold, and some silver too. He hid it all under his coat. He ran back to his tent, dug a hole, and buried his loot in the ground. No one saw what he had done.

The next time the Israelites attacked a city — just the little town of Ai — they were defeated. The soldiers of Ai chased the Israelites back to their camp. Thirty-six men were killed in that headlong flight. Joshua was thunderstruck. He lay down on the ground in front of the ark of God. "Alas, O God," he said, "Your people have run away from their enemies. Everyone will hear about this. We shall all be killed! And Your great name will be dishonored!"

"Get up off the ground," God answered. "The Israelites have sinned. They have stolen the thing dedicated to Me. Call the people together, and I will show you the man who has done this." Joshua called the people together. One by one they passed by the ark of God

— first the tribes, then the families, then man by man. And God pointed out Achan. No one had seen what Achan did; no one, that is, but God.

"Confess what you have done!" Joshua said to Achan. "I saw a beautiful coat, and gold and silver," Achan said, "and I took them. They are hidden inside my tent." Joshua sent messengers, and there, buried in his tent, just as Achan had said, were the things he had stolen from God. Then all the Israelites took Achan, and the things which he had stolen, outside the camp, and there they stoned him to death. They burned the stolen things, and buried them all under a great heap of stones.

That was a solemn day in Israel. You might almost say it was a terrifying day. For that day all Israel learned that our God is not just a God who loves. He also expects love in return. He is not only a God who gives. He also commands that we willingly return to Him whatever He asks. He is kind, He is patient beyond belief, He is forgiving. But He also requires loving obedience. He demands that we dedicate ourselves and everything we own to His service.

56
Old Clothes and Moldy Bread

Joshua 9

*U*se your head to save your neck. That was the motto of the Gibeonites. Let other people talk, if they liked, about freedom and love of your country. Let them die a hero's death if they chose. The Gibeonites had no taste for becoming heroes. What interested them was staying alive. And it was easy to see that that would take some doing.

For many years already there had been terrifying rumors about these invaders. Not that the people themselves were so fierce. They were not giants, as were some of the near neighbors of the Gibeonites.

They did not have horses, or chariots, or armor. They were not even especially known for their skill in battle, or their courage. If it was a question of ordinary courage and hard fighting, the Gibeonites were willing to match themselves with any enemy.

No, it was the God of the invaders who struck terror to the Gibeonites' hearts. No one had ever before heard of such a God. He dried up seas so His people could cross over. He sent hail and darkness and strange, unnatural death in the night to those who stood in their way. Stories like these had been filtering along the desert trails and across the mountain passes for many years now. The coward trembled when he heard them; strong men laughed at them as fables.

But there is a time to stop laughing. If you wish to stay alive, that is. For now this people, whose God was so much more powerful than any other god, had appeared on their very doorstep. Perhaps the stories they had heard were true. Perhaps not. The Gibeonites could not be sure. But they were sure about what had happened at Jericho — Jericho the powerful, Jericho fortified so strongly that no army could possibly capture it. The invaders had simply marched around the city, carrying a covered golden box, which, so men said, was the house of their God. Not a spear had been lifted; not an arrow had been shot. No, the priests had blown their trumpets, and the soldiers had raised a shout. That was all. The walls of Jericho had fallen down flat. The city had been burned to the ground, and every living person in it had been killed. The only thing left of Jericho today was a heap of smoking ruins.

Even a fool could see that this was no time to talk of courage and being a hero. Who could fight against a God that powerful? No, this was a time to think hard about how to escape the fate of Jericho. When a man cannot succeed by his strength, he will have to use his wits.

The Gibeonites selected a group of ambassadors to visit the Israelite camp at Gilgal. The men put on the oldest clothes they could find. They changed their shoes for some that were worn out, almost falling apart. They took wineskins so old that they were patched, and patched again. They found some bread that was dry and moldy. And they came to Joshua at Gilgal.

"We have come," they said, "from a far country. Even far away, where we live, the name of your God, and the marvels He did in Egypt, are talked about. Our people have sent us to make an alliance with a nation so favored as to have such a God."

Joshua hesitated. "Perhaps," he said, "you live right here among us. How then could we make an alliance with you?" But the ambassadors answered, "Oh, no! We have come from a very far country. Do you see this bread? We took it hot out of the ovens when we left home, but now it is dry and moldy. Our wineskins were new, but now they are patched and worn. Even our clothes and our shoes are worn out because we have traveled such a long way to make an alliance with you!"

Be careful, Joshua! Remember that God said you were not to make an alliance with any of the wicked, heathen people of this land. Ask God about this first, before you decide! But Joshua was not careful. He forgot to ask God. He listened to the clever story of the Gibeonites. He made an alliance with them. He swore by the name of the great God of heaven and earth that he would not do them any harm.

Three days later the Israelites learned the truth. The Gibeonites lived next door. Gibeon was one of those cities so wicked that God had commanded they be destroyed. Now they had sworn in God's name not to harm them! They could not take back their promise. A promise made in God's name was holy. Joshua called the leaders of Gibeon together. "You have tricked us," he said. "We will not kill you, because we have promised in the name of our God. But you shall not go free either. From now on, as long as you live among us, you will have to work for the house of our God. You will have to chop the wood and carry in the water." And the Gibeonites, much disappointed that their clever scheme had backfired, said, "We did it because we had heard your God had commanded you to destroy all the people of the land. We were afraid for our lives. But now we are at your mercy. Do whatever you think is good and right."

So the Gibeonites saved their lives, but not their freedom. They became slaves who helped with the hard work of caring for God's house. And Joshua learned a bitter, painful lesson. He learned to ask God before, not after he decided.

57
The People at the Oak Tree
Joshua 24

Near Shechem, in the valley between the twin mountains, Gerizim and Ebal, there stands a solitary oak tree of great age. A tree does not have eyes to see with, nor ears to hear. But if a tree could see and hear and even talk, what stories this tree could tell!

Down the hillsides into the valley creeps a lonely group of travelers: a man, his wife, his nephew, a few servants. They are weary and travel-stained, and perhaps even a little perplexed. Abraham has been traveling for years already, and still he does not know where he is going, or why — only that God has commanded him to go. To this one certainty he clings. Along the road, in a strange country, his father has died, and he has buried him there in a lonely grave, among strangers.

The oak tree offers a grateful shade in this hot land. Here the travelers set up their tents, to rest a little while before they go on. God's ways are most mysterious. He does not tell us where He is leading us, or why. Neither does He tell us when to lift up our eyes and suddenly behold His glorious presence. And so it was with Abraham. Here, beneath this very tree, God Almighty appeared to Abraham.

"Look around you," God said. "For I am going to give this country to your children." And so beneath the oak tree Abraham built an altar, and he prayed to the God who had spoken to him. What did he say? I think he must have thanked God for His protection on the long journey, and for God's gracious promise for the future. And surely here he also made a promise to God, a promise to love and trust Him all his life long.

It is perhaps a hundred and fifty years later. The oak tree still stands. Is it the same oak tree? Or is it a son, or even a grandson of the first? I cannot tell, but it is true that oak trees live to a great age, and this one stands in the same spot as the first. Another group of travelers approaches. This is the train of a rich man, with great herds of cattle, hundreds of servants, and a large family also. Jacob is returning home with his two wives, his eleven sons, and one daughter. He has been away for many years.

Not far from here is the stony hillside where he lay, alone and frightened, beneath the stars the night he ran away from home; where he dreamed of the ladder reaching up to heaven, and where God promised, "I will go with you wherever you go, and I will bring you back again to this place, for I am going to give this country to your children." Yes, Jacob, like his grandfather, Abraham, before him, can testify that God's promises are forever sure. That He does for us more even than He says He will, heaping up His measure to overflowing.

Jacob's wives and children have never seen the Promised Land before. Always they have lived in Mesopotamia, and there they have mingled their prayers to God with prayers to the heathen idols all around them. Now Jacob, like Abraham before him, wishes to dedicate himself, his family, everything most precious to him, to the God who keeps promises. He collects from all his family, and his servants' families, the idols they have brought with them from their childhood home. Jacob digs a hole beneath the oak tree, and he buries the idols deep under the ground. From now on he and his family are going to bring the sacrifices of thanksgiving to God, and God alone.

Five hundred years pass. There is still an oak tree standing in the valley between Mt. Ebal and Mt. Gerizim. I doubt that it is the same oak tree, though one cannot say for sure. Another group is approaching, this time a great multitude, almost beyond numbering. All these are the children God gave to Abraham, just as He promised so long ago. Strange and wonderful have been their experiences since that day that Jacob dedicated all he had to God. One of them has ruled the great land of Egypt, second in power only to the king himself. And then they have been slaves, building pyramids for the Egyptian rulers. For forty years they have wandered aimlessly back and forth through the wasted desert, dependent on God for every mouthful they ate, for every sip of water they drank.

They have crossed the wild Jordan River. They have besieged fortified cities, fought fearful battles, defeated whole leagues of kings. Always God has fought for them. Yes, God has given them the land, just as He promised to Abraham so long ago, as He promised again to Jacob.

Their leader, Joshua, who went with them into all these battles, is now very old. He is almost the only one in all their hundreds of thousands who remembers what it was like in Egypt. But now he hears, as it were, the voice of God calling him to come home. Have the Israelites come to hear the parting words of their great general? No, this is not why they have come. They will hear Joshua's dying words, but they have really come, like Abraham and Jacob before them, to renew their covenant with the great God of heaven and earth. To remember all that God has done for them. To tell over to each other His sure promises. To dedicate themselves and their children in grateful service to their God.

Perhaps some day you, too, will visit Palestine, and will see the oak tree that grows near Shechem. Surely this is not the same oak, though the people who live there will tell you that it is, and it does grow in the very same spot. But this *is* the very place where God talked to Abraham, and where Jacob, and, later on, the Israelites, dedicated their lives to God.

But you do not need to travel across the ocean to find a place to pledge your life to God. Any place will do, for our God is everywhere, and hears what we say even when we do not speak aloud. You, too, can pause a moment in your busy life to remember what God has done for you, and to remind yourself that His promises are always sure.

And you too, kneeling by your bed tonight, can promise to God a life of thankful obedience. You, too, can trust, as those people so long ago trusted, in the salvation God has provided in our Saviour, Jesus.

58
God Hears the Cries
of His People

Judges 4, 5

her name was Deborah. She lived in the hill country, perhaps thirty miles south of the famous oak tree at Shechem where the Israelites had dedicated themselves to serve God. That was when her grandparents were still alive.

When she was a little girl, Deborah dreamed, as little girls will, about a husband and a house full of glad children. And God — for this is God's work too — gave her a husband, and also the children she longed for. In fact, as He so often does, God gave Deborah *more* than she had dreamed about, *more* than she had longed for. He gave her unusual wisdom. When there were quarrels and bitter rivalries, Deborah knew how to put everything straight again. She gained a reputation for fairness, and people came from far away to ask her to settle their problems. Yes, Deborah became a judge in Israel. She sat on the hillside, in the shade of a palm tree, and listened to the quarrels and arguments of her fellow Israelites, and then she decided. She decided fairly and wisely.

But this was not all that God gave to Deborah. God chose Deborah to be a prophet. Now a prophet is a person who brings a message from God. Sometimes this message is a happy one. The prophet has beautiful promises to tell. He paints a delightful picture of what God has in store for His people. Sometimes the message from God is an angry message. When the people sin against God, the prophet warns them of what will happen if they do not repent.

The time in which Deborah lived was not a happy one. The Israelites — those very people whose grandparents had solemnly promised to serve God — had forgotten all that God had done for them. They had found other gods, heathen idols of brass and stone, and they prayed to these idols instead of to the true God. When they fought against the Canaanites, they no longer won their battles, because God no longer fought for them.

For twenty years God had allowed Jabin, the king of Hazor, to enslave them. Jabin was a powerful king. He had nine hundred chariots made of iron. The Israelites had no iron. Their weapons were made of copper, which was too soft to make a sharp sword or spear. And they had no chariots. A copper chariot would not be of any use at all.

These twenty years were years of slavery, of grinding poverty, of cruel suffering. At last the people remembered their God, the only true God there is. They cried out for help. They admitted their wickedness. They promised to trust only in God.

From her judgment seat on the hillside under the palm tree, Deborah sent out a messenger. She sent for Barak, who lived far to the north, north even of Hazor, where the cruel tyrant, Jabin, reigned. "God has a command for you," she said to Barak. "Collect an army together, and take up your position on Mt. Tabor. God will deliver Jabin's army into your hands."

What kind of a man was Barak? Was he a mighty hero of faith, who never knew what it was like to be afraid? No, Barak was a man like you and me. He loved God, he wanted to trust God, he *did* trust God. But it was hard to trust in God. Barak had never seen God. But many times he had seen those nine hundred iron chariots, and the cruel face of Sisera, the king's general, as he swept down upon the helpless Israelites. "You come along," he said to Deborah. "Then I will go." "I will come," Deborah promised. "But God will not deliver Sisera into your hand but into the hand of a woman!"

So there we see them, Barak, and Deborah, and their ten thousand foot soldiers drawn up rank by rank on the slopes of Mt. Tabor. And sweeping towards them, the shout of victory already ringing out, Jabin's iron chariots, with the hated Sisera at their head. "Up!" Deborah said to Barak. "God has gone out to battle ahead of you!" And that is just the way it was. The Israelites ran down the mountainside to fight, but it was God, not Barak, that defeated the enemy. The nine hundred iron chariots were thrown into hopeless confusion. Many of them were dashed into the river below.

Sisera escaped on foot, running for his life. Out of breath, and utterly exhausted, by terror as much as by his headlong flight, he came to the tent of Heber, the Kenite. The Kenites were distant relatives of the Israelites. Some of them had come along with their cousins to Canaan, and had settled there.

Jael, Heber's wife, was home alone. She opened the tent flap, and said to Sisera, "Come in and rest!" Sisera stumbled into the tent and fell exhausted on the floor. Jael took a rug and laid it over him. "Give me a drink of water," he gasped. Jael gave him a drink of milk. "Stand in the tent door," Sisera begged. "If anyone asks you, 'Is there anyone here?' tell them, 'No!'" Then Sisera fell into an exhausted sleep.

Sleep deeply, Sisera. When you awake, you will meet your Maker and your Judge. Jael looked around the tent. There was no sword or spear there. She picked up a tent stake, and the wooden mallet used to pound it into the ground. Softly she came up to the sleeping man. She raised the mallet, and pounded the stake right through his head into the ground below. So Sisera the cruel, Sisera the hated and feared, was killed by a woman.

A few minutes later Barak came panting up the hillside. "Come in," Jael said to him. "I will show you the man you are looking for." And there on the tent floor lay the great general, dead.

Then Deborah sang a song of victory to God: *I will sing praise to God. The Lord came down for me against the mighty. So let all thine enemies perish, O God.*

And God gave His people peace for forty years.

59
"Show Me a Sign!"

Judges 6

Gideon dropped the last armful of grain into the winepress, and, picking up a stick, he began to beat the grain to separate the kernels of wheat from the straw. It was slow, tedious work, but he did not dare to carry it to the regular threshing floor where the oxen could tread it out. The threshing floor was on the hilltop, and could be seen for miles around. That was how they had lost their wheat last year.

As he worked, he watched constantly for any wisp of smoke, or of dust, which would signal the approach of the enemy raiders. For seven years they had come now, always at harvest time. They appeared suddenly out of the north, sweeping down with their horses and their camels upon the helpless Israelites — so many of them that they seemed to cover the land like a plague of grasshoppers. They trampled the growing crops, stole whatever could be carried away, and burned everything that was not movable. Then they vanished again to the north. The Israelites crept out of the caves where they had hidden, to stare hopelessly at the devastated land, and to weep.

Gideon's heart was heavy as he worked. He did not see how he could feed his family till the next harvest. This troubled him, but there was an even deeper despair beneath this. *Where was God while all this happened?* That was the question that continually haunted his heart.

Sunk deep in these thoughts, Gideon forgot to watch. Suddenly he came to with a start. A stranger was sitting under the oak tree by the winepress. "God is with you, you brave and powerful man!" the stranger said. Gideon stared at him in disbelief. He was only a simple farm boy. He had never heard such talk as this. At last he said sadly, "If God is with us, why has all this happened? Where are all God's wonders that our fathers told us about? I am afraid that God has abandoned us." Even as he spoke, Gideon added to himself, "But we abandoned God first!"

And God — for the Stranger was God, though Gideon did not recognize Him — said, "Go in your power, and save Israel from the

Midianites. See! It is I Myself who send you!" Gideon was more puzzled than ever. "How could I save Israel?" he asked. "My family is the poorest in our whole tribe, and I am the least important in my family." God answered, "I Myself will go with you. You shall attack the Midianites, and utterly crush them!"

A startling new thought struggled in Gideon's mind: *This stranger was no ordinary man. Could it be?* He hardly dared to think the thought, much less to say it out loud. *Could this visitor be God?* Hesitating, half afraid to speak, he begged, "Show me a sign that it is really You talking to me. Do not leave till I have brought You a gift." God said, "I will stay until you come back."

Gideon hurried to prepare some meat, and to bake some little cakes. "Lay the meat and the cakes on this rock," God said to Gideon, "and pour the gravy over them." Gideon did so. Then God stretched out His rod and touched the meat and the cakes, and they burst into flame. At the same moment God Himself disappeared. Gideon was afraid. He prayed, "O Lord God, I am afraid, because I have seen You face to face!" "Peace!" God answered. "Do not be afraid! Though you have seen Me face to face, you shall not die."

That night as Gideon lay on his bed, turning over in his mind these unbelievable events, God spoke to him again: "Throw down the altar of Baal, which your father has built, and the goddess Asherah, which stands beside it. Build an altar to the Lord there, and offer a sacrifice to Me on it." Gideon knew that his fellow townspeople would object to this. He waited till the next night to obey God. After it was dark, he took ten of his servants and tore down the altar of Baal. Then he built an altar to God, and sacrificed an ox on it.

The next morning, when the people of the city saw what had happened, there were angry shouts. "Who has dared to do this?" they asked. And someone said, "It was Gideon!" They came in a crowd to Gideon's father. "Hand over your son!" they ordered. "He must die." But Gideon's father said, "If Baal is really a god, he can look after his own affairs." Grumbling, the people went home.

Now the dreaded bands of the Midianites have crossed the Jordan again. The people creep away to hide in caves, hoping at least to escape with their lives. But stay! The Spirit of God comes upon Gideon. He blows a trumpet, to summon the Israelites to fight. From the north and the east and the south and the west they come in answer to Gideon's trumpet.

A pitiful-looking army, clothed almost in rags, with scarcely any weapons, and surely no camels or horses! As Gideon looks at them, he is torn again by doubt. It is ridiculous to try to fight the Midianites with such an army. That is, unless God will go with them.

Once more, as always when he was afraid, Gideon turned to prayer. "O God, if You are truly going to save Israel through me, give me, I beg You, one more sign. Tonight I will lay a fleece upon the threshing floor. If the fleece alone is wet with dew in the morning, but the ground is dry, then I will know that You go with us." So Gideon spread the fleece, and in the morning the ground was dry; but when Gideon lifted the fleece, and wrung it out, a bowlful of water fell from the fleece.

Still Gideon was afraid. Once again he prayed, "O God, do not be angry with me. Give me one more sign. Tonight let the fleece be dry, and the ground wet." The next morning it was exactly as Gideon had asked. Gideon was not afraid any longer. He was ready to go out to fight, trusting not in his army, but in his God.

6O
We Do Not Fight Alone

Judges 7

Once again it was night. Gideon and his little band of soldiers were camped on the mountain slope. Below them the campfires of the enemy lighted up the night, spread across the valley as far as the eye could see. There were more of them than a man could count.

Gideon was afraid. He was so hopelessly outnumbered! During the day God had sent most of *his* army back home. "You have too many soldiers," God had said. "If you fight with an army this big, the Israelites will say, 'We won today in our own strength. We did not need God!' Send home every man who is afraid."

Too many soldiers? There were at least four of the enemy to every one of the Israelites. Gideon did not understand how he could have too many soldiers. Just as you and I so often do not understand what God commands. But though he did not understand, Gideon obeyed. The herald called the soldiers together, and Gideon made an announcement: "Any one of you who is afraid to meet the enemy can freely go home!"

The men looked at one another. Then, shamefaced, they looked away. They saw the enemy spread like a plague of grasshoppers in the valley below. They remembered the seven times before that the enemy had beaten them, and they had hidden in caves and holes in the ground to save their lives. One by one the men picked up their weapons and their bedrolls and went home. Twenty-two thousand of them slipped away. Only ten thousand were left. Ten thousand Israelites to fight one hundred and thirty-five thousand Midianites!

Then God spoke again. "There are still too many in your army. Take them down to the water pool beneath the spring, and there I will show you which soldiers to take, and which to leave behind. Those that scoop up water in their hand, and lap it up from their hand like a dog, put them on one side. Those that get down on their hands and knees to drink, and drink directly from the pool, put them on the other side." Again Gideon obeyed, though he did not understand. There were three hundred men who lapped the water from their hands, as a dog laps up a drink. And God said, "By these three hundred men I will save you from the Midianites. Send everybody else home."

So now Gideon was camped on the mountainside with his three hundred men. And as he looked down at the far-flung fires of the Midianites, he was afraid. And God looked down on His servant Gideon, who loved and trusted and obeyed God, but who was still afraid. God bent down, in His mercy, to answer Gideon's weakness. "Take your servant with you," God said, "and spy out the Midianite camp. You will hear something that will give you new courage."

Gideon and his servant slipped secretly down the mountainside, past the enemy sentries, until they walked among the tents of the hated Midianites. It was late. The fires were almost burned out. The Midianites were sleeping. Suddenly Gideon froze in his place. Someone inside a tent was talking. "I had a dream," a soldier said to his buddy.

"A barley cake came rolling down the mountain into our camp. It bumped into the tent, and knocked it flat and upside down. What ever could this dream mean?" And his friend replied, "You dreamed about the sword of Gideon. God has delivered us and all our army into his hand!"

When Gideon heard this, it was just as if scales had suddenly fallen from his eyes. In a flash he saw that if God was fighting for you, it did not matter how small your army was. In fact, the smaller your army, the more the mighty power of God would show through. Gideon was not afraid any longer. Right where he was, in the middle of the enemy camp, he bowed his head and prayed a little prayer of thanks and praise to his faithful, his promise-keeping God. Then he and his servant slipped swiftly back through the enemy tents, past the drowsing sentries, and up the mountain slope.

"Get up quickly!" he called to his sleeping men. "God has delivered the enemy into our hands." Gideon divided his three hundred men into three companies. To each man he gave a lighted torch, and a jug to hide it in. To each man he gave a trumpet. The three companies surrounded the enemy camp. Suddenly all three hundred of them blew their trumpets. At the same time they broke their jugs with a great crash, and held up their flaming torches. All together they shouted, "The sword of the Lord, and of Gideon!"

The enemy soldiers tumbled out of their tents. On all sides they heard the ear-splitting blare of the trumpets, they saw the flaming torches, they heard the Israelite shouts. Frantic with fear and confusion, they rushed in every direction at once. No man could tell who was friend or who was enemy. They turned on each other with their swords. Terror-stricken, they fled down the valley, back towards the Jordan River, the same way they had come, so short a time before, to pillage the Israelites. The Israelites came close on their heels. That night a hundred and twenty thousand of the Midianite soldiers were killed, some by Gideon and his men, many others by their own panic-stricken fellow countrymen. After this the Midianites did not come any more to steal, and to murder the people of God.

That was how Gideon, the simple farm boy, became a great hero of faith. That was how he learned that God does not need the strong, the powerful, or even the brave, to do His work. For God is so powerful that He can work mighty works even through the weak, the unimportant, the fearful.

61
God Welcomes the Stranger

Ruth 1

Naomi had never been away from home before, and I doubt that she would have left now if it had not been for the children. She was used to the simple, friendly ways of her home town, Bethlehem. Naomi had been born here. She had played with the Bethlehem children, and later married a Bethlehem boy, Elimelech.

But this summer Bethlehem was like a haunted town. The crops had failed again. The people of Bethlehem were hungry. How would they ever live through the coming winter? No man could answer this.

Naomi and Elimelech trusted God, but there was hunger in their house too. When there was no supper to put on the table at night, it was not her own empty stomach that bothered Naomi. It was the look of hopeless longing on the faces of her two little boys. And then one night Elimelech came home with a new gleam of hope in his eyes.

"There was a stranger in town today," he said to Naomi. "He says there is plenty of food in the land of Moab." "Moab?" Naomi was puzzled. "That is a long way off. What good would food so far away be to us?" Elimelech hesitated. Then he said, "We could go there." Naomi stared at him in astonishment. Her husband hurried on. "Not to stay there. Just till this famine is over, till God remembers His people again." "That would cost a lot of money," Naomi said. "I could sell my land," Elimelech said. "Sell your land!" Naomi was horrified. "Sell your share of God's Promised Land, the part that was to belong to your children forever?" And after a moment she went on, "Moab is a foreign country. We would not understand the customs of the people, not the language either. Besides, they worship idols. Can we bring up our sons among the heathen?"

"It is for the boys' sake that we *must* go," Elimelech said. "We can teach them about the true God there as well as here. And God will hear and answer our prayers even if we live in a strange land." Naomi looked around at the dear, familiar walls of her little home. And then she looked at the pale, thin faces of her two boys. "You are right," she said. "We must go."

Can you imagine what it would be like to leave behind everything that is familiar? To set out, taking only what you can carry, for a strange country, where a language you do not know is spoken, where people dress differently, and eat different foods, and perhaps even worship God in a different way? To leave behind all your toys and all your playmates?

Perhaps in your own church, or in your class at school, there are children like this. Children who have recently come from Cuba, or, a little while longer ago, from Hungary. Have you ever stopped to think what it must feel like to be a stranger? Have you ever gone out of your way to smile at these children, to include them in your games, to ask them over? If you do this — not because they are so attractive or so popular, but just because you love Jesus — if you do this, the day will come when Jesus Himself will stand up before His Father and all the angels, and will say, "Once I was hungry, and this boy, this girl, brought me something to eat. Once I was cold, and they shared their clothes with me. Once I was a lonely stranger, and they took me in." For, you see, if you have done this for the least of Jesus' children, He counts it as done to Him, Himself.

It was true, what Elimelech had heard. There was plenty to eat in Moab. The family found a place to live, and Elimelech managed to find some work. After a while they even learned to speak the language, though the boys were quicker at this than their parents. And they did not forget the promise they had made to each other and to God. They taught the boys about the one true God, and every day the family offered prayer and praise to God.

The famine back home in Canaan lasted much longer than they had expected. The truth is, Elimelech never saw Bethlehem again. He died there in Moab. The boys were grown up now. They married Moabite girls and brought them home to live with their mother. Naomi taught her daughters-in-law about the true God, and the two girls, Ruth and Orpah, joined in the family worship. Naomi's one great desire was for a grandson, but before a baby could be born, Naomi's two sons became sick. One after the other, they died too. Poor Naomi was left alone with her daughters-in-law.

It was only then that Naomi heard at last that God had remembered His people. There was food once more in Bethlehem. "I will go back," Naomi said to the girls. "God has taken away all my family. But I can at least see my home town again before I die." The two girls went along with her a little way down the road, to start her out. Then Naomi said to them, "Go back now, each of you, to your mother's house. May God be good to you, as you were good to my sons. I will pray God to send each of you a new husband." Then she threw her arms around them and kissed them. Ruth and Orpah burst into tears. "We will go along with you," they said.

"No, my daughters," Naomi said, "I have no more sons to become your husbands. You must stay here and marry again." Orpah kissed her mother-in-law again and, crying softly, she turned back home. But Ruth refused to leave Naomi. "Do not ask me to leave you," she said. "Your country shall be my country, and your God my God." Naomi saw that she could not persuade her to change her mind. So the two of them came back at last to Bethlehem. Ruth and Naomi settled down there, though they did not know who would help them, or how they could ever pay for what they needed. But God knew, and God had not forgotten them.

62
God Turns Tears to Laughter

Ruth 2-4

Every home needs a man in it — a father, or a husband, or a son. This is why the home Naomi and Ruth tried to make for each other when they came back to Bethlehem was sadly incomplete. For God had taken away all their men. Naomi had lost her husband and her two sons. Ruth had seen her husband die, and God had never given her the son she longed for. There was no man to care for them, to love them, to provide them with food and shelter and clothing.

But God had not forgotten these two women. God never forgets those who trust in Him. And God has a special love, and extra special care, for lonely women who have lost their husbands, and for children whose father or mother has died. This is one of the reasons He commands you and me to be loving and helpful to widows and orphans. He allows us to be His hands in comforting people who are unhappy.

Ruth and Naomi had no money and no way to earn any. In those days a woman could not get a job in an office or clerking in a store. Some kind soul, someone who remembered God's commands about widows, must have offered them a house. Their next most desperate need was for food. As it happened, they had arrived in Bethlehem just as the barley harvest was starting. I say *happened.* But this was not chance. This was all part of God's plan, all part of the way in which God was going to wipe away their tears, was going to give back to them something even better than those loved persons He had taken away.

If you live on a farm, or even if you have just driven through the country when the grain is ripe, you have seen the wonderful and complicated machines that are used to harvest grain today. This is not the way grain was harvested in Bethlehem. The farmers walked through the fields with a sickle that had a sharp, curving blade. As the men cut the stalks in the field, and carried them to the threshing floor, they missed some, and others fell out of their armfuls as they walked. They did not come back to rake these up later. For God had commanded that whatever was left belonged to the poor, the widows, and the strangers. These folk came behind the harvesters. They were called gleaners.

Ruth had heard about this custom. She said to Naomi, "They are harvesting barley today. Let me go to the fields and glean." So Ruth walked out to the fields where the barley was being cut. It so happened that she gleaned in the fields of Boaz. I say *happened,* but this too, though Ruth did not know it, was part of God's plan. For Boaz was a rich man and, what was more, he was a relative of Naomi's dead husband, Elimelech. Towards noon Boaz himself came to the fields to see how the harvest was going.

"Who is this girl?" Boaz asked his chief servant. "She is the girl from Moab, who came back with Naomi," the servant answered. "She asked permission to glean behind us, and she has been here all morning." God had commanded that the stranger should be allowed to glean too, as well as the poor among His own people. But there was a special reason for Boaz to feel kindly towards the stranger. For his own mother had once been a stranger too. Boaz was the son of Rahab, the woman who hid the spies when they came to the city of Jericho. Boaz said to Ruth, "Stay here, my daughter, and glean in my fields. When you are thirsty, drink from my water jugs. I have heard how you left your father and your mother and your own country, to come along with your mother-in-law. You have taken refuge under the wings of the Lord God of Israel. He will give you a full reward." As he was leaving, Boaz said to his servants, "Drop some stalks from your handfuls, and leave them for the Moabite girl." So Ruth gleaned all day in Boaz' fields, and by night she had a peck of barley.

"Where did you work today?" Naomi asked her when she came home. "In the fields of a man named Boaz," Ruth answered. Then Naomi said, "Blessed be God who has not forgotten us! Boaz is a near relative of ours." So all through the barley harvest, and afterwards the wheat harvest, Ruth gleaned in Boaz' fields.

One day Naomi said to her, "You know that Boaz, because he is a near relative, has the right to buy back the lands my husband sold when we left Bethlehem. Perhaps he would be willing to do this, and also to marry you, so that I could have a grandson. Go out to the threshing floor tonight, and lie down at his feet where he is sleeping. Then you will be able to speak to him privately."

Boaz was sleeping in the fields to protect the harvested grain from wild animals or robbers. At midnight Boaz turned over, and was startled to find a young woman sleeping nearby. "Who are you?" he asked. "I am Ruth," she answered. "Will you spread your coat over me as a sign that you will protect me, and marry me? For you are a close relative." "Indeed I will," Boaz answered. "But there is one man who is a closer relative than I am. I will speak to him first. If he does not wish to redeem your fields, and to marry you, I will do so. Sleep quietly, my daughter. Tomorrow I will arrange all this."

Boaz was as good as his promise. He talked to the nearer relative, but this man did not wish to marry Ruth. So Boaz married her, and presently God sent them a little baby boy. They called him Obed. The sorrow in Naomi's heart was healed when she held her little grandson in her arms. And Ruth, the girl who had left home to seek the protection of God, became not only a happy wife and mother, she also became the great-grandmother of King David, and among her children's children, long, long afterwards, was our Saviour, Jesus Christ Himself. The road along which God's children travel often seems to lead over rough detours. But always God leads the way. Ruth and Rahab were strangers. But God reached out His mighty hand to draw them in among His people, and He wove their lives into the great pattern of His redeeming love.

So this story, which starts with a famine and three funerals, ends with a wedding and a baby boy. That is God's way. He sometimes sends us trouble, but in the end He sends us joy. And if right now you are one of those to whom God has sent laughter, not sorrow, then He extends an invitation to you. No, He gives you a command. You are to be the hands, and the feet, that show the love of God to those who are in trouble.

63
Dedicated to God

Judges 13

When he came to the end of the row, Manoah straightened his back and wiped the sweat out of his eyes. There was a single oak tree here, and he rested a moment in its shade and raised the water bottle to cool his parched throat. His eyes searched the horizon for any sign of the enemy. His farm was so close to the land of the Philistines that he was always alert for marauding bands.

To the south and west a column of smoke stained the sky black. Manoah stared at it in horror. Which one of his countrymen had lost his home, perhaps even his life, today because he would not pay tribute to the fierce Philistine warlords? "O God," Manoah prayed under his breath, "have mercy on Thy suffering people!" And what if they came here next? What could he do to stop them? They were giants, armed to the teeth. He was only a poor farmer, with not even a sword to protect his home and his wife. "It is because of our sins that God has forsaken us," he thought as he went back along the field, stooping over the sprouting grain. "O God, our faithful God," he prayed again as he bent over the rows, "do not remember us according to our sins, but according to Thy great mercy, and Thy promise to our father, Abraham."

There were no children in Manoah's home, so his wife also worked in the fields. One day when she was alone, a Stranger came up to her. "You do not have any children," the Stranger said, "but you are going to have a son. Be careful now not to drink any wine or eat anything unclean until the child is born. The boy's hair must never be cut, for he is to be dedicated to God from the day he is born. He shall begin to save God's people from the Philistines." And before the startled woman could ask a single question, the Stranger disappeared.

Manoah's wife hurried to find her husband. "A man from God spoke to me," she said. "His face was terrifying, dazzling, like the face of an angel. I did not dare to ask where he came from, and he did not tell me his name. He said to me, 'You are going to have a son. Do not drink any wine or eat anything unclean until the child is born, for he will be dedicated to God from the day he is born till the day he dies.' "

This was good news, but it was frightening too. How could simple farmers like themselves ever know how to bring up properly so special a child? Manoah knew of just one thing to do. He must ask God to show them how. He prayed, "O Lord, let the man You sent come back again, and teach us how to care for the child You have promised." God heard Manoah's prayer. The Stranger appeared a second time to Manoah's wife as she sat resting in the fields. This time the woman hurried to call her husband. "The man that came before," she said, "is here again." Manoah went back with his wife. "Are you the man that spoke to my wife before?" he asked. The Stranger said, "I am."

Then Manoah said, "How are we to train the child?" "Just as I told your wife the first time," the Stranger answered. "She must not drink wine, or eat anything unclean. Be careful to do everything I told her." Manoah said, "Stay a little while, so we can prepare something for you to eat." For Manoah did not guess who this Visitor was. The Stranger answered, "I will not eat your bread. If you want to make an offering, offer it to God."

All this was very strange and puzzling. Manoah asked, "What is your name? If we know your name, we can remember and honor you after what you have promised happens." The Stranger answered, even more mysteriously, "Why do you ask my name? Truly, it is very wonderful!" Then Manoah took a young goat and a little grain, and he laid it on the rock as a sacrifice to God, as the Stranger had suggested. Suddenly a flame came bursting out of the rock and burned up the sacrifice, and the Stranger went up to heaven in the flame!

Manoah and his wife were terrified at what they saw. They fell on their faces on the ground and worshiped God. For now they understood that the Stranger was the very angel of the Lord. Manoah said to his wife, "We will surely die, because we have seen God!" But his wife said sensibly, "If God wished to kill us, He would not have accepted our sacrifice, neither would He have told us all these things."

They did not see the angel of the Lord again. But after a time it happened just as God had promised. They had a son, and they called him Samson. The boy grew strong and tall, and God blessed him. The Spirit of God worked in his heart, to prepare him to save God's people from their cruel masters, the Philistines. For though God's people had sinfully turned away from trusting in Him to serve idols instead, yet God was faithful. He remembered the promise He had made to Abraham that his children should inherit this land.

64
One Man Against a Thousand

Judges 14, 15

He was walking quietly among the vineyards when it happened. A young lion sprang out at him with a bone-chilling roar. You and I would have run away — as we so often run away from our enemies. But Samson, filled with the power of the Holy Spirit of God, turned on the lion. He tore the animal to pieces with his bare hands. For weaponless hands, backed by the might of God, are stronger than any enemy.

Later he came back. He found a swarm of bees had settled in the bleached bones of the lion. He took some of the honey and ate it. He gave some to his father and his mother. And this seemingly meaningless act led, in the mysterious providence of God, to another, greater proof of the strength of a man dedicated to God.

From the dead lion, and the bees, and the honey came a riddle. The riddle was told by Samson to the young men who were guests at his wedding. They were Philistine men, and the wife he married was a Philistine too. His parents objected to his marrying a Philistine woman. They did not realize that it was all God's doing. "I will tell you a riddle," Samson said to his guests, "and if you can guess it, I will give you thirty linen shirts, and thirty suits of clothes. If you cannot guess it, you must give me the same prize." The young men said, "Go ahead!" This was the riddle: *Out of the eater came forth food. And out of the strong came forth sweetness.*

The young men racked their heads, but they could not guess the riddle. At last they said to Samson's bride, "You had better get the answer out of him. Otherwise we will burn up both you and all your family." "You do not love me at all," Samson's new wife said to him. "You have not told me the answer to your riddle." Samson answered, "I did not tell my father or my mother either. Why should I tell you?" The wedding feast lasted for seven days, and for seven days Samson's new bride wept, and coaxed, and wept again. Can you guess what happened? At last Samson could not stand her tears any longer. He told her the answer, and she promptly told it to the young Philistine men. "What," the young men said to Samson, "is sweeter than honey? And what is stronger than a lion?"

Samson went down to the Philistine city of Ashkelon. In the power of the Spirit of God, he killed thirty Philistines, and took their shirts and their suits to give to the wedding guests. Then, angry that his bride had betrayed him, he went home without her. Some months later he returned to get her. Her father said, "I didn't think you wanted her, so I gave her to another man." Now Samson was really angry. He caught three hundred foxes. He tied them tail to tail, fastened a burning torch between each pair, and turned them loose into the grain fields of the Philistines. They set fire to the grain, and also burned down the olive trees.

Samson went home, and hid in the rocky hills of Judah. Soon the Philistines came looking for him. The men of Judah were afraid of the Philistines. "What do you want?" they said. "Why have you come?" "To catch Samson, and get even with him for what he has done to us!" the Philistines answered. There was not a man in Judah who had not suffered from the cruel raids of the Philistines. But did they say, "God has heard our groans, and raised up a deliverer for us! Let us ask God to forgive us for our sins, and rally behind the champion God has sent us"? No, instead three thousand of the men of Judah, cowards and idolaters all of them, hunted Samson down where he was hidden.

"Don't you understand," they said to him angrily, "that the Philistines are our masters? What ever have you been trying to do? We are going to tie you up and hand you over to them." Samson said, "Swear solemnly that you yourselves will not harm me." And they answered, "No, we swear it. We are only going to hand you over to the Philistines."

Samson let them tie him securely with two new ropes. Then the men of Judah carried him down to the Philistines. When the Philistines saw him coming, bound and helpless, they raised a great shout. Immediately the Spirit of God came upon Samson. He broke the ropes that bound him as if they had been string melted in a fire. Lying nearby on the ground he saw the jawbone of a long-dead donkey. He snatched it up, and struck about him right and left. The Philistines ran in terror in all directions, and Samson after them. He piled up his dead enemies, until at last he stopped and looked around him. Wondering to himself at the power of God, he said, *With the jawbone of a donkey, heaps upon heaps, With the jawbone of a donkey have I killed a thousand men.*

So shall all those who trust in the almighty power of God defeat God's enemies!

Samson was utterly exhausted by the power of the Spirit of God which had driven him to this prodigious feat. He thought he was going to die of thirst. He prayed to God for help, saying, "Thou hast given Thy people this great deliverance by the hand of Thy servant, and now I am going to die of thirst, and fall into the hands of the heathen!" God heard his prayer, and He opened a spring of water in the rock for Samson. Samson drank and was refreshed.

And Samson judged God's people for twenty years.

65

"The Philistines Are Upon You"

Judges 16

On the third finger of her left hand your mother wears a ring. It may be a simple gold band. Or it may be set with precious stones, and engraved with the date of her wedding. Whichever it is, that ring is a sign that your mother has pledged her love to your father.

Samson also wore a sign. His sign was his long hair which had never been cut. There is no special strength in long, uncut hair — just as there is no love in the gold band on your mother's finger. But Samson's hair, like your mother's ring, was a sign, a sign that he had devoted himself to God. He was a pledged man, a man set aside to do God's work, and to do it in God's strength.

A sign always carries a message. Samson's sign was a message to the Philistines. It said to them: *One man who relies on the living God is stronger than a thousand Philistines, giants though they be, and armed to the teeth.* Samson's hair was also a message to his own people. To the Israelites it said: *There is no enemy that can defeat you if you only trust in God. But if you forget God, and put your trust in idols, you will surely be enslaved.*

The Philistines saw the sign that Samson carried. They read its message loud and clear. The Israelites were slower to read. But the sad thing about our story is that the man who carried the sign himself forgot its meaning.

Samson fell in love with a Philistine woman named Delilah. On the outside Delilah was sweet and attractive and feminine. Inside she was heartless and greedy and calculating. Samson saw only the outside. He was so infatuated by her that he forgot his pledged life. He forgot the meaning of the sign he carried.

The Philistine leaders came to see Delilah. "Each of us will give you eleven hundred pieces of silver," they said to her, "if you discover for us what is the secret of Samson's strength." Delilah at once set about to earn that silver money. She said to Samson, "Tell me, please, I beg of you, what makes you so strong? There must be some way to bind you so as to conquer your strength."

Samson forgot that another woman had betrayed him; he forgot about the wedding feast and the riddle. He forgot that his great strength was not really his, but God's, given him to use for God's work, not for a woman's amusement. He enjoyed making a game of teasing Delilah. "If I should be bound with seven bow strings," he said, "I would be as weak as other men."

Delilah sent a message to the Philistine leaders, and they brought her the seven bow strings. She hid some of the Philistines in the room. She bound Samson with the bow strings. He thought it was a joke. "Samson!" Delilah shouted, "The Philistines are upon you!" Samson stood up. He broke the bow strings as string burned by fire. Delilah said, "You are just making fun of me. Tell me truly how you may be bound." Samson said, "If you tie me with new ropes, I shall be as weak as other men." Delilah bound him with new ropes, and again she hid Philistines in the room. "The Philistines are upon you, Samson!" she cried. Samson stood up and broke the ropes off his arms as if they were thread.

"You have mocked me, and told me only lies," Delilah said. "Tell me now truly how you may be bound." Samson said, "If you weave my long hair into the cloth of your loom, I will be weak as other men." *Samson, Samson, you are playing with fire! That hair you speak of so laughingly is the sign of your pledged life!*

That night when Samson was asleep, Delilah wove on her loom, and she wove Samson's hair into the cloth. Then she cried, "The Philistines are upon you, Samson!" Samson woke up, and he carried both cloth and loom away with him.

Then Delilah said, "How can you say you love me? Your heart is not with me. You have mocked me these three times." Day after day she teased and begged and tormented him, until at last, worn out by her nagging, Samson gave in. He said to her, "Since the day I was born my hair has never been cut, for I am dedicated to God. If my hair were cut, I should be weak like other men." Delilah knew at once that he had told her the truth. She sent for the Philistine leaders. "Come at once," she said, "for now he has told me all that is in his heart!" The Philistine leaders came, bringing the money with them in their hands. That night, when Samson was asleep, Delilah cut off his long hair. Then she cried, "Samson! Samson! The Philistines are upon you!" Samson woke up, and said, "I will get up as I did the other times, and shake myself free." He did not realize that God had left him. For the great strength was not Samson's. It belonged to God.

So the Philistines captured their greatest enemy — for Samson was now indeed as weak as other men. They put out his eyes, and set the blinded Samson to doing slave's work — grinding grain in the prison house for his enemies to eat.

66
The Lesson of Suffering

Judges 16

around, and around, and endlessly around he stumbled. The double brass chains on his legs dragged behind him. His muscles bulged with the strain of turning the giant millstone. The sweat poured down his face. Was it day? Or was it night? He did not know. His world was always dark, for the Philistines had put out his eyes.

Around, and around, and endlessly around went his thoughts as well, and the darkness inside him was worse, if anything, than the darkness outside. *Why did I do it? I have broken my vow to God. I have carelessly thrown away the gift given me to free my people from slavery! And now I am a slave myself. If only I could go back and do it over differently! Why, why did I do it?*

Around, and around, and around, while his feet wore a path in the prison courtyard, and his thoughts a path in his darkened mind. *Can I ever forgive myself? No, that is not what matters. Will God ever forgive me? It is so dark everywhere! And darkest of all because He has left me. Why did I do it?*

And while Samson stumbled in the prison courtyard, the Philistines celebrated. "We must have a great thanksgiving feast in honor of our god, Dagon," they decided. "For he has helped us to capture our greatest enemy." And so they named a day for the feast, and made all

the preparations. So many Philistines came to celebrate Samson's capture that there was not room for all of them in the great temple of Dagon in the city of Gaza. The temple itself was crowded to the doors with worshipers, and about three thousand who could not get into the building watched from the flat roof of the temple.

The priests offered many sacrifices to Dagon. The people sang songs of praise: *For thou hast delivered into our hands the destroyer of our country, who has killed many of us!* Then there was a feast, with food and drink for all, and much laughter and merriment. Someone said, "Let us have Samson brought out from the prison, so that we can laugh at him." A young boy was sent to fetch him. When the chained prisoner was led into the temple, the Philistines set up a great shout of triumph and mockery. As the blind man stumbled clumsily about, feeling with his hands in front of him to find his way, the temple walls echoed with the laughter of the Philistines.

Samson said to the boy who had led him from the prison, "Put my hands on the pillars that support the roof, so that I can rest myself a little." The boy took hold first of Samson's right hand, then of his left, and placed them on the pillars of the temple. Samson leaned against the pillars as if he were exhausted. Another shout of mocking laughter echoed through the temple.

Then Samson prayed to the one, true God: "O Lord God," he said, "remember me, I pray You, and strengthen me just this once, O God, that I may be avenged on the Philistines for my two eyes!" He put his right hand on one of the two center pillars of the temple, and his left hand on the other. Then he cried, "Let me die with the Philistines!" He bowed himself forward with all his might — with God's might, for God heard his prayer. And the roof crashed down upon Samson, and the idol Dagon, and Dagon's priests, and all the Philistines. And in his death Samson killed more of the Philistines than all those he had killed when he was alive.

Then the members of his family came to Gaza. They took Samson's body back to his birthplace, and buried him beside his father, Manoah.

When you remember Samson, do not think of him as a man who was stronger than other men, for he was not! Think of him instead as a man given great opportunities to do something for God and His people, a man who carelessly threw these opportunities away to seek instead his own selfish pleasure. Think of him as a man who suffered greatly, and who learned in the school of suffering lessons he had not learned in happier days.

Hast thou not known? Hast thou not heard? The everlasting God, the Lord, the Creator of the ends of the earth, fainteth not, neither is weary; there is no searching of His understanding. He giveth power to the faint; and to them that have no might, He increaseth strength. Even the youths shall faint and be weary, and the young men shall utterly fall: but they that wait upon the Lord shall renew their strength; they shall mount up with wings as eagles; they shall run, and not be weary; they shall walk, and not faint (Isaiah 40:28-31).

67
Hannah Gives Her Son Back to God

I Samuel 1

In your home there is one father and one mother. Elkanah's home was not like that. Elkanah had two wives, and this is just where the trouble started. Peninnah had a big family of boys and girls, and she was always boasting about this. Hannah had no children at all. She tried not to be jealous of Peninnah. She knew that it is God who gives children, and that everyone ought to be content with what God sends. She had often prayed about this. She prayed for a son, but she also prayed for patience. For Peninnah would not leave her alone.

Peninnah was jealous too. She had the children, but Elkanah, their husband, loved Hannah the most. This made Peninnah furious. Surely a man should love best the woman who gives him sons and daughters! It was not fair that Hannah should be the favorite! So Peninnah never missed a chance to remind Hannah that she was really a useless wife because she was not a mother.

Every year at harvest time the whole family packed up their things and went to spend a week at Shiloh for the thanksgiving festival. The children especially looked forward to this outing. The weather was still mild and pleasant, not cold as it so often is on our Thanksgiving. They did not rent rooms in the town. Instead their father built little shelters of green branches and leaves for them to sleep in. These little shelters reminded them of the tents their fathers had lived in while they wandered forty years in the desert. They reminded them to be thankful that God had rescued them from slavery in Egypt, and had brought them to a land of their own, just as He had promised. They ate under the open sky, as if it were one long picnic. All around them were the leafy shelters of other families who had also come to give thanks to God for the harvest, and, even more, for the faithful fulfillment of all His promises.

Of course the festival had its solemn moments too. The children stared with wide-open eyes at the tent of God. There, in the holy place, where only the high priest might go, the great God of heaven and earth, whom no man had ever seen, dwelt above the mercy seat. The family always brought a lamb with them from home to sacrifice to God. After the lamb was killed, parts of it were burned on God's altar, to show that everything they had belonged first of all to God. Parts were given to the priests, who prayed every day for all the people. And then the family sat down to share the rest in a happy feast of thanksgiving.

Father cut up the meat, and gave a part of it to each one of them. Peninnah came first — she was the children's mother. Then each boy and each girl, in the order of his age, was served. At last Father came to Hannah. Hannah's face was sad. Another year had passed, and God had not answered her prayer for a child of her own. Father cut two pieces of the very best part of the meat, and put them on Hannah's plate. "Do not be sad, Hannah," he said softly. "I love you very much. Will not my love make up to you for the sons you do not have?"

Peninnah saw the two pieces of meat her husband gave to Hannah. "Eat it and grow fat!" she said to Hannah angrily. "That is all you are good for! You cannot produce even one child to carry on your husband's name." Hannah burst into tears. She picked up a piece of the meat and tried to eat it, but she could not swallow it. Crying bitterly, she got up and ran from the table. She ran to the tent of God. No one was there at this time of the day except the old priest, Eli. Hannah kneeled down, and as the tears ran down her cheeks, she spoke to the God she knew and loved. "O Lord God," she prayed, "the God of all the earth, if You will look down on my sorrow, and remember me, and if You will give your handmaid a son, I will give him back to You to serve You all his life long!"

Hannah prayed this prayer in her heart. She did not speak out loud. The aged Eli saw her mouth moving, but he did not hear any words. He thought Hannah must be drunk. "Put away your wine," he said to her. "How long are you going to be drunk?" Hannah answered, "I am not drunk. I am a woman with a great sorrow. I have been pouring out my soul to God." Then Eli said, "Go in peace, and may God give you what you have asked Him for."

After she had prayed, Hannah felt calmer. She did not know whether God would grant her request. But she did know that God had heard her, and that He would help her. She went back to the thanksgiving feast, and she sat down and ate with the others.

The next morning the whole family was up early. They went one last time to God's tent, to offer praise and thanksgiving. And then they packed up their things and set out for home.

God remembered Hannah, and He sent her a baby boy. Hannah called the baby Samuel, because, she said, I asked God for him. When it was time again for the thanksgiving feast, Hannah said to Elkanah, "I will not go to Shiloh again until the baby is old enough to stay by himself. Then I am going to take him to God's house, that he may stay there forever." Her husband answered, "Do what you think is right. Stay here till he is older." So Hannah stayed at home and cared for the baby while the rest of the family went to Shiloh for the feast.

When Samuel was about three years old, Hannah took her little boy, and an ox to sacrifice to God, and she brought Samuel to Shiloh, to Eli, the priest. "I am the woman who stood here praying," she said to Eli. "It was this child I prayed for. God has given me what I asked for, and now I am giving him back to God, to serve God as long as he lives." And Hannah left little Samuel in God's house, in the care of Eli, the priest.

Every year Hannah made a little coat for Samuel, and brought it along when she came to Shiloh for the thanksgiving feast. And God remembered Hannah. He gave her three more sons, and two daughters.

I do not know what it is that you want most in all the world. I do not know what it is that troubles you. But I do know where you can go for help. It is the same place that Hannah went, to the God of heaven and earth, who holds all things in His mighty hand. He will hear your prayer. I cannot say whether He will give you what you ask for, or whether He will take away the thing that troubles you. But I do know you can safely trust all your life to His loving care. Hannah tried this, and proved that it is so.

68
Goɔ Calls a Chilɔ to Service

I Samuel 3

If tomorrow night, when you come home from school, your mother should say to you, "Your father and I are going out tonight. You will have to stay home and look after your younger brothers and sisters. I am sorry that you will have to miss the basketball game," I am sure your face would fall. But if instead Mother should say, "Hurry up and pack your things. Father is taking us on a trip for two weeks. Of course you won't be able to go to the game tonight," you would laugh out loud. What is one basketball game compared to a chance to see Florida or California, or Washington? What you give up would be so little compared to what you get! It would not even be worth thinking about.

That is just the way it was with Hannah, and Elkanah, and little Samuel. And that is just the way it is with every single person who gives up something for Jesus. You get back a hundred times as much as you give up. Jesus Himself has said that this is so. Hannah and Elkanah gave up their little boy. And Samuel gave up his father and his mother. But not one of them was ever sorry for what they did. God pays back those who make sacrifices for Him with a reward that is heaped up and running over.

Hannah had given her little boy to God, and every day God watched over His child. Every night too. Eli grew tired and had to sleep. But not God. God cared for Samuel every minute of the day and night. He planned and arranged all Samuel's life, even the little things, so that some day Samuel would be ready for the important work God had planned for him to do. And this is just the way God cares for you. Day and night, always watching and protecting, never sleeping, nor forgetting. He plans your life too, down to the very little things. The fun you have, and your lessons, your friends, the things you most like to do and those you find so very hard — all these are part of God's plan to train you for the important work He has for you to do. For God *has* work for you too, and it *is* important. All of God's work is important, very important.

What was it that God had planned for Samuel? Eli, the old priest, was a good man who loved and trusted God. But he had one terrible weakness. He had never taught his sons to obey God. Eli's sons had grown up to be wicked men, who did just as they pleased. They committed dreadful sins, and they did them even right in God's house. Now Eli was very old. He could not live much longer. After he died, his sons would become the priests of God. *They* would bring the sacrifices and the prayers of the people to God, in God's holy tent. God could not allow this. He was training Samuel to take Eli's place, to be a priest who obeyed and trusted God; to be a prophet who would teach God's people how they ought to live.

But Samuel did not know anything about this yet. He was still a boy. Every day he helped with the sacrifices, he listened to the prayers. But he had never yet dared to speak to God himself, all alone in his room. He had never heard God speaking to him in the quiet of his heart.

It was late at night. Everyone was asleep — Samuel, and Eli too. The lamp burning in God's tent flickered softly. And God called, "Samuel!" Samuel jumped up quickly. He ran to Eli's room. "Here I am," he said. "You called me." "I didn't call you!" Eli said. "Lie down again." So Samuel went back to bed.

God called again, "Samuel!" Again Samuel ran to Eli's room. "Here I am," he said. "You called me!" And Eli answered, "I didn't call, my son! Lie down again." Again Samuel went back to his bed. God called a third time, "Samuel!" A third time Samuel ran to Eli's room. "Here I am," he said once more. "You called me!" Now Eli understood that it was God who had called Samuel. "Go and lie down," he said. "If He calls again, answer, 'Speak, Lord, for Your servant hears.'"

So Samuel went back and lay down on his bed. And God came and stood beside his bed, and called, "Samuel! Samuel!" This time Samuel answered, "Speak, for Your servant hears."

God said to Samuel, "I am going to do something that will frighten everyone who hears about it. For I am going to punish Eli's sons for their wicked ways. And I am going to punish Eli because he did not stop their wickedness." I do not think that Samuel slept much the rest of that night. When it was morning, he got up and opened the doors of God's house. But he was afraid to tell Eli the dreadful message from God.

Then Eli called him, "Samuel, my son!" Samuel answered, "Here

I am." "What did God say to you?" Eli asked. "Do not hide anything from me." So Samuel told Eli the message God had given him. Eli said, "It is the Lord! Let Him do whatever He thinks is right!"

This was the first message God gave Samuel to deliver to God's people, but it was not the last. For Samuel became a great prophet. He led the sinful, wandering people of God back to their Saviour. He helped them drive out their enemies. And he taught them how God wanted them to live.

I do not suppose that you have ever waked up in the night because God called you by name. But He is calling you just the same. "My son, My daughter," He says to you, "give Me your heart." And God has work for you to do, just as He had for Samuel. If you listen for His voice, if you pray, as Samuel did, "Speak, Lord, for Your servant hears," then He will show you what it is He plans for your life also.

69
The Israelites Kidnap God

I Samuel 4

*e*ven as I set the words of this title down, I shrink back. The very words seem shocking, irreverent. But the really shocking thing is that they are true. They describe what the Israelites tried to do. They seized hold of what they supposed was the person of God, and they held Him for ransom.

It happened this way. For many years the Philistines had oppressed the Israelites. They came in small, marauding bands. They stole the crops and burned the houses, and punished anyone who dared to oppose them. Why did God allow the Philistines to do this? It was because God's people had forsaken God, and trusted instead in heathen idols. So God left them to the idols they had chosen, until they discovered for themselves how powerless the idols were to help them.

At last the Philistines themselves grew weary of this guerrilla warfare. "Why should we be content with loot and with tribute?" they said. "Let us exterminate this troublesome people once and for all and seize the entire country for ourselves." So they marched on Israel. In desperation the Israelites collected an army of their own. They did not have the weapons, nor the discipline, nor the fighting experience of the Philistines. But they were fighting for their homes and their families.

The battle was fierce. After it was over, four thousand Israelites lay dead on the field. The rest of the army fled in terror back to the camp. Here they held a council of war. "Why in the world has God treated us like this in front of our enemies, the Philistines?" they asked each other. And then someone thought of the kidnap scheme. "Let us get the ark of God, and bring it into our camp. Then God will have no choice. He will *have* to save us from the Philistines."

If you listen carefully, I think you can hear God's mocking laughter as He heard these words. But the Israelites were not listening. They did not hear God laugh from the heavens above.

The ark, you remember, was the very heart of God's tent. It was the beautiful golden box kept in the holiest part of the tent. On its golden cover two cherubim overshadowed with their wings the mercy seat, the place where the great God of heaven and earth lived among His people in a blinding light of glory.

It was a long time since the Israelites had troubled themselves about what God did, or where He was, or what He wanted them to do. Even when God showed them quite plainly, in the life of Samson, how one man could kill a thousand of his enemies if he only trusted in God, still they did not pay any attention. And now, after this terrible defeat, not one man in that camp asked, "Is God displeased with the way we live? Is He trying to tell us something by what has happened? Ought we, perhaps, to burn our idols? Ought we to bow before the true God in shame and in repentance that we have forgotten Him all these years?"

No, they were not interested in what God was saying to them. They were not interested in how God wanted them to live. They were only interested in what use they could make of God. Perhaps you have sometimes sung the song, "I'll go where you want me to go, dear Lord." The Israelites had another kind of song. It was — I hardly dare say the words out loud — it was, "You'll go where we want You to go, dear Lord." They planned to force God to bless them in spite of their wicked lives.

And, like many heathen people, they had a superstitious regard for the outward forms of religion. It was the ark, wasn't it, that the priests held when the water of the Jordan River was piled up in a heap so the Israelites could cross over on dry ground? It was the ark, don't you remember, that we carried around the city of Jericho, and the walls fell down. If we only fetch the ark, God will *have* to help us.

And so they fetched the ark. Eli's two wicked sons, Hophni and Phinehas, brought the ark into the camp. When they saw the ark, all Israel shouted with so great a shout that the very ground rang with the echo.

"What is the shouting in the Israelite camp?" the Philistines asked each other. And someone said, "Their God has come into the camp of the Israelites!" Then the Philistines were terrified. "Woe is us!" they said. "Such a thing has never happened before! Who will save us from this God? This is the same God who smote the Egyptians with all those terrible plagues!" But the Philistines did not turn and run as perhaps the Israelites had hoped they would. Instead they said to each other, "Be strong today, and fight like real men, O Philistines! Otherwise you will become slaves of the Israelites, just as they have been our slaves."

The Philistines fought with the fierceness of terror. There was a fearful battle. Thirty thousand Israelites died that day. The two wicked priests, Eli's sons Hophni and Phinehas, were among the dead. *And* the ark of God was captured by the Philistines!

Eli was a very old man by now, and he was blind. He sat waiting by the side of the road, trembling because his sons had taken away the ark of God. At last a man came running. "I am running away from the battle," he said to Eli. "Israel has fled before the Philistines. There has been a great slaughter. Your two sons are dead also. And the ark of God has been captured." When Eli heard about the ark of God, he fell off his seat backward. His neck broke, and he died.

That was a dark day in the history of God's people. Thirty thousand homes had lost a husband, or a brother, or a father. Their army had been utterly routed. And the ark of God, the symbol of His loving, protecting presence among His people, was in Philistine hands!

70
The Dead God
Meets the Living God

I Samuel 5, 6

*T*he Philistines carried the ark of God to their capital city of Ashdod, and placed it in the temple of their god, Dagon, as a thank offering for their great victory over the Israelites. But they were quite mistaken about the cause of their victory. It was not due to the power of Dagon. It was instead a punishment for the sins of the Israelites.

The next morning, when the priests of Dagon opened the temple doors, they were horrified by what they saw. For the statue of Dagon had fallen on its face before the ark of the living God. Carefully, reverently, the priests lifted up the idol and set it back in its proper place.

The next morning when they opened the temple doors, Dagon had again fallen down before the ark of God. This time both the head and the hands of the idol had broken off, and they lay on the threshold of the entrance to the temple. Ever after that shocking event, the priests of Dagon stepped carefully across the threshold of the temple entrance, not wishing to set their feet down on the sacred spot where Dagon's head and hands had lain!

There were two gods there in that heathen temple, and it was quite plain which one was alive, and which one was dead; which one was powerful enough to help His worshipers, and which one was helpless. But still the Philistines did not understand.

The hand of God was heavy also on the people of the city of Ashdod. God sent terrible boils to the people who had dared to lay careless hands on His holy ark. Then the people of Ashdod said, "The ark of the God of Israel shall not stay here in our city, for the hand of their God is heavy on us, and on our god Dagon." They called a meeting of the Philistine leaders. "What shall we do with the ark of the God of Israel?" they asked. And the leaders suggested, "Let the ark be carried to the city of Gath."

So the ark was brought to Gath. Now the people of Gath began to suffer from boils, boils so terrible that many of them died. And at the same time their crops were devoured by a plague of mice. The people of Gath said, "The ark of the God of Israel shall not stay in our city." So they carried the ark to the city of Ekron.

When the people of Ekron saw the ark of God coming down the road, they cried out, "They have sent the ark of God here to kill us all! Send away the ark of God, before we all become dead men!" For God had afflicted the people of Ekron so severely that their cry went up to heaven.

Then the Philistines called together all their priests and wise men and magicians, to advise them what to do in this terrible calamity that had come upon their land. The priests and the wise men and the magicians consulted together. At last they said, "If we are going to return the ark of God to the Israelites, we must not send it back empty. We must send along with it an offering to the God of the Israelites, to pay for our sin in carrying off His ark."

"What offering shall we send?" the Philistines asked. The priests and the wise men said, "Send five golden boils, and five golden mice, one for each of our cities. For the same plague has been on all of us. Make golden images of our boils, and of the mice that destroy our crops, to the honor of the God of Israel. It may be He will lift His heavy hand from off us and our land. We must not harden our hearts against Him, as the Egyptians and Pharaoh did, when they would not let the Israelites go.

"Prepare a new cart, and fasten to the cart two milk cows that have never been harnessed before. Put the ark of God on the cart, and beside it, in a little box, the golden jewels we are sending as an offering for our sin. Take away from the cows their young calves, and then let the cows pull the cart wherever they wish. If they go straight to the land of Israel, we will know that it is the God of the Israelites who has sent this great evil upon us. But if they go somewhere else, we will know it is not His doing, but merely a coincidence."

The Philistines did as the priests advised. They prepared a new cart, and on the cart they placed the ark which had brought them not triumph but only bitter grief. Beside the ark, in a little box, they put the golden offerings of the images of their boils and of the mice that devoured their crops. They fastened two milk cows to the cart, and took away their calves. And, wonder of wonders, the cows did not follow their calves. Instead, they went straight down the road to the land of the Israelites, mooing as they went, and did not turn aside to the right hand or to the left. The leaders of the Philistines followed at a little distance, to see what would happen.

The Israelites were reaping their wheat. When they looked up and saw the cart, with the ark of God on it, they were very happy. For all Israel had mourned the loss of the ark of God. The cows came to the field of a man named Joshua. The Israelites lifted the ark off the cart carefully. There was a great rock standing there, and they set the ark on the rock. Beside it they set the golden offerings sent by the Philistines. Then they offered sacrifices of thanksgiving to God, who had brought back to His people His holy ark. When the Philistine leaders had seen all this, they turned and went home.

71
The Stone That Points Two Ways

I Samuel 7

*T*he old man now sat most of the time by the door of the house, soaking up the sun. His legs were too stiff and his back too bent to work in the fields. During harvest time, when the mother helped in the fields, he kept an eye on the small children. When the children tired of their games, they would sit in a circle on the ground around him, and say, "Tell us a story, Grandfather. Tell about how it was when you were young." Or, asking for their favorite story, "Tell about the stone."

"There were so many stones," he said, remembering. "I used to think I would never be finished with picking them up." "Father says," the oldest boy interrupted, "that I will soon be big enough to help pick up stones." Grandfather smiled at him. "Soon," he agreed. "But there is one stone you must not move. This stone is special. It is a sign. It points two ways.

"Those were dark days for our people," Grandfather went on. "We were really no better than slaves to our cruel enemies, the Philistines. They trampled our crops. They burned our houses. They stole our cattle. They tortured those they captured."

"But God had not forsaken you," the oldest boy said. "Father says God never forsakes those who trust in Him." "No, God had not forsaken us," Grandfather said sadly. "We had forsaken God. We had forgotten all the wonderful things He had done for us. We were God's own people. He had brought us from Egypt with great signs and wonders. But had we learned to trust in Him? No, we trusted in idols made by men out of wood or stone. And when men refuse to listen to the words God speaks to them in love and mercy, then God speaks in thunder and in judgment."

"The Philistines were God's thunder?" the oldest boy asked. "The Philistines were God's thunder and judgment," Grandfather said. "For forty years we held our hands over our ears so that we would not hear what God was saying. For forty years we suffered under the Philistines. God looked down on us from heaven. He saw our obstinacy. He saw our suffering. And He remembered the promises He had made to

Abraham and Isaac and Jacob. He reached right down from heaven and thrust aside those hands we held over our ears. In His great mercy God *made* us hear. He opened our ears. He sent us a teacher.

"The teacher's name was Samuel." All the children smiled in delighted recognition. They loved to hear stories about Samuel. "Samuel said to us," Grandfather went on, " 'If you get rid of the idols in your houses and in your hearts, and return to the one true God, and serve and trust Him only, then God will save you from the Philistines.'

"We listened to Samuel. We put away our idols. We threw away, like the rubbish they were, those false gods made of wood and stone. They had not answered the prayers we made to them. They had not helped us in our troubles. All of us came together right here at Mizpah. We took water and poured it out before God, as a sign that we poured out our hearts in bitter sorrow for our past sins. We did not eat, as a sign that we were so grieved with our own faithlessness that we could not bear to swallow one mouthful. We said to God, 'We have sinned. Forgive, we pray Thee, our great sin!'

"Even while we were praying we were interrupted. The Philistines had heard about our coming together to pray. They came with a great army. They said, 'In one battle we will exterminate this troublesome people.' We saw that great army bearing down on us. The ground shook with the thunder of their horses. The air rang with the clang of their armor. Even today," Grandfather said to the oldest boy, "you will find broken pieces of that armor as you cultivate the fields."

"Go on," the children urged. "Do not stop now." "We had thrown away our idols," Grandfather went on. "We had said we would trust only in the true, living God. But now we were afraid. It is not easy to trust in the God you cannot see. We said to Samuel, 'Cry to God for us, that He will save us from these Philistines! Cry hard! Do not stop crying even to catch your breath.'

"Samuel took a lamb, and offered it as a sacrifice. He cried to God. And the living, unseen God heard him. God thundered with a fearful voice out of heaven. The Philistines fled in terror. We chased after them. We utterly defeated them. Then Samuel took the stone, and set it in place. He called it Ebenezer, or the Stone of God's Helping. For, he said, 'So far God has helped us!' And there the stone stands today," Grandfather said, "to remind us that God, the unseen God, hears the cries of those who trust in Him."

"But how does it point two ways?" the littlest one asked. "It points backwards," Grandfather said, "to the day when I was just a boy, no bigger than you are, the day when God heard our cries and delivered us from our cruel enemies. And it points ahead. For it is a sign you can see with your eyes, and touch with your hands, a sign that God delivers from their enemies all those who put their trust in Him. That is why it must never be moved. For God does not change. He remains faithful forever."

72
God Chooses a King

I Samuel 9, 10

Saul was the kind of person who is always popular wherever he lives. He was taller than most fellows, and very handsome. He was modest, and friendly, and generous. He was a farmer, as his father had been before him. Like farm boys everywhere, he was busy that spring with the plowing.

This happened quite a long time after that night when God stood beside the bed of Samuel and called him. Samuel was now an old man. He had had a busy life, and a happy one — with that true, lasting happiness that can come only to those who are busy about God's work. If you have watched a Western on TV, you know about the old circuit judges who traveled from town to town to bring law and order to the frontier country. There were circuit preachers in those days too, though you do not often see them on TV. They also traveled from place to place, preaching, teaching God's Word, baptizing children, and serving the Lord's Supper to lonely men and women hungry for the food of life.

Samuel was both a circuit judge and a circuit preacher. He went from place to place all his life long. He settled quarrels, explained the law, decided who was guilty, imposed punishment. And he preached

God's Word, and led the people in prayer, and offered sacrifices of repentance and thanksgiving. And then the next day he was off again to another little town, to teach and judge and pray for the people there.

Now he was old. He was tired from so much traveling about, sleeping almost every night in a different place. His two sons were helping him now with the work. Boys who have a godly father ought to try to imitate him. But how often they do not! Samuel's sons were not good men. They did not enforce the laws with fairness. They decided each case in favor of whoever offered them the biggest bribe, and so they lined their own pockets.

The Israelites came complaining to Samuel. "Give us a king," they said, "like all the other nations. You are getting old, and your sons do not follow in your ways. We need someone to lead us when we go out to fight. It is because we do not have a king of our own that we are so often beaten in battle."

The people of God did have a King. God Himself was their King. It was He, and no one else, who went before them into battle — and who sent them good and honest judges, and priests too. But they had again forsaken God. And so God had forsaken them.

Samuel was troubled. He talked to God about this. "Do not feel bad," God said. "It is not you they have rejected. They have rejected Me. They do not want Me to be their King. I will give them a king of their own, since that is what they want."

Meanwhile young Saul had been interrupted at his spring plowing. His father's donkeys had broken out from their pasture and wandered away. Saul and a servant were sent to find them. They searched for many days, but they could not find the donkeys. At last Saul said to his servant, "We had better go back home, or my father will stop worrying about the donkeys, and start worrying about us." "There is a man of God in this next town," the servant answered. "Perhaps he can tell us where to look for the donkeys." "A good idea," Saul answered. "Let us go and ask him."

As they came near the town, they met Samuel himself, who was on his way to offer a sacrifice. God spoke to Samuel in his secret heart. "This is the man," God told him, "who is to be king over My people." "Tell me," Saul asked Samuel as they came near, "where we can find the prophet." "I am the prophet," Samuel answered. "Come and eat with me. And do not worry about your father's donkeys. They have already been found." Saul stared at him in surprise. How did this stranger know about the donkeys? Samuel did not explain. He took Saul along to the sacrifice, and afterwards he gave him the seat of honor at the table, and offered him the best piece of meat. And then he took him home with him to the house where he was staying that night.

Early the next morning Samuel and Saul set out for home. As they left the city streets behind them, Samuel said, "Tell your servant to go on ahead. I have a message for you from God." Then Samuel took a little pitcher of oil and poured it on Saul's head. "God has chosen *you*," he said to the astonished young man, "to be king over His own people. When you leave me, and come to the next town, you will meet a band of prophets. At that moment the Spirit of God will come powerfully upon you, and you will be changed into another man. This is a sign to you that God is with you."

All this happened just as Samuel had said. When Saul finally got back home, and told his family he had seen Samuel, they asked him, "What did Samuel say?" And he answered, "He told me that the donkeys had already been found." But Saul did not tell anyone what Samuel had said about his being chosen king.

Not long after this, Samuel called all the Israelites together, and said to them: "God has faithfully saved you from your enemies, but you have rejected God, and have demanded a king. Now then, march past me tribe by tribe, and God will point out the man He has chosen." So the people filed past Samuel, and God chose Saul from among all the thousands of the Israelites. And when Saul had come forward, and the people saw how tall and handsome he was, they all shouted, "Long live the king!" And Samuel wrote down in a book how the king was to rule God's people. Then everyone went home again. Saul too. He went back to his plowing, to wait till God should show him what to do next.

73

Saul Makes a Good Beginning

I Samuel 11

It is spring. In the fields outside the little town of Gibeah, a man is busy with the plowing. He follows the team of oxen back and forth across the field. He is a good farmer. The furrow he makes is straight and true. But if you look closely, you will notice that his mind is not on what he is doing. His brow is wrinkled, as if his thoughts trouble him. Sometimes his lips move. Perhaps he is praying. Perhaps he is asking God to help him in his problems, whatever they may be.

If today, as you are walking home from school, hurrying a little perhaps so that you can help Father with the chores, a fancy car pulls up beside you, and if some important people get out and say to you, "You have been chosen to be king over this whole country. You are to lead the army into battle, to make the laws, to decide who has broken them and how he must be punished" — how would you feel? What would you say? I know what I would say. I would say, "I am not good enough, or brave enough, or wise enough to do these things. I am afraid to be a king."

Perhaps that is the way King Saul felt as he walked behind the oxen. Perhaps that is why he looked so troubled. His country was in bad trouble. There were enemies outside, and enemies inside. The next-door kings were just waiting to pounce on the Israelites. They hated these people who had moved into their country. And the Israelites themselves quarreled with each other, instead of uniting against the invading armies. Their public officials were crooked. Worst of all, the people had forsaken God. They prayed for help to idols of wood and stone, instead of to the true God. This was the real cause of all their troubles. For God does not answer prayers prayed to idols.

Saul was only a farm boy. He did not know how to rule God's people. He did not know what to do first. But God had chosen him. And when God calls, no man can say no. Now he would have to wait for God to show him what to do. Meanwhile there was work to do. Saul must get the fields ready for the seed. No man, not even a king, is too important to work. Saul worked all day, right through the heat.

At last, as the sun was setting, he turned his oxen's heads towards home. Some distance from the little town he heard a strange sound. It was a sound like crying, but not just one person's grief. It sounded as if the whole town were crying. There is no more dreadful sound than the weeping of grown men.

"What ever is the matter?" he asked a man on the edge of the crowd. "There were messengers here," the man answered, "sent by our brothers who live in Jabesh. The Ammonite king has attacked them. His army was so strong they saw it was useless to fight. So they offered to surrender and become his slaves. But the king of Ammon has mocked them. He said, 'I will let you live only if I first put out the right eye of every one of you!' He has given them seven days to look for help. That is why we are weeping."

When he heard these words, Saul was filled with a holy anger. The Spirit of God came powerfully into his heart. He was still just Saul, a simple farm boy. But now he was no longer troubled and afraid. For he was no longer trying to solve the problems of his country by himself. Now God was working through him. He took his oxen, and he cut them into pieces. He called messengers and sent the pieces through all the land of Israel.

"Whoever," he said, "does not come to fight with Saul and with Samuel for our brothers in Jabesh, his oxen shall be cut to pieces just as these oxen were!" The fear of God filled the heart of every man who heard this message. From all directions they came to join the battle. Saul counted the volunteers. There were three hundred and thirty thousand of them altogether.

Then Saul called the messengers from Jabesh. "Go back," he said, "and tell the men who sent you, 'Tomorrow, by the time the sun is hot, you will have help.'" Can you imagine how the men and the women and the children in Jabesh felt when they received this message? How at first they could hardly believe it, and then at last they almost wept for joy? And then they sent a message to the king of Ammon. "Tomorrow," they said, "we will come out, all of us, and you can do to us whatever you wish."

The next morning the Ammonite soldiers lined up to watch the men of Jabesh file out of their city. They laughed cruelly as they thought of what they were going to do. But their laughter did not last. For Saul's army attacked them from three sides at once. They found themselves surrounded. The battle raged fiercely all morning, till there were not two of the Ammonite soldiers left together.

Can you guess what the people of God did next? Did they spend the night in looting the enemy, in drinking and wild feasting? No, they declared a solemn feast of thanksgiving to their faithful God. They confessed their sins, they offered sacrifices, they prayed for forgiveness, and for guidance and help in the future. And God heard their prayers, and He looked down on them in mercy and in love.

74
The Test of Obedience

I Samuel 13, 15

*Y*ou sing, you pray, you listen as the minister reads the Bible. And then the deacons pass the collection plate around. You put in it whatever you wish to give to God. What happens to that money? The deacons count the money, and they put it in the safe. And what then? Do the deacons use the money to buy themselves a new car, or to take a vacation? "Oh, no!" you say, shocked. "That money does not belong to the deacons. That money belongs to God." It is used to pay the missionaries, to care for the poor, perhaps to repair or heat the church building. The deacons have it in trust, to use only as God wishes. And if the deacons should use it for themselves, they would lose their job. They might even go to jail.

That was the way it was with Saul. He had been a poor farm boy. Now he was a rich king, with many servants to wait on him. Whatever he said was law. But all these things did not really belong to Saul. He had them only in trust, just as the deacons have your offerings. This money and power were not for his own pleasure, but to use as God directed. God was the real King. Saul was only His deputy. He must follow God's orders. Otherwise he would lose his job.

It is easy to say thank you (and really mean it) when you receive a wonderful present. Especially if it comes as a complete surprise, as Saul's becoming king did. It is a good deal harder to remember to be thankful after you have had the present for some time; and it is a good deal harder, after you are rich and powerful, to remember that this is all a gift, given to you in trust, to be used only as the Giver directs. Could Saul remember this? God was going to test him.

Saul's biggest job, the one for which God had especially chosen him, was to fight the Philistines. This fierce, cruel people continually harassed God's people with sudden raids. "Go to Gilgal," Samuel had commanded Saul not long after he was made king, "and wait there for me. I will come and offer sacrifices to God, and I will also tell you what it is God wants you to do next." These were God's commands, not Samuel's. For Samuel too, like Saul, was God's deputy, taking orders from God.

Saul raised an army of about three thousand men. But when he came to Gilgal, the test turned out to be much harder than it looked. For the Philistines had raised an army too. Perhaps they had heard about Saul's army. At any rate, their army was much, much bigger than Saul's. They had thirty thousand chariots, and six thousand men on horseback, and so many infantrymen you could hardly count them.

When the Israelites heard about the Philistine army, they were so frightened that they hid in the caves and in holes in the ground. Saul waited for Samuel to come, as God (and Samuel) had commanded. But every day his little army grew smaller, as his terrified men deserted. He waited one day, and two, and three. He waited four days, and five, and six. His army kept shrinking. He waited seven days. Seven was the number of days Samuel had said he must wait. Still Samuel did not come.

Saul decided not to wait any longer. If he did, he was afraid he would have no army left. He took the animals which were prepared and ready, and he himself offered the sacrifice. He had hardly finished when Samuel arrived. "What have you done?" Samuel asked. Saul was quick to make excuses. "My soldiers were all running away," he said, "and there was this big Philistine army. You did not come. I was afraid the enemy might attack before I had asked God for His blessing. I did not want to offer the sacrifice, but I forced myself to do it."

"You have been foolish," Samuel answered. "If you had obeyed God, He would have established your children as kings over His people forever. But now your children shall not rule after you. God will find Himself a man after His own heart."

This was a sad lesson for Saul to have to learn. Oh, yes, he still won the battle. A big army, or a small one, does not matter to God. He can win even with a tiny handful. Saul had only six hundred men left, but God gave him the victory. But the taste was ashes in his mouth, because God had ruled that Saul's beloved son, Jonathan, would not follow his father as king.

Saul fought many wars. Did he learn to obey, as God helped him in one battle after another? Years after that first test, which Saul had failed so sadly, God tested him again. He sent Samuel with another command. "God commands you to destroy the Amalekites," Samuel told him, "every one of them, even their sheep and cattle and camels." The Amalekites were the nation that had attacked God's people almost as soon as they escaped from Egypt. God had said then that He would surely punish the Amalekites.

Saul called his army together, and he did as God commanded. He utterly destroyed the Amalekites. But he saved alive the best of their cattle, and also Agag, the Amalekite king. As he returned from this battle, Samuel met him. "I have done what God commanded," Saul said. "What then is this bleating of sheep and lowing of cattle that I hear?" Samuel asked him. "The people spared the best of the animals to sacrifice them to God," Saul excused himself.

"To obey God is better than to offer sacrifices," Samuel answered. "Because you have disobeyed God, God has rejected you as king over His people."

And what about you and me? God has not chosen us to be king over Israel. But He has given us many gifts, many talents. Not for our own pleasure, but to be used in His service. Do we listen for His voice, and try always to follow His commands? Or do we follow our own desires instead?

75
God's Arithmetic

I Samuel 14

From the beginning we were so outnumbered that only a fool would,have tried to fight at all. But then perhaps the man who trusts in the unseen God will always seem a fool to the man who depends on iron chariots, and swords, and spears, and the sheer weight of great numbers of soldiers.

There were many among God's own people who were certain that the fight was hopeless. When they saw that Philistine army, they shook with fear. They deserted King Saul in large numbers. They hid in the caves, and in the thickets, and in the old cisterns left by people who had lived in these wild hills long ago.

There had been three thousand of us to begin with — and even that number was pitiful compared to the unnumbered host of the Philistines. But now we had only six hundred soldiers left. We were camped at the edge of a steep cliff, and the Philistines had set up their tents on the edge of the opposite cliff. The two armies were near enough to each other to hear what was said in the enemy camp; and yet between us there lay a deep canyon, with walls so precipitous that it was all but impossible to scale them.

My master was Jonathan, the king's oldest son. He was a young man, and a brave man, but, more important, a man who trusted in God. This was his first real battle. I was his armor-bearer. There were not many armor-bearers in our army, for the simple reason that only the king and his son had real weapons to fight with. The Philistines had seen to this. They had the only smiths who could forge weapons; and though they were willing enough to sell us forks and shovels and plow-shares and any other such farm tools for a price, they would not sell us swords or spears. Except for King Saul and Prince Jonathan, our soldiers had to fight as best they could with sharpened wood cudgels, or bow and arrow, or slingshots loaded with stones.

It was my duty to accompany my master into battle, carrying his weapons for him. I handed him whatever he needed, and helped him in his brave fight against the Philistines. I suppose you could say we

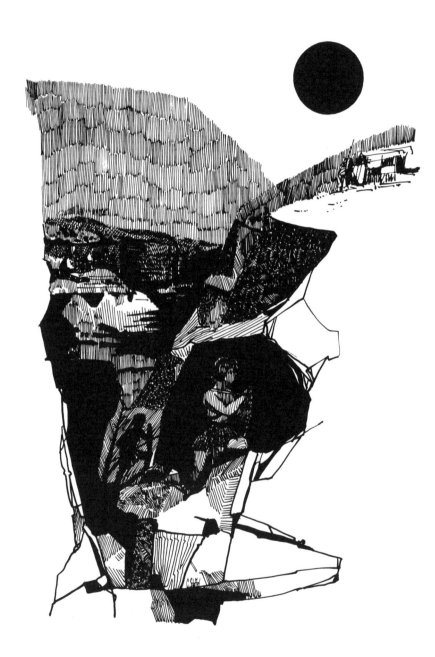

fought as a team, but it was Jonathan who supplied the daring, and the cunning, yes, and the trust in God. I followed where he led.

We had been camped this way across from the Philistine army for some days. Day after day pitiful stragglers came limping into our camp with tragic stories of Philistine raids on the countryside, of houses burned, and crops and animals stolen, and children murdered. King Saul listened to the reports with helpless rage. For what could six hundred soldiers do against the thirty thousand war chariots of the Philistines?

And then one morning Jonathan said to me, "Come, let the two of us go over to the camp of these heathen. It may be God will fight for us. For God is able to save by a few just as well as by many." I answered, "Do whatever your heart tells you to do, for I am with you all the way."

So we slipped quietly out of the camp. We told no one where we were going, not even King Saul nor our friends. We went to the very edge of the cliff. Jonathan said to me, "We will ask God to give us a sign. We will show ourselves to the enemy. If they say, 'Wait there. We are coming over to you,' then we will know it is God's sign that we should not attack them. But if they say, 'You fellows come over here,' then it will be a sign from God that He has delivered them into our hands."

When the Philistines saw us, they said, "Look! The Hebrews are creeping out of the holes where they have hidden themselves!" And they called out to us, "You fellows come over here, and we will show you something worth seeing!"

It was the very sign we had asked God to give us. Jonathan said to me, "Follow close behind me." So together we clambered on all fours down the rock wall on our side, and up the rock wall on the further side. And suddenly we fell upon the Philistines. The Philistines were so thunderstruck when we appeared in their very camp that they turned and ran, like mice instead of men. In a few short minutes the two of us had killed more than twenty of them. This caused a panic in the Philistine camp, men running frantically in all directions. Our God Himself struck terror into their hearts.

On the other side of the cliff, the Israelite soldiers heard the panic in the Philistine camp — though, of course, my master and I did not find this out till afterwards. "Count quickly, King Saul said to his officers, "and find out who is missing." And so they discovered that

Prince Jonathan and I, his armor-bearer, were not in the camp. The king called for the priest. "Inquire of God," he said, "whether we should attack." But even while the king talked to the priest, the tumult in the Philistine camp became so violent that the king said, "No, we will not wait to cast lots." And so he and all our army followed Jonathan and me across the canyon and up the further side of the cliff.

So that was how God saved His people. For my master, Jonathan, was right — and those who said that only a fool would attack against such odds were themselves the fools. The might of our God is so great that He can save by two men — or even by one, if He should so choose.

76
"Senð for the Youngest!"

I Samuel 16

David was the youngest of eight sons. If you are the youngest in your own family, you will know that it is not always easy to be the youngest. There are so many interesting things your older brothers and sisters can do, but not you. It seems they are always saying to you, "You are too young!" David found this out too. He was not as hand-some as his brother Eliab, not as tall as his brother Abinadab, not as quick of speech as some of the other boys. But mostly he was just too young. Whenever anything exciting happened, there were seven older boys who had the first chance at it. "You are still young," his father Jesse would say. "Your chance will come later."

And so David was sent off to tend the sheep in the hills. Of course, someone had to look after the sheep. David knew this. Tending sheep was important work, even if it was not very exciting. It was lonely up there in the hills with only the sheep for company. There was a lot of time to think, too. David did not waste this time in grumbling because he was the youngest and had to look after the sheep. There was one thing David knew for certain. God was taking care of him. God was planning his life. And because he trusted in God, he was sure that his chance would really come some day. Every child of God can be sure of this. God does not make mistakes when He plans your life. If you wait patiently for Him, your chance will surely come.

When he felt lonely, David would pick up his harp and play little tunes he had made up. And he would sometimes sing songs he had thought of too, songs of praise and prayer to God. And even tending sheep had exciting moments. Sometimes a bear or a lion would sneak quietly into the flock and snatch up a helpless lamb. The mother sheep would bleat piteously when this happened. David was so sure of God's care that he never stopped to be afraid. He whispered a little prayer for help as he ran after the lion. And God heard his prayer. With God's help — he could never have done this by himself — he caught hold of the lion by his beard, and killed him with his bare hands.

And so David sat on the hillside above Bethlehem, guarding the sheep, playing his harp, and waiting for God to show him God's plan for his life. Sometimes it seemed as if the whole country were just sitting and waiting, though not all of them had David's confidence in God's plan. King Saul sat brooding in his palace. He knew that he was a failure as king of God's people, and the knowledge filled him with a wild fury. He sat silent for hours, and then he flew into violent rages.

You would never have recognized the brave, handsome first king of Israel if you saw him now. God had given Saul an extra measure of His Holy Spirit when he became king. But Saul had rejected the gift. He had hardened himself against the leading of God. He had disobeyed again and again. And so the Holy Spirit had left him, and now he was torn to pieces by evil spirits who filled his heart with anger and hatred and suspicion and cruelty.

Even the great Samuel, who had judged God's people so many years, sat at home waiting. Samuel was grieving over Saul's failure — for Samuel had loved Saul. And Samuel was worrying about what would happen to God's people now that they no longer had a king who was led by the Spirit of God.

Only God was still working — as God is always busy working, while you and I sit waiting in anger, in sorrow, or just patiently till God shows us the way. "How long," God said to Samuel, "are you going to sit there feeling bad about Saul? Come! There is work to be done. You are to go to Bethlehem, to the home of Jesse. I have chosen a new king from among his sons."

"How can I go to Bethlehem and anoint a new king?" Samuel asked doubtingly. "If Saul hears about it, he will kill me." Yes, this is Samuel speaking, the man who had trusted and served God all his life, ever since his mother left him as a tiny boy in God's house. Never suppose, my young friends, that it is only young people who have to learn lessons in faith. We must all go on learning all our life long. "Take a calf with you," God said. "Call the people to a sacrifice. Invite Jesse and his sons too. I will show you the one I have chosen."

And so Samuel went to Bethlehem, where he invited the people of the town to a sacrifice and a feast to God. One by one the seven sons of Jesse arrived. When Samuel saw Eliab, the oldest, he thought to himself, "Surely this handsome young man is the one God has chosen." But God said to him, "Do not consider how handsome he is. I, the Lord, do not judge as man judges. A man looks at the outside appearance, but I look at the heart." Then Abinadab, the second son, came, but God had not chosen him either. Nor had God chosen Shammah, Jesse's third son. One by one the seven boys passed by Samuel. Samuel said to Jesse, "God has not chosen any of these. Are these all your children?"

"There is still one more, the youngest," Jesse answered. "He is looking after the sheep." Samuel said, "Send for him. We will not sit down to the feast until he comes." So Jesse sent for David. And when David at last came in, God said to Samuel, "Get up! Anoint him! This is the one I have chosen." So Samuel took the oil and poured a little of it out on David's head. And even as Samuel made this outward sign, the inside reality — which the sign stood for — happened too. The Holy Spirit of God came mightily into the heart of David.

77

In the Name
of the Lord of Hosts

I Samuel 17

If you look closely, you can see them — the two armies lined up for battle on opposite mountains. On one side are the Israelites. All the best fighting men in the nation are there. In the middle of the camp stands the royal tent of King Saul himself. Across the valley on the other side stand the ranks of the Philistines, ancient enemies of the people of God. The trumpets sound for the advance, but neither side goes forward.

But look! Someone is separating himself from the Philistine army. A man steps out in front of the line of soldiers. But would you call this a man? This is a giant! He must be all of ten feet tall. He is dressed in dazzling armor made of brass, from the shining helmet on his head down to the greaves which protect his legs. His weapons are all giant-size too! He carries a spear whose handle is like a tree trunk. A javelin hangs from his shoulder, and a giant sword by his side. As he strides forward, an ordinary man, who looks like a pygmy beside him, runs ahead of him, carrying his shield.

The hearts of the Israelite soldiers are filled with unreasoning terror as they watch. Finally the giant stands still. His fearful voice roars out across the valley to the Israelite army on the opposite slope. "Who do you think you are," he bellows, "that you dare to fight against the Philistines? Choose a champion for yourselves. Let him come out and fight with me. If he wins, we will all be your slaves. But if I kill him, then you must become our slaves." There is no answer from the other mountain. The Israelites stand frozen in their places. They would like to run and hide, but who could outrun such a man? At last the giant turns, and laughing mockingly, goes back to his camp. But the next day he comes out again to mock the terrified Israelites. And the next. And the next.

No one comes forward to take up his challenge. King Saul offers a reward to anyone who dares to fight him. He promises to make that man rich, to give him the king's own daughter as a wife. No man cares to try for the reward. What good will money and a princess do if you are already dead? For forty days the giant comes out each morning. For forty days the Israelites slink trembling back to their tents as soon as Goliath leaves.

Several miles away there is a quite different scene, a peaceful scene. Young David is sitting on the hillside, watching his father's sheep. He has an eye out for wild animals that might endanger the flock, or for a sheep that might stray and get lost. As he watches, he whiles away the time playing on his harp.

But today he must find someone else to watch his sheep. His father has sent him on an errand. He has sent him to carry food to his three older brothers who are in Saul's army. It is not a very long journey, and soon David comes to the Israelite camp. The soldiers are lined up again on the mountainside. Just as David arrives, Goliath comes out again to mock the frightened Israelites. David listens to the threats of the giant. He alone, of all the Israelites, is not frightened. The giant is powerful, but God is far more powerful. "How does this heathen dare to defy the armies of the living God?" David asks the soldiers. The soldiers stare at him in surprise. Then they bring him to King Saul's tent.

"I will go and fight this giant," David says to Saul. "You couldn't possibly," Saul answers sadly. "You are only a boy, and he is an experienced soldier — and a giant besides." "When the lion and the bear attacked my father's sheep," David answered, "God helped me to kill them. God will help me kill Goliath also." "Go!" Saul said, desperately clutching at this little hope, "and may God be with you!" Saul gave David his armor — for only the king and his son had armor among the Israelite soldiers. David tried the armor on, but it was much too heavy for him. So he went out unprotected to fight Goliath. He took with him his slingshot, and five stones which he picked up on the bank of the little brook in the valley. But he was not really alone. God went with him, and David was not afraid, because he trusted in God.

When Goliath saw David, he was insulted that such a young boy should dare to come out against him. "Am I a dog," he shouted, "that you come out to fight me with a stick? Come then! I will give your body to the birds and the wild beasts to devour." David answered calmly, "You come to fight me with a sword, and a spear, and a javelin. But I come to fight you in the name of the Lord of hosts, the God of the armies of Israel, whom you have defied. God will deliver you into my hand this very day!"

David ran bravely toward Goliath. He took a stone and put it in his slingshot. He pulled back his hand, and let it go. He hit Goliath right in the center of his forehead. The giant fell down on his face onto the ground. Then David ran forward. He took Goliath's own sword, and cut off the giant's head. When the Philistines saw their champion was dead, they ran away. With a great shout the Israelites ran after them. That day they won a great victory over the Philistines.

David trusted in God, and God honored his trust. He answered David's prayer for help. If you trust in God, He will hear your prayer also. No matter what your trouble or your difficulty is, God will help you. Nothing is too small to take to Him for help. Nothing that troubles you is so big that God cannot defeat it. He will give you everything you need to do what He wants you to do. "Call upon Me in the day of trouble," He has promised, "and I will deliver you." He delivered David. He will surely deliver you too.

78
The Education of a King

I Samuel 16, 18

*T*his story is about two men to whom God assigned lessons to be learned. One of them refused to learn. He came to an unhappy end. The other worked patiently, faithfully, willingly, even though he sometimes wondered why he had to learn these things, why it took so long before he graduated. He became an instrument useful in God's hand. In the school these two men attended, and through the lessons that God assigned, their lives became strangely intertwined. Both of the men were kings. The one who refused to learn God's lessons, who repeatedly rejected God's commands, was Saul. And so at last God rejected the king who had rejected God. For the man who will not obey, who refuses to learn, cannot rule God's people. Unknown to Saul, God sent the prophet Samuel to Bethlehem to anoint David as the new king.

And so David's lessons began. Where would you learn to be a king? Where better than at the court itself? The Holy Spirit of God had left Saul. For this is what happens to every man who refuses to learn, who resists God's teaching. At last God leaves him to the life he has chosen. Now Saul was tormented by an evil spirit. His conscience reproached him. He brooded bitterly about the loss of the kingdom. He wondered with fierce jealousy who had been chosen to take his place. He became suspicious of everyone who was successful as a soldier, or popular among the people. He flew into violent rages, or sank into moods of deep depression.

His servants were troubled by the king's black moods. There are doctors to heal a broken leg or an aching tooth, but no doctor to cure a sick soul. But men have long known that music can soothe a man who suffers the darkness of despair. "Let us search out a man who is a skilled player on the harp," Saul's servants said to him. "When the evil spirit torments you, he can play soothing music, and you will be restored." And Saul, sunk in deep despair, said, "Find me such a man."

So David came to the king's court. Saul loved the handsome young shepherd boy. He made him his armor-bearer, and David accompanied the king, carrying his weapons when they went into battle against the Philistines. And when the king's violent moods came upon him, David played sweet music on the harp, and the king's dreadful sickness was relieved.

Before this, David had lived a solitary life, caring for his father's sheep. Now he lived the busy life of the king's court. He met important people. He discovered how the country was run, and what the king's duties were. He became a brave soldier — the boy whose previous battles had been against the bears and lions that threatened his father's sheep. Saul set David as an officer over a troop of soldiers. David learned how to handle men, and how to lead them in battle. And he was successful in everything he did, because God was with him. Soon the whole country knew and loved the young soldier-musician.

These were all important parts of David's education. But I want you to notice that David himself did not understand why he must learn all these things. Perhaps he sometimes wondered when, or how, God was going to give him the kingdom. Perhaps he sometimes thought he must have dreamed that day in Bethlehem when Samuel anointed him with oil as king of God's people. But he went faithfully about the tasks God assigned from day to day. He walked in trust, believing that God had planned his life.

When the army returned from war against the Philistines, the women of Israel came out to meet the soldiers. They sang a chant of victory: *Saul has killed his thousands, and David his ten thousands.* When King Saul heard these words, he was very angry. A bitter suspicion haunted his darkened mind. Was it possible that this young nobody, David, whom he himself had promoted from being only a sheep-tender to the life of the court — was it possible that this was the new king, chosen by God? "They say," he muttered to himself, "that I have killed thousands, but David has killed ten thousands. What more could he have but the kingdom itself?" From that day on Saul hated David with a jealous hatred.

The next morning the evil spirit attacked Saul. He raved violently as he stormed about the palace. David played, as he usually did, on his harp. Saul stared at him with maddened eyes. "I will fix his ambitions," he thought. "I will pin him to the wall with this spear." And he flung his spear at David. But God averted the spear. David was not harmed. Was this, too, part of David's education? Yes, I think it was. This was a lesson in trust. It was a lesson David was going to have to learn over and over in the next few years.

79
"The Lord Watch Between Me and Thee!"

I Samuel 19, 20

In the center of the throne room, sitting on the great throne itself, King Saul stared unseeing at the walls, his eyes blinded with hatred and jealousy. He was a failure as king of God's people, and he knew it. This bitter knowledge filled him with a wild fury. He sat silent for hours, and then he flew into violent rages. It was dangerous to come near him when this happened. But even more maddening to the king than his own failure was the success of this young upstart, David. "Only a shepherd boy when I was first kind to him," the crazed king said to himself. "And now he is so brazen as to pretend to the throne itself. If it is the last thing I ever do, I will prevent that. He shall never be king. I will kill him first!"

Yesterday David had been summoned, as he often was, to play his harp to quiet the raving king. And for the second time Saul had thrown his spear at the young musician. For the second time he had missed. He, Saul, who never missed his target! David had escaped to his house. There his wife, Michal, had let him down from a window under cover of darkness. Then she quickly took the teraphim, the household idol, and put it in the bed. Over the idol's head she draped a goatskin, and pulled the covers carefully up. When Saul's soldiers arrived to seize David, Michal said innocently, "He is sick in bed." The soldiers went back to King Saul. The king became more furious than ever. "Bring him at once," he commanded, "so that I can have the pleasure of killing him with my own hands. Bring him here even if you have to carry him in his bed!" So the soldiers tramped into the bedroom itself. Did they laugh when they saw the idol with its goatskin hair in bed? Probably they did not dare to laugh. King Saul was too dangerous in these evil moods.

David escaped to Jonathan. "What have I done that is wrong?" he asked Jonathan. "Why does your father wish to kill me?" Jonathan was Saul's oldest son. He had far more reason than Saul did to be jealous of David. For Jonathan was the crown prince. He had expected to be the next king ever since he was a little boy. But Jonathan loved David. From the first time they saw each other, the two had become fast friends. They had even sworn a solemn oath that they would always be friends, and had called on God Himself to witness their pledge.

True love does not know envy or jealousy. If you really love a person, you want to do something for him — not to have him do something for you. Love is not self-seeking; it is self-giving. This is a pretty good test of whether any love is the real thing, or only a poor imitation. Who was to be the next king? Jonathan and David were content to let God decide this. They would trust in His direction, and always, whatever happened, they would remain faithful friends.

"Tomorrow," Jonathan said to David, "is the feast of the new moon. You should be present at that feast. If my father asks where you are,

I will say you have gone to Bethlehem for a family sacrifice. I will be able to tell from the way he answers whether or not your life is really in danger." "How will you let me know?" David asked. "You hide here in the field," Jonathan answered. "I will come out here to practice shooting. If I say to the boy who picks up my arrows, 'The arrows are beyond you,' you will know that God has sent you away from here to a safer place. Promise now that if something happens to me, you will be kind to my children." David made a solemn promise, calling on God as witness, that he would always be kind to Jonathan's children.

The next day David's seat was empty at the feast. The king stared angrily at the empty chair, but he said nothing. The second day of the feast he shouted, "Where is that David?" Jonathan answered, "He asked my permission to go to a family sacrifice." Then Saul stood up, trembling with fury. "You are no better than a traitor," he shouted at Jonathan. "You love that worthless shepherd boy more than you do your own crown. Don't you see that you will never be king as long as he is alive?" Then Saul picked up his spear, and flung it at his own son. Again the spear did not hit its mark. Jonathan got up from the table in fierce anger. He refused to eat at the same table as his father.

The next morning Jonathan went out to the field. He took along a little boy to pick up the arrows he shot. He shot his arrow, and said to the boy, "Hurry! Don't be so slow! The arrow is beyond you." Then he gave his bow and arrows to the boy, and said, "Carry them back to the city."

Then David came out of his hiding place. The two friends threw their arms around each other, kissed each other, and wept the bitter tears of parting. Jonathan said to his friend, "Go now in peace. God watch between you and me forever. And between my children and your children. For we have sworn an oath of everlasting friendship."

Jonathan turned and went back to the city. David went to the wilderness, to look for a hiding place where he could be safe from King Saul and his spies. But David did not forget his solemn pledge to Jonathan and his children.

80

The Lesson of Waiting

I Samuel 24

Perhaps at some time or other it has happened to you yourself. Suddenly, without warning, you find yourself in big trouble. You are face to face with great danger. There is no time to think, no time to get down on your knees, even. You can only whisper under your breath, "God, help me!" and then you have to act. But God hears your simple prayer. He does help you. And when it is all over, you have learned a lesson in faith, a lesson you will not forget.

But what about those other times when, day after day, everything seems to go wrong? You pray, and pray, but you get no answer. Nothing changes. What then? Do you still believe the promises of God? Is your trust steadfast? Are you able to wait for God?

The truth is, waiting is much harder than fighting. Any soldier will tell you that. It takes more courage, more strength, more faith. Waiting for God is what we call patience. You and I do not care much for patience. Perhaps just because it is so very hard. Too hard, it often seems to us. But in God's way of figuring, patience, waiting for God, ranks very high. Sooner or later, if you are really a child of God, your life is going to include lessons in patience. And these lessons are never easy.

David had already learned the lesson of faith in great danger. He had learned it when the bear and the lion burst into his flock of sheep. He had learned it when he fought against Goliath. But he still had to learn the lesson of waiting for God. It took him ten years to learn this lesson. This is how patient our God is with His stumbling, slow-to-learn children.

After Jonathan warned him to escape, David became an outlaw, a fugitive. He fled from place to place, always just one step ahead of Saul's soldiers. He hid in caves, and in wild desert places. He rarely had enough to eat, and almost never a roof over his head. He had one narrow escape after another. Other outlaws, men who were in trouble, or in debt, joined him, until at last David had a band of six hundred men with him, all of them running away from Saul and his soldiers.

God had promised that David would be king. But for ten years God waited to fulfill this promise. And slowly, painfully, David learned to wait for God, to go on trusting God even though God allowed all these troubles to happen to him.

In the southern part of Judah, along the shores of the Dead Sea, is a wild, mountainous area, filled with steep rocks, and threaded with numerous caves. Here the wild goats play on the rocky slopes. Here, even today, outlaws hide from the officers of the law. Here David, too, found a hiding place when he was hunted by Saul. Saul was the king, and he had a big army at his command. Poor David had only his six hundred fellow outlaws. But David was really more powerful than Saul with all his soldiers. For David had God on his side. God is more powerful than all the armies in the world.

David and his friends were camped in the dark, secret recesses of a big cave. Saul was scouring the mountainsides to find them. The soldiers stopped just outside David's hiding place. David and his friends could see them as they stood in the light outside the entrance to the cave. And then Saul came into the cave alone. He took off his coat and sat down. The men in the dark corners held their breath, but Saul did not see them.

David's men whispered to him, "This is your chance. Kill him now, and you will be king." What went through David's mind at this moment? Long ago in Bethlehem God had anointed him to be king in Saul's place. David had already waited many years for God's promise. Was this really his chance? Had God sent Saul here to this very cave at this very moment so that he could kill him?

But Saul had been anointed by God as king too. It was wrong to harm the man God had anointed as king. It is never right to do something God forbids, not even to bring about something that is right. So David did not kill Saul. He secretly cut off a little piece of Saul's coat. Saul did not see him. Presently the king got up and left the cave. David waited a minute to let him get ahead. Then he followed him.

"My lord the king!" David called after him. Saul turned around, startled. David bowed low before his king. "Why do you listen to those who tell you lies about me?" David asked. "See! Today God delivered you into my power. My friends urged me to kill you. But I would not harm God's anointed. Look! Here is a piece of your coat in my hand!"

Saul's heart was moved by what had happened. "You are a better man than I am," he said. "I have done you harm, but you have returned only good to me. God will reward you for this. And now I know that you are going to be the next king of Israel. Promise me that when this happens, you will not harm my children."

David promised. Saul went back home. For the moment he gave up trying to capture David. And David went back to his hiding place. For he knew only too well that Saul's change of heart would not last. Meanwhile he waited with patience for God Himself to fulfill what He had promised.

81

A Woman's Good Advice

I Samuel 25

Mind your own business! I know what I am doing. If I want your advice, I will ask for it! Have you ever said this? Or at least thought it in your secret heart? You and I know we are not perfect. But how we hate to have anyone point out our mistakes! When someone offers us advice, often we do not even stop to listen before we start to make excuses.

We search our Bible to hear the voice of God. But God also speaks to us in our daily lives. Sometimes He speaks to us through the advice other people offer us. Through these people He himself reminds us of something we have forgotten, or warns us that what we are planning to do is wrong. The boy or girl, the man or woman, who is willing to listen to advice will save himself heartache, grief, and vain regrets. Heartache, and vain regret, and haunting guilt are exactly what David saved himself when he listened to the advice of a beautiful woman, a woman sent by God Himself to warn David.

David and his men were no longer hiding in the caves near the Dead Sea. They were now camped in the wilderness mountains of southern Palestine. No one actually lived in this area. But there was a large flock of animals pastured here — three thousand sheep, and about a thousand goats. These animals belonged to a rich man called Nabal, who lived some distance away. Many bands of guerrillas live off the countryside. They simply help themselves to whatever grain or cattle they need for food. But not David. Instead of stealing from him, David protected Nabal's shepherds from other wandering outlaw bands.

The shepherd's year comes to its climax with the shearing of the sheep. Then the owner provides a great feast for all his workers, to celebrate a successful year. Then, too, it is the custom to give gifts of food to the poor. David sent a message to Nabal. "Peace be to you!" he said. "Peace to your family, and all your household! I hear that you are going to shear your sheep. Your shepherds have been with us all season in the fields. We did not harm them in any way, and we stole nothing from them. If you ask them, they will tell you that this is true. Now, I beg you, share with your son David some of the food provided for the feast."

Nabal was both stingy and surly. He answered rudely, "Who is this David? There are many runaway slaves wandering around the countryside. For all I know, he may be one of them. Am I to take food provided for my men and give it to someone who comes from I do not know where?" David's messengers returned and told him what Nabal had said. David was angered by this insulting message. But he only said, "Every one of you put on his sword." So the men picked up their weapons and set out for Nabal's house.

One of Nabal's servants hurried meanwhile to tell his mistress what happened. Abigail was just the opposite of her husband. She was beautiful and sensible and generous. She loved God and trusted in His care. She knew that David was going to be king some day, and she knew, too, that Nabal's rudeness would anger David. Abigail quickly collected a present for David. She took two hundred loaves of bread, five sheep, a bushel of roasted grain, two wineskins filled with wine, a hundred clusters of raisins, and two hundred cakes of dried figs. She loaded all these on donkeys, and set out for David's camp. She did not say anything to her husband, who was busy gorging himself on the food provided for the feast, and drinking himself drunk on the wine.

Suddenly, as Abigail came around the corner of the mountain, she came face to face with an angry David and his men. For David had said to his men, "Why did I bother to protect this fellow's cattle in the wilderness? He has paid me back evil for good. By tomorrow this time I will not leave alive so much as one man-child of all of Nabal's family!"

When Abigail saw David, she got off her donkey, and bowed low before David. "I pray you," she said to David, "let me speak a word in your ears, and be so gracious as to listen to what I say. Do not pay any attention to the foolish rudeness of Nabal. Today God has kept you from murdering your enemies. And God will surely continue to protect you, and will keep His promise to make you king of all Israel. When that day arrives, you will be glad that you have not revenged yourself, and shed your enemy's blood. And now allow me to give this small present I have brought to your young men."

Did David answer, "Mind your own business! I don't need your advice!"? No, David listened to Abigail's advice. He said, "Blessed be God, who sent you to meet me! And may God bless you also, for today you have kept me from the guilt of murder, and from revenging myself with my own hands. For surely, if you had not come to meet me, by tomorrow morning there would not have been one man-child of all Nabal's family left alive!" David took the present she had brought. "Go home in peace," he said to Abigail. "I have listened to your advice."

Abigail returned home. She found her husband so drunk that she could not even talk to him. The next morning, when he awoke from his drunken sleep, she told him what she had done. When he heard it, Nabal was struck down by a stroke, and was paralyzed. Ten days later he died.

David did not forget the beautiful God-fearing woman who had given him such good advice. After a while he sent her a message asking her to become his wife. So Abigail married David, and later God sent them a little son.

82
The Wages of Sin

I Samuel 28, 31

The sentry stood motionless, listening. Was that the tramp of many feet he heard? He leaned forward, straining to see better. Then he turned and shouted, "They are coming!" Every man in the Israelite camp dropped what he was doing and came to see for himself. Yes, they were coming, their ancient enemy, the Philistines. Rank after rank they marched through the mountain pass and down the valley. The sun shone on their heavy armor as if on a thousand mirrors. Their five kings were there, and every man in the nation old enough to throw a spear or aim an arrow. For this was no brush-fire war they planned. This was an all-out war of extermination. They were going to destroy the people of God once and forever.

"There are more of them than there are of us," one of the Israelite soldiers said doubtfully, "and they are better armed." "Yes," his companion replied, "they are much stronger than we are, but God is stronger than they. Look, these fields there below us are the very place where Gideon defeated a hundred and thirty-five thousand Midianites with only three hundred men by the help of God. If the trees and rocks down there could speak, they would tell you to trust in God. They saw *that* battle!" "If only our God fights with us!" his companion answered. "They say He does not answer the prayers of King Saul."

"Where is the king?" another soldier asked. "He is in his tent," someone else said. "He is afraid. There is no message from God, and he does not know where to turn for help."

The Israelites were camped on the slopes of Mt. Gilboa. The Philistine army set up its camp in the valley below. It was dark by this time. Soon there was nothing to be seen but hundreds of little glowing fires. The men huddled around the flames, trying to thaw out the cold fear in their hearts, even as they warmed a little food.

In King Saul's tent there was no supper. Saul had not eaten any food that day. His servants tried to tempt him with roasted meat. "You will need your strength for the battle tomorrow," they said. Saul sat crouching in the corner. "God does not answer me," was his only reply. "What must I do?" Unhappy Saul! Long ago he had chosen to walk his own path instead of God's way. Now he found the way he had chosen was bitter; it led only to death. But it was still not too late. It is never too late to repent of our wicked deeds, to throw ourselves on God's mercy. God never despises the brokenhearted prayer. But Saul was not sorry for his sins. He was only sorry for the bitter wages his sins had earned him. Suddenly he sprang up, a wild gleam in his eye. "If God will not answer me," he exclaimed, "I will force the dead to speak!"

By now it was quite dark. The fires had burned down to ashes. The soldiers lay sleeping on the ground. Only the call of the sentry disturbed the quiet. Three figures slipped out of the king's tent, muffled up to their ears in heavy coats. They slipped past the sleeping soldiers, past the guarding sentry. They made a wide circle around the Philistine camp. They came at last to a lonely hut. An old woman answered their knock. She did not recognize the king in his disguise.

"I want you to bring someone back from the dead for me," Saul said. "You will get me into trouble!" the woman objected. "The king has forbidden such things." "No," Saul promised, "you will not have any trouble. Bring me up Samuel." The old woman crouched on the floor of the hut and worked her magic spells. Presently she cried out in terror. "What do you see?" Saul asked. "It is an old man, wearing a long robe," she answered.

And now Samuel's voice spoke: "Why have you disturbed me?" "The Philistine army is upon us," Saul cried out desperately, "and God no longer answers my prayers!" "Why come to me?" Samuel answered. "You abandoned God long ago. Now God has abandoned you. You will lose this battle. By this time tomorrow night you, and your three sons, will be with me among the dead!"

At these dreadful words Saul fell full length upon the ground, as if he were already dead. The old woman and his two servants struggled to get him up again, and they persuaded him to take a little food before he started on his sad trip back to his own camp.

Did all this happen as Samuel said it would? Indeed it did. The battle started early the next morning. The Philistines pressed hard against the Israelite army. They killed many, and many others fled before them in terror. Saul saw that the battle was lost. His three sons had already been killed. He said to his armor-bearer, "Draw your sword, and kill me, so that I do not fall into these heathen hands." The armor-bearer shook his head in horror. He, too, was afraid of the Philistines, almost too afraid to speak. But he could not raise his hand against his king. Saul saw that the Philistine soldiers were almost upon him. He took his own sword, and fell upon it, so that he died. Then the terrified armor-bearer also fell on his sword. So Saul and his three sons and his armor-bearer and almost the whole Israelite army died that dreadful day.

When David heard what had happened, he did not rejoice that at last his relentless enemy was dead, and he could become king. No, he sang a sad song of mourning for Saul and Jonathan:

> *How are the mighty fallen!*
> *Thy glory, O Israel, is slain.*
> *Saul and Jonathan were lovely in their lives,*
> *And in their death they were not divided.*
> *I am distressed for thee, my brother Jonathan:*
> *Thy love to me was wonderful,*
> *Passing the love of women.*
> *How are the mighty fallen!*

83

The Circle of God's Mercy

II Samuel 4, 9

When President John F. Kennedy was assassinated, Vice-president Lyndon Johnson was sworn into office immediately, without an hour's delay. It was done secretly, on an airplane, and under heavy guard. This was because no one knew whether the assassination was the act of an isolated madman, or whether it was part of a widespread plot to take over our whole government. In many other countries today, when the ruler dies, a fierce struggle for power follows. Those who emerge victorious from this struggle promptly imprison, or even kill off, all their rivals, to ensure their own position.

It is that way today, and it was that way long ago in Palestine. The first thing a new king did was to murder all the sons of the previous king, even if they happened to be his own brothers, to protect himself from revolt and civil war. This is what many new kings did. But it is not what David did.

In the terrible battle of Gilboa, Saul and Jonathan and Jonathan's brothers, the other heirs to Saul's throne, died a violent death at the hand of their ancient enemies, the Philistines. Though Saul had been his bitter enemy, David did not rejoice when he received this news. He grieved over it, and sang a sad lament for Saul and Jonathan. Not long after Saul's death, the people of Judah made David their king. But the ten tribes to the north were not ready for this. They still felt a sense of loyalty to the family of Saul. There was one son of Saul who had not been in the terrible battle. His name was Ish-bosheth. The ten tribes crowned Ish-bosheth as their king. Now a tragic civil war followed, the followers of David fighting against their own brothers, the followers of Saul's family. And, as so often happens in a civil war, there was plotting and intrigue on both sides.

One day two of the servants of King Ish-bosheth plotted together to murder their king. They expected that David would reward them handsomely for this. While Ish-bosheth was sleeping, in the hottest part of the day, they slipped into his room. They cut off his head, and carrying this grisly proof of what they had done with them, they escaped under cover of darkness to the south. When they were admitted to David's presence, they unwrapped their trophy. "Look!" they said, "Here is the head of Ish-bosheth, the son of Saul, your enemy. God has avenged you on Saul and on Saul's children."

David was shocked by their cruel deed. "You are wicked men!" he said. "You have murdered an innocent man in his own house while he was asleep. I will require his blood from you!" And then David commanded his soldiers to execute these heartless murderers. And he had the head of Ish-bosheth buried properly in a grave.

Then King David remembered the solemn pledge he had made to Jonathan. For he had sworn, calling God Himself to witness, that he would be kind to the children of Jonathan forever. "Is there anyone of the family of Saul left alive," he asked his servants, "so that I may show him kindness for the sake of my friend Jonathan?" One of Saul's servants named Ziba answered, "There is still one son of Jonathan. His name is Mephibosheth. He was just a baby at the time of the terrible battle when his father and his grandfather were killed. In terror for his life, his nurse snatched him up and ran to hide him. But she dropped him, and ever since he has been lame in both his legs."

"Bring him to me at once," King David commanded. So they brought Mephibosheth to the king. Mephibosheth was afraid. He thought that surely David had sent for him to kill him too, so that the last of Saul's family would be safely out of the way. When he came limping into the king's audience chamber, he fell on his face before the king. David said, "Mephibosheth?" And he answered, "I am your servant, O King." David said, "Do not be afraid! I will surely treat you kindly because of my love for your father Jonathan, and my solemn pledge to be kind to his children forever. All the land that belonged to your grandfather, King Saul, shall be restored to you. And you yourself shall live in my palace, and eat at my table with my own sons." Mephibosheth could hardly believe his ears. He had not expected anything like this. Again he bowed low before the king. "Who am I," he said, "that my lord the king should trouble himself about me!"

Then David sent for Ziba, and said to him, "Everything that belonged to Saul I have given to Mephibosheth. You and your sons are to look after his property for him, and to farm the land, and bring the fruits to your master's son. Mephibosheth himself is to live here in my palace with me, and eat at my table with my own sons." Ziba answered, "Everything the king has commanded I and my sons will do."

So David remembered the love between himself and Jonathan, and his solemn pledge not to forget Jonathan's children.

For the mercy of God is like a circle. The circle starts always with God Himself. God shows mercy to David, to you, to me, although we have not earned His mercy, nor do we deserve it. But those who receive God's mercy must close the circle. David was merciful to Jonathan's lame son. And you and I must show mercy to others around us, without asking whether or not they deserve such kindness. For if we do not show mercy to others, God will withdraw the mercy He has shown to us.

84
David Learns About God's Holiness

II Samuel 6

Johnnie was puzzled. He peered up at Mother's face. She seemed so strange today. Usually she was all smiles. Now she was sober and quiet. At last he asked, "Is something wrong, Mother?" Mother seemed startled. She looked at Johnnie, smiled just the tiniest little bit, and reached out her hand to pull him close to her side. "No, Johnnie," she said, "there is nothing really wrong. It is just that God has given me a hard lesson to learn. You know how it is when you have an arithmetic problem and cannot find the answer, or a Bible verse you cannot seem to remember." Johnnie was more puzzled than ever. "But you are too old to go to school, Mother," he said. "Not really," Mother said. "You see, God goes on teaching His children lessons just as long as they live." After a moment she added thoughtfully, "I suppose that perhaps even in heaven we shall go on learning lessons. We shall go on forever learning more and more things about our wonderful Saviour."

David had known and loved God since he was a boy no bigger than

Johnnie, since he made up songs to sing to God as he sat on the hillside looking after his father's sheep. He was a grown-up man now. But he was still learning God's lessons. And some of them were hard.

Saul had been dead for seven years now, and at last David was king over all Israel, just as God had promised he would be. He had captured the city of Jerusalem and made it his capital. He had built himself a fine palace there. But in all this beauty of his capital city there was something missing. There was no house of God where He could be worshiped. This troubled David. "I must bring the ark of God to Jerusalem," he said.

The ark, you remember, was that beautiful golden box containing the two tablets of stone on which God had written the Ten Commandments with His own finger. On its golden cover was the mercy seat, and this was the place where the great God of heaven and earth lived among His people. Long ago, almost seventy years before this, the Israelites had carried the ark with them into battle, and the Philistines had captured it. They did not keep it long, for in whatever town they put it, God sent dreadful sickness to that place. So the Philistines sent the ark back to Israel, and ever since then it had been in the house of Abinadab in Kiriath-jearim, forgotten and neglected.

David planned to make the bringing of the ark to Jerusalem a great celebration. He invited thirty thousand of the most important men in the country to serve as an honor escort. He collected a whole orchestra of musicians, harp players, cornet players, trumpet players, cymbalists. He himself wrote songs of praise to God, and he trained choirs of singers to take part in the triumphal procession. He had enough food prepared so that every single person in his capital could share in the feast.

But you are forgetting something, David, forgetting the most important thing of all. You are forgetting to ask God for direction. Yes, David forgot, as you and I sometimes forget, that God is holy, and that man is sinful. And it is dangerous, terribly dangerous, for a sinful man to come into the presence of a holy God. Such a man will surely die. Only God can prevent that, and it will take a miracle even then — the miracle of God's Son dying on the cross.

Long before this, God had set up careful directions for the moving of the ark. He gave strict orders that it must be carried by specially trained Levites, and that they must touch only the poles that were threaded through the rings on the side of the ark. The Levites must carry the ark on their shoulders. No man must ever touch it, or he would surely die. David knew all this, but in the excitement of his big plans, he forgot.

And so they brought a new cart, and hitched up two oxen, and set the ark on the cart. The musicians played, and the choirs sang. Ahio, one of Abinadab's sons, drove the cart, and Uzzah, his brother, walked beside it. They had not gone far when the oxen stumbled. Uzzah stretched out his hand to steady the ark. And in that very moment God struck him dead. Can you imagine what confusion there was in that grand procession? The musicians stopped playing, the choirs stopped singing; everyone stared at one another in horror.

That day David was afraid of God. He was afraid to have the ark, God's dwelling place, in Jerusalem. Hastily, carefully, the men lifted the ark off the cart and carried it to the nearest house, the house of Obed-edom. The ark stayed there three months. God blessed the family of Obed-edom because they took such good care of the ark.

David mourned over Uzzah, and grieved, too, for his own sin, that he had been so bold as to think he could rush into the presence of a holy God without coming in the way God Himself had provided. At last he took heart again. He trusted in God's forgiveness. Again he set out to fetch the ark. The orchestra and the choirs went along. But this time David took great care to follow God's directions. He set up a tent in Jerusalem, like the original tent built as God had commanded so long ago in the desert, all ready to shelter the ark.

And so they brought the ark to Jerusalem. It was a grand procession. The Levites carried the holy box on their shoulders. David took off his royal robes, and, in a simple undergarment, he danced before God. And as they came through the city gates, the choirs sang:

> *Lift up your heads, O ye gates:*
> *And the King of glory will come in.*

A second choir answered:

> *Who is this King of glory?*

And the first singers replied:

> *The Lord of hosts,*
> *He is the King of glory.*

They carefully set the ark in the tent which David had prepared. They offered sacrifices to God, peace offerings they called them, because they symbolized the fact that God Himself had somehow provided a way for peace to be restored between sinful man and a holy God. And then the whole nation celebrated in a great feast of thanksgiving. For each man had only to lift his eyes, and, once again, he could see the very tent of God where God lived among His people.

85
The House That Lasts Forever

II Samuel 7

he is the Lord of heaven and earth. Heaven and the heaven of heavens are not big enough to hold Him. And yet, so great was His love and His tender care for His people that, when they wandered forty years in the wilderness, He declared that He would live among them in a tent, as they lived. And so He taught them to build not a *house* for God, but a *tent* — the tent of meeting they called it, for here the great God met with His people.

This happened long before David lived. More than two hundred years had already passed since the Israelites settled down in their Promised Land of Canaan. The people no longer lived in tents. They lived in comfortable houses. And David, who was now king of Israel, just as God had promised he would be, lived in a beautiful palace built of costly cedar wood brought from the mountain slopes of the kingdom of Tyre to the north. But the place where God lived among His people was still a tent.

This troubled David. He spoke to the prophet Nathan about it. Nathan said, "Go! Do what is in your heart, for God is with you." But that very night God gave Nathan a different message for David. "Thus says the Lord," the message said, "are you going to build a house for Me to live in? I have not lived in a house since the day I brought the children of Israel out of Egypt. From that day to this I have walked among My people in a tent. And never in all these years did I ask any of the children of Israel to build a house for Me of cedar.

"I took you, David, from following the sheep, and made you king over My people Israel. I have gone with you wherever you went, and have cut off all your enemies from before you. And I will give you, and all My people, rest from their enemies, so that they may live in their own place, and be moved no more.

"Are you going to build a house for Me, David? No, I am the one who is going to build a house, a house for you. Not a dead house of cedar wood, but a living house. When your life is finished, and you rest with your fathers, I will set your children after you on your throne. Your family and your kingdom shall be made sure forever. As for this house that you wish to build for Me, your son, who shall reign after you, shall build Me a house. If *he* does what is wrong, I will send troubles to him to teach him what is right, but I will not take My loving-kindness away from him, as I took it away from Saul. And this kingdom which I am going to give you, and this living house which I am going to build for you, shall be made sure forever!"

Forever! It is as if God wished to seal His promise with a threefold seal. For He repeated three times that tremendous word, "Forever!"

It was David's son, Solomon, who was going to reign after him, who would build the temple for God. But God's "Forever!" was not just for Solomon, and certainly not for Solomon's temple which was going to be destroyed less than four hundred years after it had been built. No, that "Forever!" was for you, and for me, and for everyone who trusts in God, from the very beginning to the very end of the world. For the king of David's family who was going to rule forever was no one else but our Saviour Jesus Himself. And what God wanted David to see was that this Saviour, Son of God and son of David both, would truly be God living among His people. Jesus was the wonderful living house in which God lived in all His glory, and in all His love for those who trust in Him, and in all His tender, protecting care.

David listened quietly to the message Nathan brought him. When he had heard it all, he was quite overwhelmed by God's goodness. He went into the tent where God lived, and he bowed low before God. "Who am I," he prayed, "O Lord God, and what is my family, that You have brought me this far? And now this was only a small thing in your eyes. You have also spoken of my family for a great while to come. O Lord God, what can David say in answer to such goodness?

You are great, O Lord God! There is none like You! You brought Your people out of Egypt with great wonders, and became their God, choosing them to be Your people forever. And now, O Lord God, do as You have said. Bless the family of Your servant David, and let this living house, that You have promised to make for me and for Your people, be blessed forever!"

David knew that the promises of God are trustworthy. He knew this from the many long years when Saul hunted him like a wild animal from one hiding place to another. In all those years God never forsook him. And in the end He gave David the throne and the kingdom, just as He had promised.

And you and I — have we, too, experienced the faithfulness of God's promises? Did God keep that tremendous "Forever!" which He promised to David, and to us as well? Nearly a thousand years later, when the temple Solomon built for God had long since been burned down to a rubble, a messenger from God appeared to a young girl who was a member of David's family. "Do not be afraid, Mary!" the angel said. "You are going to have a son. You are to call Him Jesus. God is going to give Him the throne of His father David. And He shall reign forever, and of His kingdom there shall be no end!" And so He was born at last in Bethlehem, the living house promised to David, the house of God who chose to live among His people. And His glorious reign shall indeed last forever!

86
The Bitter Fruit of Envy

II Samuel 11, 12

a breathless hush lay over the whole assembly. "And now," the principal said at last, "will Tom please come forward. Tom has won the first prize!" You clapped just as loudly as anyone when Tom went up to the platform. But you were not really glad. Inside your heart someone — could it have been Satan himself? — someone whispered, "You should have won that prize instead of Tom! You are just as good as he is! And you need that ten dollars a lot more!"

Perhaps it was not Tom's prize you envied. Perhaps it was his popularity, his friends. Or his skill at hitting home runs, while you always strike out. Or some girl's snappy clothes. Or the fact that she was always chosen first in games on the playground.

"Can I help it," you answer, "if Satan whispers in my heart? I clapped just as long as the others. I even congratulated Tom after the assembly!" No, you cannot help it. Even Jesus, you remember, suffered from the wicked whispers of Satan. But if you allow envy to *grow* inside your heart, it will never stay on the inside. It always breaks out into acts of sin — acts that later on you would give anything you own to take back. And that, of course, is just what Satan is hoping for. There is not a single Christian who could not tell you stories about the bitter fruit envy has brought into his life. Even people we think of as great heroes, as saints. Even David!

The day had been warm, but now it was evening. There was a cool breeze blowing. David had gone up to the roof of the palace. From there he could see all his capital city, and, beyond the walls, the lovely hillsides, green with olive trees and grapevines. Something caught his eye. It was a woman standing in the courtyard of one of the houses of the lower city. This woman was beautiful, so beautiful that the king's eyes were dazzled. He stood staring down at her. And at that very moment Satan whispered in his heart.

When Satan whispered to Jesus, Jesus sent him away at once. "Get behind me, Satan!" He said. But not David. David called a servant. "Who is that woman there in the courtyard?" he asked. The servant answered, "That is Bathsheba, the wife of Uriah." Uriah was one of David's best soldiers, one of his "Mighty Men," the heroes who were famous for the example of fearless daring they set the ordinary soldiers. Right now he was with the rest of the army fighting the Ammonites.

And so Satan whispered in David's heart, "Why should Uriah have such a beautiful woman as his wife? You are the king, after all. She should be your wife!" David turned this idea over and over in his mind. After a little he sent a message to his general, Joab: "Put Uriah in the front of the army, where the fighting is the fiercest. Then, when the enemy counterattacks, retreat, and leave him up there in front, so he will be wounded and killed."

Joab was a soldier. He did not question this strange message from the king. He commanded his soldiers to storm the city walls, and he stationed Uriah in the front rank. The Ammonites rushed out to defend their capital. The archers stationed on the wall joined in. At this point Joab commanded his men to retreat. Several Israelites were killed. Uriah was one of them.

When the news of this battle reached Jerusalem, Uriah's wife went into mourning for her dead husband. A little later David sent for Bathsheba. He married her, and she became his tenth wife. Presently David and Bathsheba had a baby boy.

But the thing David had done displeased the Lord.

Nearly a year passed by. It was not a happy year for David. The beautiful Bathsheba was his wife — the very thing he had wanted so much. And they had a darling baby, a child that had twined himself around David's heart. But David was not happy. He was tormented day and night by the memory of what he had done. He was haunted by the echoing of the laws of God in his heart — *Thou shalt not covet thy neighbor's wife,* and *Thou shalt not kill.* His prayers did not seem to reach God any longer. God seemed far away.

One day the prophet Nathan came to the palace. "I have a problem," Nathan said to the king. "There were two men who lived next door to each other. One was rich, the other poor. The rich man had great flocks of sheep and cattle. The poor man had one little orphaned lamb. He had held it in his lap when its mother died, fed it from his own plate, and his children had made a pet of it. One day the rich man had company. He did not kill one of his own sheep. He stole the poor man's lamb, and roasted it, to feast his guests."

David grew angry as he listened. "The man who has done such a thing deserves to die!" he exclaimed. "He shall give back four lambs for the one he has stolen!" Nathan answered, "You are that very man! Thus says the God of Israel: 'I made you king of Israel. I saved you from Saul. And if this wasn't enough, I would have added still more blessings. Why have you despised My law? You have killed Uriah, and stolen his wife. Because you have done this, the sword will never depart from your family!' "

David's heart melted within him, and he cried out in bitter repentance, "I have sinned against the Lord!" "Because you have confessed your sin," Nathan said, "and are sorry for it, God will forgive you. But the child, your baby and Bathsheba's, will surely die!"

And it happened just that way. The baby boy died within a week. Not as punishment — God had forgiven David. God never punishes a Christian, for Jesus bore all our punishment on the cross, every single bit of it. No, the child died as a lesson to David, as a bitter reminder of the wickedness which lived in his own heart, which only God could conquer. And later three other of David's sons died a violent death.

87

The Man Who Was
Nearly Perfect

II Samuel 15-18

Chuck wears glasses. Kathy has braces on her teeth. Tom has hay fever; he gets shots every summer. Susie has ankles that turn over when she tries to ice skate; she needs special reinforcements in her skates. And so you could go on. Each of us has some flaw or imperfection that we have to learn to live with. None of us is perfect.

And yet once in a while a person is born who seems to be nearly perfect. He is strong and healthy and handsome and clever and popular. If you know such a person, do not envy him. For to be nearly perfect does not make you happy, nor does it make you good. Being nearly perfect is like being very rich — it is terribly dangerous. Nearly perfect people often come to a tragic end.

Such a person was Absalom, King David's favorite son. Absalom was tall and straight and handsome. His beautiful long hair fell down onto his shoulders. He did not need glasses; his teeth did not have to be straightened; he did not have hay fever or ankles that turned easily — you could not find a flaw in Absalom anywhere. David loved this handsome son of his, loved him too well for David's own good, and much too well for Absalom's good.

Absalom was ambitious. He did not mean to spend all his life in his great father's shadow. He had his eye on the throne itself, and he did not plan to wait, either, till his father died, to seize the kingly power. He bought himself a chariot, pulled by high-spirited horses, such a chariot as only a king has a right to ride in. Fifty men ran in front of Absalom's chariot whenever he went out to drive. David could not bring himself to say anything to his favorite son about this royal chariot.

Early in the morning, on the days when the king held court, Absalom would stand just outside the palace gate. People who came in from the country would bow low before the king's favorite son. But Absalom would always stop them. He would put his arm around the stranger, and kiss him, and ask, "What city do you come from?" And when he had listened patiently to the man's problem, he would say, "You have a good case. You are certainly in the right. It is too bad the king is too busy to help you. Oh, if only I were judge! I would see that every man got a fair hearing!" So, day by day, and month by month, Absalom stole the hearts of the people.

About four years after he had started this, Absalom said to his unsuspecting father, "I have made a vow to God, to offer a sacrifice in Hebron." Naturally, David said, "Go, and fulfill your vow in peace." Then Absalom sent spies through all the land, and told them, "As soon as you hear the trumpet being blown in Hebron, shout, wherever you are, 'Absalom is king in Hebron!' " And that is how it went. As soon as the report spread that Absalom had been proclaimed king in Hebron, more and more of the Israelites, those Israelites whom he had so carefully flattered in the past, flocked to join him. Soon Absalom had a powerful army at his command.

David was shocked when he heard this news. He said to his servants, "Let us escape quickly, before Absalom comes and destroys the whole city of Jerusalem." So David, and his wives and children, and the six hundred loyal men who had fought by his side when Saul was hunting for him, left the city. They set out for the wilderness to hide from Absalom. They walked barefoot, their heads covered to show their grief, weeping as they went. For David remembered what he had done to Uriah, and the judgment of God, "The sword shall not depart from your family." The priests followed David, carrying the ark of God. But David said to them, "Take the ark of God back to the city. If God is gracious to me, it may be He will bring me back again, and will again show me the place where He lives among His people. But if not, here I am. Let Him do to me as seems good to Him."

As news of the revolt spread, many of the Israelites joined David. Some of his friends brought supplies to feed the men. Soon David, too, had a large army. David wanted to lead his men out to fight against Absalom. But his friends would not allow this. "You are worth ten thousand of us," they said. "You must stay in the city, and be ready to come to our help if you are needed." So David stood beside the gate as his soldiers marched out to battle. "Deal gently, for my sake," he commanded his general Joab, "with the young man Absalom."

The two armies met in wild forest country. There was a terrible battle. Twenty thousand of Absalom's soldiers were killed. Some fell before David's men, but even more met death in the wild gullies and ravines of the forest. Absalom was riding a mule, and as the mule ran under a tree, Absalom was caught by his hair — that beautiful long hair of which he was so vain! — caught up into the branches of the tree. The mule went on from under him, and Absalom hung there helpless.

One of the soldiers said to Joab, "I saw Absalom hanging in a tree." Joab was angry. "Why did you not kill him?" he asked. "I would have given you ten pieces of silver for it." The soldier answered, "If you gave me a thousand pieces of silver, I would not kill him. I myself heard the king command you to deal gently with him." Joab took three darts. He went to the tree where Absalom hung and drove them right through Absalom's heart. The young men who carried Joab's armor cut Absalom down from the tree, and buried him there on the battlefield. They heaped a great pile of stones over his grave.

David sat by the city gate waiting for news of the battle. At last a messenger arrived, running. "Good news, O king!" he said. "Today the Lord has avenged you of all those who rebel against you." But this was not what David most wanted to hear. "Is the young man Absalom all right?" he asked. The messenger answered, "May all your enemies be as that young man is now!" Then David turned away and went up to the room above the gate. And as he went, he wept, saying, "O my son Absalom, my son, my son Absalom! Would that I had died for you, O Absalom, my son, my son!"

V

THE FORK IN THE ROAD

I have set before thee life and death: . . . therefore choose life, that thou mayest live (Deuteronomy 30:19).

88
"Long Live King Solomon!"

I Kings 1

*U*sually the palace was busy with hurrying servants, filled with the coming and going of the young princes and princesses, with their laughter and their talk. But not today. Today all was hushed and sad. For the aged King David lay dying in his bedroom. He trembled with cold as his life grew weak within him. His servants heaped his bed with blankets, and the only sound in the room was the king's heavy breathing and the soft footsteps of his nurse.

Outside the bedroom door Prince Adonijah stood listening. Now that Absalom was dead, Adonijah was the oldest of the royal princes. He meant to be the next king. He knew that he was not his father's favorite. David had promised the throne to his youngest son, Solomon. For Solomon was a special son. He was the living sign of God's love and forgiveness. Solomon was the baby God had sent as a gift to David and Bathsheba after their first child had died. But Solomon was only a boy, scarcely out of his teens. And David was dying. Besides this, Adonijah had powerful friends on his side — Abiathar the high priest, and Joab, general of all the king's armies.

"He cannot live much longer," Adonijah said to himself. "We must not wait. Tomorrow may be too late." He called a servant. "Invite all the king's sons to En-rogel," he said. "Prepare a feast, with plenty of roasted meat and wine. Invite the captains of the army too. But, if you

269

value your life, do not say anything about this to my brother Solomon, or to his mother Bathsheba."

And so that afternoon, while his father lay dying, Adonijah entertained all his brothers — all of them, that is, except Solomon — at a truly royal feast. The army officers were there, and Abiathar, the high priest, and Joab, the general, too. After they had eaten till they were full, and drunk over and over from the cups the servants always filled again, someone picked up the cry, "Long live King Adonijah!" And soon they were all shouting, till the hills echoed the cry back again, "Long live King Adonijah!"

Back in the deserted palace, Queen Bathsheba had a visitor. It was Nathan the prophet. "Have you heard what Adonijah is up to?" he asked her. "Both you and Prince Solomon are in danger of your life, for, if this plot succeeds, Adonijah will stop at nothing. You must go to see the king. Remind him of the promise he made about Solomon. Tell him what Adonijah is doing. While you are talking to him, I myself will come in and back up your story."

So Bathsheba went into David's room. The dying king peered at her from his bed. "What is it you want?" he asked. And she answered, "My lord, you swore by God Himself that our son Solomon should be king after you. But now Adonijah is ruling without your knowing about it. He has invited all your sons except Solomon to a royal feast. All the people look to you, my lord, to tell them who should be king after you."

Even while she was talking, Nathan came in. He bowed low before King David, and said, "My lord, did you say Adonijah should be king? He has invited all the king's sons, and the army captains, and Abiathar and Joab to a feast, and they are all shouting, 'Long live King Adonijah!' But he did not invite Prince Solomon."

With an effort David sat up. He said to Bathsheba, "As the Lord lives, who has saved me in all my troubles, surely your son Solomon shall be the one to sit on my throne." Then he turned to Nathan: "Take Zadok the priest, and the holy oil from the tent of God. Put Solomon on my own royal mule, whom no one but the king may ride. Take him to Gihon, and there anoint him king of God's people. Blow the trumpet, and say, for all the people to hear, 'Long live King Solomon!'"

And that is just what they did. Solomon rode on King David's own royal mule. They poured the sacred oil on his head, anointing him as God's king to rule over God's people. As they came back to the city, a great crowd followed the procession. The trumpets sounded, the flutes played, and all the people shouted, "Long live King Solomon!" The very ground shook with the joy of their shouting.

Even the guests at Adonijah's banquet heard the noise. "What is going on?" Joab asked. "The whole city seems to be in an uproar." And someone who had just arrived said, "King David has made Solomon king. Solomon has ridden on the king's own mule, and Zadok has anointed him with the holy oil, and all the city is celebrating. That is the noise you hear. Even now Solomon is sitting on the royal throne. All the king's servants are bowing down before him, and saying, 'God make your name even more famous, and your throne even greater, than your father David's!' "

When Adonijah's guests heard these words, it was as if an icy wind blew through the banquet hall. One by one, in a great hurry, they got up and disappeared.

Solomon was now king. He had not planned this great honor. He had not raised so much as a finger to bring it about. God had done it all, and Nathan, Bathsheba, and King David had been God's instruments. Nor have you and I deserved the many blessings God has sent to us. They are all free gifts from our God.

Free gifts, yes, but not random, haphazard, purposeless gifts. Every single one of these gifts has a purpose, a meaning. Each is part of the preparation for the work God has specially planned for you to do. And the gifts are so carefully planned, so exactly calculated, that no other person in all God's creation could do the work God has waiting for you. Perhaps that is one of the very greatest of God's gifts — that He allows you and me to do something for our great King.

O Lord Jesus, make each one of us ready for our work, for Your work. For we wish to yield ourselves, our time, our talents, entirely to You, to be instruments in Your hand, to do Your work!

89
What Do You Want Most?

I Kings 3

Ask what you wish, and it will be given to you!" Perhaps you have heard of kings who talked like that. That is what King Ahasuerus said to Queen Esther, and what King Herod said to his niece who had danced at his birthday party. But no king has ever said anything like that to you. Probably you do not even know any kings. But you may have wished in your secret heart that some day someone would give you just one wish.

What would you ask for? I once thought the thing I wanted most in all the world was a pony. Perhaps you would choose a new bike instead. Or a whole collection of skirts and sweaters. Or would you ask for friends, and popularity, and being elected class president? Or to be chosen captain of the basketball team?

"Ask what you wish, and I will give it to you!" Once there was a man who heard those very words. He was sleeping when he heard them. He heard them in his dream. He was a young man. Perhaps not as young as you are, but still, young and inexperienced. Perhaps nineteen, perhaps twenty. He had been thrust rather suddenly from his loving home to the lonely place on the throne. And now his father was dead. There was no one to advise him, no one to help him make decisions. All around him were enemies, rivals; even his brothers, who hated him, envied him and plotted to kill him.

All around him, too, was the great nation of God's own people. Solomon's carefree, careless days of youth were gone forever. Every word he spoke must be carefully weighed. For at his word hundreds, perhaps thousands, of men would live or die. This awful responsibility frightened Solomon. And that was good. Solomon's youth, his inexperience, his fear were not accidents. They were tools in God's hands, tools to drive him to God. There is only one Person who can help the man who sits on a lonely throne — or, for that matter, the man who sits at a lonely desk in the White House — and that is the One who has said, "My strength is made perfect in weakness." Yes, the very fear Solomon felt was worked in his heart by the Holy Spirit of God.

"I will start my reign," Solomon said to his doubting heart, "by asking for God's help." He called the heralds. "I am planning a great national day of prayer," he said. "Carry the invitations to the farthest reaches of my kingdom. I want every man of importance to be there, the captains of the army, the judges of the courts, the princes of each tribe, all the heads of each family. We will all of us assemble at Gibeon, and ask God's blessing on our nation."

That was a sight to see! On the top of the mountain there was a beautiful brass altar. All around, reaching down the slopes of the mountain as far as the eye could see, were the thousands and thousands of God's people who had come to pray for the new king, and for their country. Solomon offered a thousand sacrifices to God. This was a lot of sacrifices. But it was nothing compared to the blessings God had heaped upon His people during the long reign of King David. Israel had become a great nation whose power reached out in every direction. God had given them peace from all their enemies. Solomon's heart was so filled with love and gratitude that even a thousand sacrifices could not begin to express what he felt. And after the sacrifices there was a great feast, just as we have when we celebrate Thanksgiving Day.

Late at night, after the last worshiper had left, Solomon lay down to sleep. That night he dreamed a dream. God Himself appeared in his dream. He said to Solomon, "Ask what you want most, and I will give it to you." What does a young king, who has just become ruler, want most? Does he want to be rich? Or, perhaps, to be powerful? Or to live a long time? Or to see all his enemies defeated and dead? I am sure that Solomon wanted all these things. But they were not what he wanted most.

Solomon felt overwhelmed that God had appeared to him with this offer. "O God," he said, "You have been so good to my father David all his life long! And now You have made me king. I am no wiser than a little child. I do not know how to be a good king. And here I am, in the middle of the people You have chosen as Your own people, so many people no one could count them all. Give me an understanding heart, so that I may know how to rule this great people of Yours."

God was pleased with the choice Solomon had made. "Because you have asked for this," He said, "and did not choose riches, or honor, or long life for yourself, I will give you what you asked for. You shall have a wise and an understanding heart, so that not now, nor ever afterwards, shall there be anyone as wise as you are. And I have also given you the things you did not ask for, both riches and honor. All your life long there shall not be any king as rich and as honored as you are. And if you walk in My ways, as your father David did, I will give you a long life also."

Then Solomon woke up, and it was a dream. But he knew that God had really spoken to him as he slept. God kept the promise He made to Solomon. Solomon really became the wisest man that ever lived. Even today, if you visit the part of the world where Solomon lived, you will hear old men, as they sit around the fire at night, tell stories about Solomon's wisdom.

Solomon said many things so wise that they have become proverbs. His proverbs have been written down for us, so that you and I might learn some of Solomon's wisdom too. "The fear of the Lord," Solomon said, "is the beginning of knowledge." He did not mean that you and I are to be afraid of God. He meant that we must love and reverence God for all His blessings to us. If we do not do this, all our studying and going to school are wasted. Solomon also said, "Remember your Creator in the days of your youth." This is what Solomon himself did. He started his life's work with prayer and offerings to God. God, you know, remembered you when you were just a baby. He thought about you even before you were born. And God wants you to remember Him. He wants you to love Him, as Solomon did. He wants you to offer Him something. Not a thousand sacrifices, as Solomon did. He wants you to offer Him something even more precious. God wants your heart. And He wants you to pray to Him for wisdom to do well whatever it is He calls you to do.

90

The House of God

I Kings 6, 8

*t*he Israelites had been at war for almost three hundred years, ever since they crossed the Jordan River to take possession of their Promised Land. During those long, weary years of seemingly endless fighting, the people had found time to build houses for themselves, and King David had even built himself a palace of costly cedar wood. But God had declared He would not live in a house until the day arrived that His people were at last at peace. Until that time He would continue to live in a tent, as He had ever since the Israelites left Egypt.

Now the happy time of peace had come. And so one of the first things Solomon did was to build a house for God, a wonderful temple, where the great God of heaven and earth could meet with His people. What was it like, this marvelous temple that, even hundreds of years after it had been destroyed, was still remembered by the Jewish people with homesick longing?

It was not like the churches you and I are used to. The temple was not a comfortable auditorium to shelter the worshipers while they listened to God's Word. It was a house for God, not for the people. The building was made of stone, and the stone was covered with fine cedar wood, and the wood, on the inside of the building, was completely covered with gold which was engraved in beautiful flower designs. There were two rooms in the building. The larger room, called the holy place, was where the priests offered to God the worship of the people. There were ten golden lampstands along its walls, and ten golden tables, on which fresh loaves of bread were placed every Sabbath as a sign that the people received their daily bread from God. Just in front of the closed doorway to the smaller room was the golden altar of incense. Here sweet-smelling perfume placed on the hot coals rose constantly to God as a picture of the never-ceasing prayers of God's people.

The smaller room, the holy of holies, was completely dark. It had no windows and no lamps. Its only furniture was the ark, the beautiful golden box which contained the two tables of stone on which God had written the Ten Commandments with His own hand. Solomon did not build the ark, of course. Moses had done that. Solomon simply moved it to the temple from the tent where it had been until now. He did make two great golden cherubim for the holy of holies. These angelic creatures spread out their wings to shelter the ark.

Outside the temple itself was a courtyard for the priests, surrounded by a low wall. Here Solomon built a great altar on which sacrifices to God were burned, and also an enormous brass "sea," a huge basin, fifteen feet across, standing on twelve brass oxen, in four groups of three facing in four directions. The priests used the water in the sea to wash themselves before they offered the sacrifices to God.

Beyond and below the courtyard of the priests was another, larger, courtyard, also surrounded by a low wall. This was where the people gathered, to pray and to offer sacrifices to God. There was no roof over their head, only God's sky. And there were no benches or pews to sit on. The people stood up.

It took seven years and thousands of workmen to build this golden temple. After it was all finished, the priests carefully carried the ark from the tent which had sheltered it for three hundred years, and placed it in the inner room, the holy of holies. And then God Himself came down into the temple, into the holy of holies just above the ark, in a cloud of blinding light, a light so dazzling that the priests were unable to go on with the service.

Solomon called all the people of Israel together to dedicate God's house. They came from far and near, and all of them crowded into the courtyard. Solomon had built a brass platform in the courtyard, so that everybody could see and hear him. He kneeled down on this platform, raised his arms to heaven, and prayed a long, beautiful prayer. And part of what he prayed was for you and me, who live so long afterwards.

"Will God actually live on the earth?" Solomon prayed. "Behold, heaven and the heaven of heavens are not big enough to hold God. How much less this house that I have built! But now, hear my prayer, O Lord my God. Let Your ears be open towards this house both day and night, to listen to the prayers of Your people." Solomon prayed that God would hear the prayers of the people for rain, for good harvests, for healing from sickness, for victory over their enemies. But most of all he prayed that God would forgive their sins, for, he said, "there is no man that does not sin." And then Solomon thought of you and me. "And if," he said, "the foreigner who comes from a distant country hears about God's great name, and His outstretched arm, and prays to You, then hear in heaven, Your dwelling place, and answer his prayer, so that all the people on the earth may learn to know and trust You!"

God heard Solomon's prayer, and He promised to do what Solomon asked. And that is one reason why today, three thousand years after Solomon built the beautiful temple, you and I can turn to God in prayer and know that He will hear and answer. That temple is long since destroyed. But we do not miss it. For we know about Jesus, who is God Himself, actually come to live among us as a man. We do not offer sacrifices any longer, for Jesus offered to God the perfect, the complete, sacrifice to pay for our sins when He died on the cross. But our prayers still go up to God, as the incense did in that temple long ago. And today the great God, whom heaven and the heaven of heavens are not big enough to contain, makes His home not in a building of stone and cedar and gold, but in the hearts of all those who trust in Him.

91
The Sign of the Golden Temple

I Kings 8

I was just a boy when all this happened. And, now I am an old man. But I have never forgotten. For I saw it with my own eyes.

We lived in the country then, and a visit to the city was a rare treat. One month out of every three Father was gone, working on the king's building projects. While he was away, my mother had to manage the farm as best she could with what help we children could give her.

It took seven years to build the house for God, and though we children had never seen it, yet we were sure we knew exactly what it looked like, for Father reported to us each time he came back from the city how the building was progressing. "When it is finished," Father would always end his latest account, "you must all be there to see it dedicated." It seemed to us that day would never come. But at last it really did. We were up before it was light that morning, and we got the chores done in a big hurry. Then we washed and put on our best clothes. Mother had breakfast ready, but none of us was hungry. It was as if there was such a big lump of excitement in my throat that I couldn't swallow. "You must eat something," Mother insisted. "It is a long walk to the city, and it will be afternoon before the ceremonies are over, and the feast begins." But Father laughed. "Let them alone, Mother," he said. "Today they can live on excitement. For this is such a day as God's people have never seen before!"

Even the country roads were crowded with people, and when we got to the city, we found the streets so jammed that we could hardly push through. But because Father had worked on the building, there was a special place saved for us.

That day there was a grand procession through the streets of Jerusalem. The priests came first, blowing their trumpets as they marched. Behind them came the Levites, playing harps and cymbals and psalteries. Then the great choirs, singing, "Praise the Lord, for He is good; for His loving-kindness lasts forever." Then King Solomon in his royal robes. After him, all the royal princes. And then we fell in, the thousands and thousands of God's people, all singing the praises of our God. I don't know if you have ever shared an experience like that. There is something exciting about being part of a great crowd of people, all of them worshiping God together. I was only a boy, but I felt as if my heart was going to swell up and burst with love and praise to God.

We marched through the streets till we came to the place where King David had set up the tent of God when he brought the ark from Kiriath-jearim to Jerusalem. Carefully the priests lifted the ark of the living God to their shoulders. And then we marched back again, with music and singing. Only now the king offered sacrifices to God as we went along the streets. And so we came at last to the beautiful temple. It was everything Father had said it was, but that is not what I remember best about that day. The priests carried the ark into the innermost room, which we call the holy of holies. And that was when it happened! The glory of the unseen God came down from heaven and settled above the ark. It was so dazzling a sight that no one of us could stand to look at it. Even the specially consecrated priests had to leave the holy place.

After it was all over, the sacrifices, and the prayers, and the feasting, we went home. We had seen something no one of us would ever forget — the visible sign that God lived among His people. We were quiet at first on the way back, remembering. But at last my brother said, "But God lived among His people even when the ark was in the tent, didn't He?" "Yes," Father said, "the tent itself was God's gracious sign that He was among us." "But why a tent?" my sister asked. "I have never seen a tent before. Nobody lives in a tent any more. Today everyone lives in a house. Even Grandfather and Great-grandfather had houses to live in." Father smiled at her. "At first, Ruthie," he said, "all our people lived in tents. We had to, because we were traveling from Egypt to the land God had promised us. God's tent was a measure of the wonderful love of our God. He stooped down from heaven to live among His people in the way they had to live. *God* lived in a tent because *we* had to live in a tent."

My little brother began to cry. "My feet hurt," he sobbed. Father picked him up and carried him. "Soldiers still live in tents," I said. "Yes, Joseph, that is right," Father agreed. "A tent is where soldiers live. One reason God lived so long in a tent is because His people were still at war. It is almost as if He was trying to tell us that even God could not rest until His people were at peace." We were all quiet for a long time, thinking about this.

After a while I said, "A temple is made of wood and stone and gold. It is safer and more permanent than a tent. Perhaps the temple is God's sign that He will always live among us, forever and ever." Father's face was sober. "God will always live among those who put their trust in Him," he said. "But we must be very careful, son, that we do not put our trust in stone and wood and gold. God will not live among wicked men, temple or no temple."

"Everybody sins some time or other," Ruthie said. "But you have always said that God forgives our sins." "Yes," Father said, "God is patient, and He does forgive our sins. I don't know how He can be so patient with weak, stumbling people like us, but He is. But not forever, Ruthie. There is an end even to the patience of God."

After a little he added, "All of you children saw the dazzling sign that God was present in the house we built for Him. But the temple could easily become another, quite different kind of sign, a dreadful sign. For if we turn away from God, then the day will surely come when this temple will be destroyed, and people who see what is left of it will say in astonishment, 'Why has God done this?' And others will shrug, and say, 'This people forsook their God. That is why He has brought this evil upon them.'" He spoke so solemnly that all of us were frightened. Then he smiled. "The temple is beautiful," he said. "But do not put your trust in wood and stone, but in the promises of our faithful God. These will stand forever and ever!"

And so at last we reached our home, so tired that we fell asleep almost before we had time to take off our clothes.

92
Solomon in All His Glory

I Kings 10

far to the south, more than a thousand miles from Solomon's kingdom, the great peninsula of Arabia hangs like a giant pear, swaying softly in the waters of the Indian Ocean. It is not a friendly land. Its shifting sands, fanned always by the hot breath of the equator, see no human figure for years on end. Only a few hardy souls work the gold and silver mines in the interior. A stranger who wanders into these trackless dunes rarely comes out again alive.

Along the coast here and there a spring of water creates a life-giving oasis, and a small town appears. In one of these towns, a tiny strip of green between the threatening desert and the stormy sea, the great queen lived. Though nearly all the country she governed was barren sand, the queen was rich. She had few subjects of her own, but her power was felt to the very edges of the civilized world. For every caravan of camels that carried spices and perfumes, gold and silver northward had to pass through her capital town. And from every caravan the queen levied tribute. Every fleet of ships that tacked up the Red Sea, carrying rare woods, pearls, emeralds, and ivory, had to pass her front door; indeed, had usually to anchor in her harbor, to wait for favorable winds on this dangerous strip of water. And every ship paid well for the privilege.

So it had been as long as anyone could remember. But now suddenly the queen's power was challenged. There were strange ships sailing her seas, strange drivers manning the caravans that passed through. And these strangers told wild stories. Far to the north, they claimed, was a great king, their king. This king was the richest man there had ever been. So rich that he ate only from solid golden dishes. So rich that peacocks from far-off India, and monkeys from mysterious Africa played in his palace gardens. So rich that he sat on a gold and ivory throne protected by fourteen golden lions.

The Queen of Sheba did not believe these stories. Sailors, and camel drivers too, are well known for their wild, boastful tales. No doubt their master was rich. His large, skillfully built ships, which she could see from her front door, proved that. And any king who owned so many caravans carrying rich trade goods was plainly powerful. But there was something else that interested her more than these fairy tales about gold and ivory. The sailors claimed their king was not only the richest man in all the world — he was also the wisest. And this wisdom was a special gift from his God. They told endless stories of his skill in discovering the truth hidden beneath the surface. Yet he claimed no credit for all of this. The skill lay not in himself, he said, but in God. It was God's name that must be honored.

The Queen of Sheba was a woman. And women are notoriously curious. One day, as she stood in her garden watching Solomon's ships, a thought came to her. "I will go myself," she said in her heart, "and see this wise king. I will find out for myself!"

She summoned her servants. A great train of camels was made ready. Enormous bales of provisions were loaded — it must be more than a thousand miles to the land of the wisest man that ever lived. And gifts were prepared, rare spices, gold, emeralds, pearls.

It was a long, hot, monotonous journey. How long does it take a camel to travel twelve hundred miles? I do not know. But I wonder if more than once the queen, weary from the dust and heat, and sore from the long riding, did not ask herself, "What ever am I doing here?" But she did not turn back. And so they came at last to Jerusalem.

King Solomon entertained her royally. This wisest of men rejoiced that the knowledge of the Lord of heaven and earth had reached even to dark, heathen Arabia. The queen asked him hard questions. He answered them all. She told him dark riddles — a favorite way of testing wisdom in those days — but no riddle was too hard for him to solve. And always the great king gave honor to God, who had answered his prayer for wisdom so many years ago.

There were parties too, of course. The Queen of Sheba sat at Solomon's grand banquet table, ate sumptuous food from the golden dishes, drank from the golden cups, and walked in the palace gardens, playing with the monkeys and marveling at the beauty of the peacocks.

All visits have to end, and so, at last, it was time for the queen to go back to her own land. She brought out the gifts she had prepared, and presented them to King Solomon. And Solomon gave her gifts in return, rich gifts from his own fabulous wealth. The queen said, "It was a true report I heard in my own land of your wisdom. I did not believe it until I came and saw it with my own eyes. But now I have to admit

that even the half of your wisdom and your riches was not told to me. Happy are your people, who stand in your presence, and hear your wisdom every day. Blessed is your God who delighted to set you on the throne, to rule over His people Israel, whom He so loved!" And so she went back to her own country.

Later on Solomon wrote a song about all this. Speaking of God's king, he said: *The kings of Sheba and Seba shall offer gifts. Yea, all kings shall fall down before him.* He was not speaking about himself. He was speaking of God's great King, our Saviour, Jesus. There were kings who brought Him gifts, too, you remember. And the Queen of Sheba, though she did not understand this herself, was only the first in a great chorus of praise to God for Jesus, our King.

93

Torn Into Pieces

I Kings 11

Zeruah stood in the doorway, her eyes searching each face, as the column of men marched down the village street. And then at last she saw him. Jeroboam smiled, and waved his hand at his mother as he came opposite her, but he couldn't step out of the ranks. She followed him with her eyes, staring after him until at last the men vanished in the distance. Then she turned sadly back into the house. There were many sad mothers in the tribe of Ephraim that day, but none sadder than Zeruah, the widow.

But Jeroboam was not sad. Being drafted into the labor battalion would give him a chance to see the world. Jerusalem lay ahead, the city where they said silver was as common as stones in the street. He would see the king's palace, maybe even the gold and ivory throne, and the wonderful temple of God. He was going to work hard, to make something of himself. Jeroboam did not mean to be a farmer all his life.

As for the king, he always had need of men who were willing to work hard. The palace and the temple were finished, but there was still much building to be done. Jeroboam was set to working on the city wall. This eager, industrious young man quickly attracted the attention of his supervisors. And then one day King Solomon himself, as he was inspecting the work, noticed Jeroboam. "That is a likely worker," he said to the supervisor. "Put him in charge of the laborers drafted from the two tribes of Joseph."

Jeroboam was elated. It was a first step up. It would not be the last! "There is always room at the top," he thought to himself. As he planned and checked the work, he kept eyes and ears open. Not all the workers had been as ready to leave home as Jeroboam was. Some had wives and small children to support; others worried about aged parents. There was a lot of grumbling. "One month out of every three for the king! It is too much! How is a man to feed his own family?" one of them complained. And another answered, "Yes, and the heavy taxes besides!"

Still another man dared, in a whisper, to criticize the king himself: "A thousand wives! And hardly one of them chosen from his own people!" The workers glanced furtively over their shoulders. There, across the valley, right opposite the beautiful temple built for God, smoked the altars to heathen idols Solomon had built to please his foreign wives. There were ugly rumors in Jerusalem about what went on at those altars, about newborn children being thrown into the fire to please Moloch.

"Some say," another man added, "that the king has received a message of judgment from God." Another answered, "What would you expect? Will God support the man who bows down to Ashtoreth?" And still another, "You remember God's warning. If we serve idols, He will make this beautiful temple a heap of ruins, so that everyone who sees it will stare at it in horror. Why should the tribe of Judah sit on the golden throne? You and I come from the tribe of Joseph. Joseph was a far better man than Judah ever was."

Jeroboam listened, and stored all he heard in his memory. And King Solomon sat on his ivory throne. He ate from his golden dishes. He walked in the garden with his foreign wives, and watched the peacocks and the monkeys. And he actually went with those foreign wives, and bowed himself in front of the altars of Moloch and Ashtoreth. O yes, he went to the temple of God too. "The other is just to please my wives," he explained to his conscience. And so he tried to close his eyes to the warnings of God.

But God never closed His eyes. He saw all that Solomon did. God was angry. He had showered blessings on Solomon. He had given him peace, and wealth, and wisdom, and power. God Himself had appeared twice to Solomon to talk to him, to answer his prayers. Solomon had been warned, warned by God Himself.

One afternoon Jeroboam walked in the fields outside the city. There he met the prophet Ahijah, who was wearing a new coat. When he saw Jeroboam, Ahijah took off his coat, and right there in the fields he tore the coat into twelve pieces. He said to Jeroboam, "Take ten pieces for yourself. For thus says the God of Israel: 'I will tear the kingdom out of the hand of Solomon, and will give ten tribes to you, Jeroboam, though I will still leave two tribes to him, for the sake of My servant David. This people have worshiped Ashtoreth and Moloch, and have not kept My laws. I will not do this while Solomon lives, for David's sake. But after he dies, I will give ten tribes to you. And if you, Jeroboam, listen to My commands, and walk in My ways to do what is right, I will be with you, and you shall be king over My people.'"

Jeroboam was amazed. He had looked longingly at King Solomon's golden throne more than once. He had even dreamed of sitting on it. But he had never imagined that God Himself would promise him that throne. He was amazed, but he did not hesitate. He did not say, as David, and even Solomon did, "O Lord God, I am not good enough or wise enough to rule Your people!" Modesty was not a quality of Jeroboam. He did not wait, either, for God to make His promise come true. He went straight back to Jerusalem and collected other dissatisfied workers from his own tribe, and together they planned a revolution.

What happened then? Well, someone told the king. Jeroboam was forced to run for his life. He escaped to Egypt, and he did not dare to set foot in his own country again until Solomon was dead. And the promise of God? God's promises are sure; no man can unmake them. When Solomon died, just as God had promised, Jeroboam became king of ten of the tribes. Rehoboam, Solomon's son, ruled over the other two. The great kingdom of David and Solomon was torn into two pieces because Solomon worshiped the idols of his foreign wives.

94
Jeroboam
Reaps a Bitter Harvest

I Kings 14

If tomorrow on the way home from school you should see a dog without any head running around the street, you would stare in disbelief. Such a dog would be useless for hunting and no good as a watchdog. Indeed, a dog without a head could not run around at all.

A nation without a capital city is almost as absurd. And that was Jeroboam's problem. He had ten tribes to govern. Rehoboam, Solomon's son, had only two. But Rehoboam had the beautiful capital city, Jerusalem, with its palaces and gardens, and, most important of all, the temple where God lived among His people.

There were plenty of cities in Jeroboam's ten tribes. He could easily choose one for his capital, and build himself a palace. Not as fabulous as Solomon's palace, perhaps, but a palace just the same. He could extend and strengthen the city walls. But he could not duplicate the temple of God. "If my people," he said to himself, "go to Jerusalem to worship, soon they will remember that the citizens of Jerusalem are their brothers. The next thing will be that they will want to join them again. Then it will be all up with me. At all costs I must prevent their going to Jerusalem."

Stop a moment, and think, Jeroboam! How did you get to be king? It was God's doing, was it not? You did not even have to draw your sword from its sheath. And God promised that if you were faithful, He would be with you, and establish your sons, and their sons, on the throne. Why do you not trust God's promise?

But Jeroboam was not a man to trust in anyone or anything except his own clever schemes. And so he made two golden calves. He set one up at the southern border of his kingdom, at Bethel, and one in the north, at Dan. "Jerusalem," he told his people, "is just too far away for you to have to go there to worship. Look! These calves will be your gods. It is these calves that brought you safely out of Egypt to this land of plenty. Bring your offerings and your prayers to these calves."

A proud man thinks he is master of his own fate. He laughs at talk of trust in God. He schemes and plots his own way into power and wealth. But there is one thing beyond the power of the smartest man. That is the power over life and death.

In the palace that Jeroboam built in his new capital city there was a little prince. Of all his father's sons this boy was the favorite. He was such an attractive, winning child that he was a favorite, too, with all the king's subjects. And there is something more, something much more. This little boy, who lived in a wicked, idol-worshiping family, loved and trusted the true God. And God loved the child. As God loves all those who trust in Him.

The little prince fell sick — not just a childish upset, but desperately sick, so that his parents despaired of his life. Where now, Jeroboam, are all your clever schemes? Can you scheme your son back to health again? Jeroboam thought he could. He called his wife. "Put on a disguise," he said to her, "so that no one will guess you are the queen. Go to Shiloh, to the prophet Ahijah, the one who told me I would be king. Take a present for him; not a royal present, such as a king might give for his son's life, but a few loaves of bread and a little jar of honey, such as a poor man might bring. Perhaps if the prophet does not know who you are, he will be willing to pray to God for our son's life."

The queen put on the ragged clothing of a poor woman. She took with her the meager gifts of a poor man. And she set out to trick the prophet. Or was it God that Jeroboam hoped to fool?

Ahijah was now so old that he was blind. No doubt Jeroboam counted on this to make his scheme succeed. But someone else visited Ahijah before the queen arrived. God spoke to Ahijah. "The wife of Jeroboam is coming," God said. "She will pretend to be someone else." And so, when Ahijah heard her footsteps, he said, "Come in, wife of Jeroboam. Why do you pretend to be somebody else? I have sad news for you.

"Go and tell Jeroboam, 'Thus says the Lord: "I took you from among the common people, and made you king over My people. I tore the kingdom away from the family of David, and gave it to you. But you have not obeyed My law, and trusted in My promise, but have thrown Me behind your back. Because My people have worshiped idols, I will root them up from this good land, and scatter them beyond the river. And because you have made My people sin, I will bring evil on you, and on your family. Every man-child of yours I will sweep away, as a man sweeps rubbish out of the door. Not one of them shall even have a decent burial. Those that die in the city, the dogs will devour. Those that die in the country will be devoured by the vultures.

"And now, go home. When your feet enter the city, your little boy will die. All Israel will mourn for him. He only, of all the sons of Jeroboam, will come to a peaceful grave. For I, the Lord, have looked into the heart of this child, and found love and trust in his heart." ' "

So Jeroboam's wife got up and went back home with heavy, stumbling feet. As she stepped back into the palace, her little boy died. All the people assembled to bury this child whom they had loved, and to mourn for him, exactly as God had foretold they would.

And so Jeroboam, the schemer, came to a bad end. And he dragged his sons down with him into disgrace and everlasting sorrow. But the little boy, he who alone of all that family loved and trusted God, was caught up into everlasting joy and happiness. Do not grieve over the shortness of his journey, or his early death. For the things God had prepared for this child were so wonderful that your eyes have never seen anything like them, nor your ears heard their equal, neither could you possibly imagine in your mind how marvelous they were. But as for Jeroboam, he reaped exactly what he had sown.

95
The Secret Place of God

I Kings 17

*T*he new capital city, Samaria, was truly a sight to see. The king had built it on a mountaintop, and the view from its rooftops was spectacular. To the north the great plain stretched as far as the eye could see, edged by the dimly seen peaks of Mount Carmel and Mount Gilboa. Here Deborah had fought, and Gideon, and here King Saul lost his life in the great battle against the Philistines. To the west the blue waters of the Mediterranean broke on the shore.

On the topmost peak of the city the king had built himself a palace, with a great pillared entrance way, and a pool that was a sheet of shining water in the courtyard, and beautifully carved ivory panels on the walls. And if some day you yourself visit Israel, and climb that mountain where Samaria once stood, you can see for yourself the great double walls that protected the city from attack, the pillared entrance, the pool in the courtyard, yes, and even the ivory wall panels King Ahab looked at so long ago.

There was an ivory throne in the palace too. King Ahab sat on that throne, but it was Queen Jezebel who ran the country. She was so domineering, so violent, that the king bent before her as grass bends before the wind. Solomon is famous for his wisdom. Jezebel is remembered for her wickedness. Her great dark eyes, circled with black paint to make them look even larger, were cruel and fierce. And her exquisitely manicured hands, with their golden rings and bracelets — those hands, if you could see them for what they really were, dripped with other people's blood.

Jezebel was not herself an Israelite. She came from Sidon to the north. Her father was the king of Sidon, and his throne, too, was stained with blood. He had murdered his own brother to seize the royal power. Jezebel's father was also a priest of Baal, that monstrous idol unto whose flaming altars the worshipers flung their screaming children. Jezebel was her father's true daughter. When she came to Israel, as King Ahab's bride, she brought with her her father's carelessness about murder, and also his devotion to Baal. Ahab built her a beautiful temple to Baal, and the king and queen together kneeled to worship the idol.

But not even this satisfied Jezebel. She demanded that Baal be the only god worshiped in Samaria. Her secret agents were on every city street, in every little town, ceaselessly hunting down any person bold enough to defy the queen and worship Jehovah. Hundreds of the prophets of the true God had already died a martyr's death, and gone to their reward in heaven.

Meanwhile the halls of the ivory palace ring with merriment, with music, and even with drunken brawling. The nobles, dressed in rich clothing, speak flattery as they fawn before the king. Their wives, perfumed and jeweled and painted, join in the revels. Who of all these people remembers God and His holy law?

Or is this, perhaps, the day of judgment? For who is this that comes through the pillared gate into the beautiful ivory halls? The man's beard hangs down upon his chest. His eyes are stern and piercing. His only clothing is an animal skin slung across his shoulders. This is some wild man, such as lives in the desert. He does not belong in a palace. Let the servants throw him out! But no one moves to lay a finger on the stranger. Every eye in the hall is fixed on him.

The man steps boldly forward to face the king and queen. He does not prostrate himself on the floor before them. He speaks no words of idle flattery. "As the Lord God of Israel lives," Elijah thunders, "before whom I stand, there will be no dew nor rain for years — not until I give the word!" He turns abruptly, and strides out of the palace. A dead silence follows. Many a painted face seems pale beneath the paint. And then the voices start again. Who is afraid of this wild man? After all, Baal is the god of sunshine and rain, of fertile fields and rich harvests. They will offer another sacrifice to Baal, and all will be well.

But Jezebel stares angrily after the man who has dared to defy her. She is not afraid. She is furious instead. She cannot wait to get her lovely fingers on Elijah's neck, to spill his blood on the ground, as she has spilled the blood of so many others of the prophets of Jehovah.

Where, oh, where, can Elijah hide? No man will dare to take him in, to give him shelter and food, now that the queen's agents are hunting for him. But Elijah does not need to be afraid. He has done God's work. God Himself will hide him. He will feed him too. "Go eastward towards the Jordan River," God says to His faithful servant, "to the brook Cherith. Hide there." In the gully of the brook Elijah finds shelter, under the shrubs that grow there. There is fresh water to drink in the little stream. He lies down to sleep. In the morning he wakes up rested. And then what do his startled eyes see? Ravens circling overhead come closer and closer. At last they settle down on the rock beside Elijah. They lay before him bread and meat. And then they fly away. That night they come again, again bringing bread and meat. And so they do the next day. And the next.

Where do the bread and meat come from? Who trained the ravens to bring it to the prophet here? It was God who sent them — God who created both man and birds, both bread and meat, and who still commands and controls even the birds of the air.

While Elijah rests secure in the care of God, Jezebel's police have searched for him far and wide. Day after day the sun blazes fiercely on the land. There is no drop of rain, not even a little cloud to offer comforting shade. Frantic sacrifices to Baal bring only dead silence, never any answer. For Baal is not the god of sunshine and rain. He is only a brazen idol!

96
The Widow's Story

I Kings 17

How can I explain to you, who are young and surrounded by friends, what it is like to be a widow? The loneliness is the worst, knowing that there is no one who cares whether you live or die. And the constant battle to get enough food to keep body and soul together — for in our world there is little honest work a widow can do. And if you have a child to care for, this is double anguish. It is one thing to go to bed hungry yourself. It is another, and much worse thing, to see your little son grow thinner and more listless every day.

I would have given way to despair long before this if I had not discovered that there *is* a God who cares what happens even to the widow and the fatherless. Not the god of my people, you understand. My people worshiped the cruel idol, Baal, who cared only to see his followers cut themselves with knives to show him honor, and to have little children used to feed his altar fires. But south of us there lived a people called the Israelites. Their God was one who showed love and mercy to His worshipers, and who had a special care for the woman who had lost her husband, and the child who had lost his father. It is true, I was not one of His chosen people. I was a stranger; I had no claim on this God. Still I threw myself on His mercy. I dared to put my trust in Him.

And then there came the dreadful famine. Day after day the sun shone with relentless glare. Week after week, month after month, there was no drop of rain. Food became so scarce that even the rich felt the pangs of hunger. What hope could there be for a friendless widow? There came a day when there was only a handful of flour left in my bin, only a few spoonfuls of oil in my jug — and no way to get any more. I could hardly bear to meet the pleading eyes of my little boy. I took a basket, and went out to gather a few sticks to build a fire. I would bake one last cake for the two of us, and then we would die together. There was no other way. Perhaps, I thought despairingly, it was best that he should die young, that he should see the last of this hard world.

And right then, when I had no hope left, right then I learned that for the true God no situation is hopeless. No one is so insignificant that He does not look down on him in pity. No one so friendless that He does not reach out His arm in loving care. As I was picking up a few sticks — I would not need more than one or two — a stranger appeared, a severe-looking man dressed in an animal skin. His face was stern, but his voice was kind. "Will you get me a drink of water?" he asked. "I have traveled all night, and am thirsty." I wondered why anyone should choose to travel in the dark, to risk the dangers of wild animals and wilder criminals. I went to the well to draw a little water for him when he called, "Bring me a little bread, too!" I looked at him sadly. I could see he came from the land of Israel. I had heard the famine there was even worse than among us. I said to him, "Truly, as the Lord your God lives, I do not have any bread, but only a handful of flour and a few spoons of oil. I was even now collecting two sticks so that I could make one last bite of food for myself and my little son. After that we will have to die of hunger."

The stranger smiled, a smile that lighted up his whole face. "Do not be afraid," he said. "First make me something to eat, and then make something for yourself and your little boy. For I have a message for you from the Lord God of Israel. It is this: 'The flour in your bin shall not be used up, nor shall the oil in your jug be gone, until the day that I, the Lord, send rain upon the earth again.'" It was like a message from heaven itself. It *was* a message from heaven itself. I had dared to put my trust in the God of Israel, and He had not failed me. I made a cake for the prophet. I made a cake for myself and my son. We ate, and were filled. And it happened just as he said. No matter how many days we ate, the three of us, there was always flour and oil left for tomorrow.

Elijah lived with us for many months, and even years. I did not tell anyone he was in our house, for the king of Israel sent messengers to every country to hunt him down and kill him. He told me many things about his God — *my* God, too, now! He told me about wicked King Ahab, about God's power to stop the rain, about how God had hidden him, and sent great black birds with bread and meat to feed him. He told me how the brook had at last dried up. And then God, who sees and cares for all who trust in Him, said to His servant, "Go north, to the country of Sidon. There is a widow there, and I have commanded her to feed you." My little boy sat in Elijah's lap listening with wide-open eyes. It was almost like a fairy story, and yet it was true.

Never again, I used to think to myself, will I doubt the loving care and the almighty power of God. And then God showed me something still more wonderful about His power. It all came about in a strange way. It started with a tragedy. My little son grew sick. And then he died. Beside myself with grief, I cried out to Elijah, "Have you been telling God about my sins? Is that why my son has died?" He did not reproach me for my lack of faith. He saw that I was heartbroken. "Give me the child," he said. He took him out of my arms, and carried him to his own room and laid him on his bed. He stretched himself out on the child and prayed, "O Lord God, I pray You, let this child's soul come back into him again!" And, wonder past believing, God heard his prayer. My son coughed, and then he sat up and smiled. The prophet brought him back to me. "See!" he said, "your son is alive!" And I, overcome by amazement that God controls even life and death, said to Elijah, "Now I *know* that your God is the true God, and that you are His faithful servant."

It was hard to lose my husband. Hard to be alone and friendless. Hard to face the hunger of the terrible famine. Hardest of all to see my son die in my arms. But could I have learned these precious truths about my God in any easier way? I wonder.

97

The Fire of God

I Kings 18

Not one drop of rain! Day after day, week after week, month after month, yes, year after year, no rain!

Perhaps you yourself have lived through a severe drought. Or heard your father or your grandfather tell about one. A drought that lasted so long that people came to special church services to pray for rain.

How long did *this* drought last? It did not rain for more than three years. The grass dried up and died. When the farmer tried to plow his field, he worked in a cloud of dust. Every little breeze blew the precious topsoil away. The cattle had to be slaughtered. There was just no grass to feed them. For a little while there was a glut of meat, except that no one had the heart to eat it, with the future so dark and uncertain. The price of grain climbed higher and higher. People fainted in the streets for hunger. And still the relentless sun blazed down upon the cracked, dying earth.

There must have been prayer meetings aplenty. Not church services like ours, but frantic sacrifices offered to Baal, the god of rain and harvests. Perhaps even human sacrifices, with the priests shrieking wildly as they whirled about the altar drowning out the victim's screams. But still it did not rain.

Ahab's people were starving. But the king was more concerned about his horses. Only a handful were left of the two thousand proud war horses, each trained to pull a chariot in battle. If only he could save this little remnant! Just a little grass to keep a few animals alive!

And that is how he met Elijah. Suddenly he came face to face with this man he hated more than any other man. This man he had hunted for three and a half years, threatening the life of anyone who dared to shelter him. He stared, unbelieving, at the prophet, as if he saw a ghost. And then he cried out, "Is it you, O troubler of Israel?" Elijah answered quietly, "I have not troubled Israel. You, Ahab, caused this drought by forsaking God and worshiping Baal. Now call all your people to Mount Carmel. The four hundred and fifty prophets of Baal, who eat at Jezebel's table, must come too. For God has a message for His wandering people."

High up on the mountain slope there was a level place almost like a tabletop. Here Elijah took his stand on one side. The king and the four hundred and fifty prophets of Baal stood across from him. Below them, on all sides, reaching far down the mountain, stood the people, God's people, who had forgotten Him, and put their trust in idols instead. It was to the people that Elijah spoke; to the people that God had sent him.

"How long," he said, "are you going to stumble back and forth from one side to the other? If the Lord is God, then serve Him! But

if Baal is god, then follow him!" The people did not answer. What they really wanted was to worship both Baal and God. That was the safe way. The more gods you had on your side, the better! "Give us two young bulls," Elijah went on. "The four hundred and fifty prophets of Baal shall take their pick of the two. Each of us will cut up the sacrifice, and put it on the altar, but put no fire under it. Then we will each call on our own god. The god that answers with fire, let him be God!" All the people answered, "You speak well. It is a good plan."

The two animals were brought. "You may try first," Elijah said to the prophets of Baal. The prophets cut up the sacrifice and put it on the altar. Then they circled around the altar, shouting, "O Baal, hear us! O Baal, hear us!" All morning long they cried to their god, but there was no voice from heaven, nor anyone that answered. Elijah made fun of them. "Call louder!" he urged. "Maybe he is thinking about something else, or he has gone on a journey, or perhaps he is sleeping, and must be waked up!" The prophets whirled faster and faster in a wild frenzy. They shouted till they were hoarse. They took knives and cut themselves until the blood streamed down their bodies. But there was no voice from heaven, nor anyone that answered.

At last Elijah said to the people, "Come nearer, so you can see and hear clearly." Then he rebuilt the long-ruined altar of God. He dug a deep trench around it, and laid wood for the fire on top of the rocks. He cut up the sacrifice, and placed the pieces on the wood. Then he said to those standing nearby, "Fill four jars with water, and pour them over the sacrifice." Then he said, "Do it again." And then, "Do it a third time." The water drenched the sacrifice, and the wood, and ran down the altar and filled the trench Elijah had dug.

And then Elijah prayed. He did not shriek, or jump, or cut himself. He just talked quietly to the God he trusted, the God who answers prayer. "O Lord God!" Elijah said, "let it be known this day that You are God. Hear me, O God, and turn the hearts of these people back to Yourself." And even while he was speaking the fire of God fell on the altar. It burned up the sacrifice, and the wood, and even the stones of the altar, and it licked up the water in the trench. When the people saw this, they fell on their faces in terror and cried out, "The Lord, He is God! The Lord, He is God!"

"Catch the prophets of Baal!" Elijah called to them. "Do not let one of them escape!" And so they brought the wicked, lying prophets of Baal down the mountain to the brookside, and there they killed them all.

298

Elijah went up to the top of the mountain. He sat down on the ground, and put his head between his knees, and prayed. Then he said to his servant, "Go, and look towards the sea." The servant went, and looked, and came back. "There is nothing to see," he said. Elijah said, "Go and look again. Go seven times." The seventh time the servant came back and said, "There is a little cloud coming up out of the sea, no bigger than a man's hand."

"Go and tell Ahab," Elijah said, " 'Hurry! Get your chariot ready! Get back to Jezreel as fast as you can. For it is going to storm.' " In just a little while the sky grew black with clouds and with wind, and there was a terrible storm. Through the rain — the first in more than three years — Ahab drove his chariot back to his palace in Jezreel. And the hand of God was on Elijah, giving him strength and swiftness no man could ever have by himself. Elijah tucked up his robe, and he ran before Ahab's chariot all the way to Jezreel — a distance of about fifteen miles.

98
The Still, Small Voice

I Kings 19

Jezebel's face was twisted with fury. "You mean that man dared to raise his hand against *my* prophets?" "Raise his hand?" Ahab said. "That was the least of it. He murdered them, all four hundred and fifty of them, on the banks of the brook!" "And you did nothing to stop him?" Ahab shrugged. "Nobody could have stopped him after what happened there on the mountaintop." Jezebel looked scornfully at her husband. "Are you the king of Israel or are you not?" she asked. *"I* would have stopped him. I will stop him yet!" She summoned a servant. "Take this message to Elijah at once: 'The queen says, "May the gods take away my life if by this time tomorrow I do not murder you just as you murdered my prophets! I solemnly swear it!" ' "

When Elijah received this message, he was afraid. Late as it was, and dead-tired as he was from all that had happened, he set out at once for the southern kingdom of Judah, taking only his servant with him. He traveled two days and two nights without stopping to rest or to eat. At last he reached Beersheba, the last city on the border of the desert. He left his servant here, and he himself went on, one more day's journey into the wilderness. Here he sank exhausted to the ground under the shade of a bushy tree. "I have had enough, O Lord," he said to God. "Take away my life now. I am not a success as a prophet. I am a failure!" Then he sank into an exhausted sleep.

After a time an angel touched him, and said, "Get up, and eat." And there beside him was a little fire of hot coals, and a small loaf of bread baking on the coals, and a little jug of water. Elijah was so worn out that he did not even stop to wonder that God should have sent an angel to build a fire and bake bread for him. He ate the bread, drank deeply of the water, and fell asleep once again. After he had slept a long time, the angel came again. Again he touched him on the shoulder, and said, "Get up and eat, because the journey you must make is too great for you." So Elijah ate again, and drank deeply, till he was satisfied. And that food from heaven sustained him for forty days.

For forty days he wandered in the desert of the Sinai peninsula — the very desert where the Israelite people had wandered forty years because they would not trust in God. At last Elijah came to the mountain of Sinai, where God had made a solemn covenant with His people, to be their God and to adopt them as His people, speaking to them out of the fire and the thick darkness. Here Elijah found shelter in a cave. Was it the same cave where Moses had stood when the glory of God passed by, and God protected him by holding His hand over him? It may have been. However that is, God spoke to Elijah as he sat discouraged and heartsick in that cave on the slope of Mt. Sinai.

"What are you doing here, Elijah?" God asked. And Elijah answered, "I have been very busy protecting the honor of God. For the Israelites have forsaken the covenant You made with them, and have wrecked Your altars, and killed Your prophets, until now I am the only one left that trusts in You. And they are hunting for me, to kill me too." God said, "Go out and stand on the mountain before God."

Then a fearful wind roared across the mountain, breaking to pieces the great rocks. But God was not in the wind. After this an earthquake shook the mountain, till the ground beneath Elijah's feet trembled. But God was not in the earthquake. And then came a fierce, raging fire. But God was not in the fire. Then, last of all, Elijah heard a still, small voice. He recognized that God was speaking to him — not in the terrifying wind, or the earthquake, or the fire (though all of these were signs of God's power). No, God was calling him by a still, small voice. He went and stood in the opening of the cave. He wrapped his coat around his face, for he was afraid to look at God.

"What are you doing here, Elijah?" God asked him a second time. Again Elijah answered, "I have been very busy protecting the honor of God. For the Israelites have forsaken the covenant You made with them, and have wrecked Your altars, and killed Your prophets, until now I am the only one left that trusts in You. And they are hunting for me too, to kill me." Under the words was the unspoken wish: "It is enough! I want to die!" And the unspoken thought, "Why does not God rain judgment down from heaven on this wicked nation?"

God said, "Go back to your work. There are still many things I want you to do for Me. You must anoint Hazael to be king over Syria, instead of Ben-hadad; and Jehu to be king over Israel, instead of Ahab; and Elisha to be prophet when you have finished your work for Me. And remember that there are still seven thousand people in Israel who *have kept* My covenant, and have never bowed before Baal, nor kissed his image."

It was a gentle reproof; and yet it was a reproof. For Elijah had allowed his own disappointment and pride to get in the way of God's glory. Angry that all he had done did not turn the Israelites back to God, he wanted God to call immediate judgment down on their heads. And if God did not do as he expected, then he wished to die. Perhaps, as he stood there on the mountainside, his face hidden in the folds of his coat, he remembered what God had said to Moses at this very same spot after the Israelites had sinned by worshiping the golden calf: "I am a merciful and gracious God, slow to anger, abundant in loving-kindness, keeping love and kindness for thousands, forgiving their sins, even though I will at last judge those who refuse to repent."

Yes, He is a God of tender mercy, a God who is marvelously patient with us, His wayward children, a God who forgives the sins of all those who trust in His Son Jesus. There was still time for the Israelites, for Ahab, even for Jezebel, to answer His call, to turn back to Him, and live. There is still time for each of us. But if we will not listen, if we refuse to trust and obey, then at last we, too, must come to judgment — as did Jezebel, and Ahab, and the Israelites.

99

God's Last Message to Ahab

I Kings 22

The helicopter sets down on the White House lawn. The important visitor — sometimes a prime minister, but today it is a king — steps out. Our president greets him. A cannon booms out a salute. The army band plays the Star Spangled Banner, and then the national anthem of the visitor's country. The two men walk between rows of soldiers, drawn up stiffly to attention, to a little platform. Our president says a few words of welcome. The king replies. Tonight there will be a state dinner at the White House, the tables set with the finest of china and silver and crystal, to honor the visiting king. And after all the ceremonies are over, the president and the king will sit down together to talk about the troubled areas of our world.

If you have seen TV pictures of such a scene, you can easily imagine what the public square before the great gate of Samaria looked like that day. For Jehoshaphat, king of Judah, has come to visit Ahab, king of Israel. For almost a hundred years, ever since the death of Solomon, these two Israelite kingdoms have been enemies. But now a treaty of alliance has been worked out, and, to cement it, Jehoshaphat's son has married Ahab's daughter. So this first state visit between the two is very important. Ahab has had a platform built just inside the gate, and on it two thrones. The two kings sit on the thrones, dressed in their splendid royal robes. Behind them stand the soldiers in their dress uniforms, drawn up stiffly at attention. In front the princes and nobles and generals and judges of Israel come to bow low in greeting. And then, after the ceremonies are over, the two kings talk over the troubled areas in their world.

"Do you know," said Ahab, "that our city of Ramoth-Gilead is still in Syrian hands? Ben-hadad promised to return it when he signed a peace treaty with me three years ago, but he has not kept his promise. Will you go with me to recapture the city?"

Jehoshaphat answered, "Count my people as if they were your own people, and my horses as your horses. But before we go, let us ask the Lord what we should do." There was nothing that interested Ahab less than what God wanted. But he was reluctant to admit this to his new ally, who still worshiped the God of their fathers. He summoned his four hundred prophets — *his* prophets, not God's. For these men were in the pay of the king of Israel, and they said whatever they thought would please him most. "Shall we go to Ramoth-Gilead to fight, or not?" Ahab asked the prophets. They all said, "Go! For the Lord will give you the city." Jehoshaphat was suspicious of this great crowd of fawning prophets. "Don't you have one single real prophet of God in your country," he asked, "so that we can find out from him what to do?" "There is one left," Ahab answered. "His name is Micaiah. But I hate him, for he never brings me good news, but only bad." "Do not say such things," Jehoshaphat protested.

The messenger who was sent for Micaiah said to him, "All the other prophets are speaking good things to the king. You must do as they do, and also give him good news." Micaiah answered, "As the Lord lives, I will speak what God tells me to speak, and nothing else." And so they came to the great square where the two kings sat on their thrones. Ahab said to Micaiah, "Shall we go to Ramoth-Gilead, or not?" Micaiah answered scornfully, "Go! For the Lord will deliver it into your hands." Ahab heard the sarcasm in those words. He grew red with anger. "How often must I command you to tell me only the truth?"

"I saw all Israel scattered on the mountains," Micaiah said quietly, "as sheep with no shepherd left to lead them. And God said, 'These people have no leader any more. Let them all go back to their own homes.' " The king of Israel turned to Jehoshaphat: "Didn't I tell you he would bring only bad news, not good?" Micaiah went on: "I saw God sitting on His throne, and all the hosts of heavenly messengers standing on His right hand and on His left. The Lord said, 'Who of you will persuade Ahab to go to Ramoth-Gilead, where he will die?' One of the messengers suggested one thing, the next, another. And then one said, 'I will persuade him.' God asked, 'How?' The messenger said, 'I will put lying words in the mouths of his prophets.' And God said, 'Go and do so!'

"Now, Ahab, listen well. The words spoken by your prophets are lies. If you listen to them, you will surely die!" *Yes, listen well, Ahab. For this is the last, the very last warning God will send you, the very last chance you will ever have to turn back to God!* But Ahab will not listen. He does not wish to hear God's solemn warnings.

Then one of Ahab's paid prophets came up to Micaiah and slapped his face. "Which way did the Spirit of God go to speak to you after He had spoken to me?" he asked sarcastically. Micaiah answered, "You will see for yourself. For the day will soon come when you will frantically try to hide in your inside room." King Ahab said to his servant, "Imprison this fellow Micaiah, and feed him bread and water, until I come back victorious." Micaiah answered, "If you come back victorious, the Lord has not spoken through me."

So Ahab and Jehoshaphat went out with all their armies to fight against Syria. Though he pretended to laugh at Micaiah's prophecies, Ahab was troubled by them. He said to Jehoshaphat, "I will disguise myself as an ordinary soldier, but you can wear your king's robes into the battle." Now the king of Syria had commanded his thirty-two captains, "Fight against no one, either small or great, except the king of Israel." When the captains saw Jehoshaphat in his royal robes, they said, "Surely this is the king of Israel." They surrounded his chariot. Jehoshaphat cried out, and his God, in whom he trusted, heard his cry, and helped him. He turned away the Syrian captains.

But an archer, a common soldier in the Syrian army, drew his bow at random, and shot an arrow. That arrow flew straight to King Ahab, and pierced his armor. Ahab said to the man who drove his chariot, "Turn around, and get me out of this battle, for I am wounded badly." The battle grew more violent. His servants propped Ahab up in his chariot, so that the Israelite soldiers would not know their king was wounded. As the sun set, King Ahab died. Then there ran a despairing cry through the army, "Every man back to his own city, and his own country!" The Israelite soldiers fled in panic. They carried Ahab back to Samaria, the beautiful capital city he had built, and there they buried him. And Jehoshaphat returned to his own capital city of Jerusalem in peace.

100
Elisha Picks Up Elijah's Coat

II Kings 2

The road was narrow and rocky, continually climbing up and down. There was no one in sight except the two men. One of them was old, though he still walked upright and with a firm step. This was to be his last journey, and he knew it. You and I walk forward with the future always hidden. No one of us knows the hour of his own death. But Elijah knew. God Himself had told him. Only for Elijah it was not death, but life, that waited at the end of the road.

The second man was younger. He was a gentle, affectionate person. For several years he had lived with Elijah as his pupil and his helper. He had learned to know the stern, mysterious prophet. He had learned to love him.

But Elisha knew, too, that this was the last time he would walk beside his master. God had told him also that Elijah was going to be taken away, taken back to his Maker, God Himself. How can I describe the heart of a man that knows that grief lies straight ahead? It was not just that he loved Elijah, and now must part from him. That was surely sorrow. But Elijah was so much more to him than just a friend. He was an inspiration, an ideal, a pattern for his own life, a teacher in the ways of God, strength and meaning in the confusion of everyday events. Happy is the man or woman, happy is the boy or girl, to whom God has given such a friend. Perhaps it is your father or mother, your pastor, or teacher, or grandfather. But how your heart is troubled when you must part from this friend, must walk the confusing paths of life without your guide!

Elijah would have liked to spare his friend the pain of that parting. "Stay here," he said. "God has sent me to Bethel." But Elisha could not be persuaded to part from Elijah. "As the Lord lives," he replied, "and as your soul lives, I will not leave you!" And so they went on, side by side, up and down the rocky road, until they came to Bethel.

Outside that town a little group of friends were waiting for them. These were the sons of the prophets, students at the little school Elijah had started there in Bethel. They, too, had heard the sad, yet happy message from God, "Elijah's journey is finished. He is going to leave you. He is coming home." It was a blow to them, but a worse blow, they knew, to Elisha. "Do you know that God is going to take away your master today?" they asked Elisha sympathetically. And Elisha answered, "Yes, I know. Hold your peace."

Again Elijah spoke to his friend. "God has sent me to Jericho. I beg you, Elisha, stay here." Elisha replied as before: "As the Lord lives, and as your soul lives, I will not leave you!" So they went on till they came to Jericho. Here they were met by a second group of the sons of the prophets. "Do you know," they said to Elisha, "that God is going to take away your master today?" And Elisha answered, "Yes, I know. Hold your peace."

One last time Elijah suggested to Elisha, "You stay here. God has sent me to the Jordan River." Elisha answered as before, "As the Lord lives, and as your soul lives, I will not leave you." Fifty men of the sons of the prophets followed them at a little distance to watch what would happen.

So they came to the Jordan River. Elijah took off his prophet's coat. He folded it in his hands, and struck the water of the river with it. Immediately the water divided, right and left, and the two men went across on dry ground. Then Elijah said to Elisha, "Ask what you want me to give you, before I am taken away from you." Elisha answered, "Let a double portion of your spirit be on me!" "That is a hard request," Elijah answered. "But if you see me when I am taken away, it shall be as you ask." And even then, as they walked and talked together, there appeared, coming down from heaven, a chariot of fire with horses of fire. The flaming chariot drove right between Elijah and Elisha, and separated them. And Elijah went up to heaven in a whirlwind. Elisha stood staring after him, and he cried out, "My father, my father! The chariots of Israel, and the horses thereof!"

Then he turned in bitter grief, and tore his clothes. But even as he did so, he saw, through his tears, Elijah's prophet's coat, which had fallen from him as he was caught up to God. He picked the coat up and stared at it. He knew that he must now take Elijah's place as God's prophet. But somehow he knew, too, that he did not need to be afraid. The very God who called him to service would give him the strength and courage he needed, even as He had given these things to Elijah.

He went back to the riverside and struck the water with Elijah's coat. "Where is the God of Elijah?" he called out trustingly. And immediately God answered him. The water of the river separated on each side of him, and he went across to the other shore. The sons of the prophets were waiting for him there. "The spirit of Elijah has come to rest on Elisha," they said. And so it was. For God always gives His Holy Spirit in rich measure to those who ask for it in simple trust.

Elijah was the only person in all the world, except Enoch at the very beginning of things, who went to heaven without dying. This was not only for his sake, but for our sakes as well, that we might know for certain that what we call dying is really the entrance into life itself. For the end of our journey here on earth is the beginning of a new and far more glorious life in the very house of God. The fiery horses and chariot are a figure of the angels of God who catch up to heaven the soul of every person who dies trusting in Jesus. And so when you yourself have to part from someone you love, like Elisha you may grieve for the parting. But do not grieve for your friend. He is with God Himself. And may God in His mercy bring each one of us there too, in His own good time!

101
God Wakes the Dead

II Kings 4

He was just a small boy, about eight or nine years old. His father was a farmer, but they did not live on their farm. Their house was in the village. I do not even know the boy's name. And yet something amazing happened to him. He died, and then he came back alive again. An unheard-of thing!

It all began even before the boy was born. I do not know whether you have brothers and sisters at home. Perhaps you are the only child in your family. Perhaps you have wished for a baby brother or sister; you may even have prayed for one. In this boy's home there was no child at all, not even one. His father and his mother had been married quite a long time. Can you imagine how those parents wished and prayed for a son or a daughter in their home?

God did not answer their prayers. In their lonely home there was no shouting, no children's laughter, not even a single boy or girl. But though it was a lonely home, it was not really an unhappy one. These parents loved and trusted God. They desperately wanted a child, but they believed that what God chose for their lives was best. They did not become bitter or rebellious. They accepted God's will. And they loved each other. Any home where love rules is a happy home.

During the daytime the father went to the fields to work. The mother stayed at home, so she naturally felt the dreadful quiet the most. She did not mope about it. Instead, she looked around for work to do. If she could not raise a child for God's kingdom, there must be some other little thing she could do. One day she discovered what it was.

God's prophet, Elisha, often passed through the village, as he came and went among God's people. The mother invited him into their home for supper. After that, whenever the prophet was in Shunem, he ate supper with the man and his wife. They became close friends. The little house seemed less empty than before.

One day the woman said to her husband, "Couldn't we make a room for the man of God on the rooftop? He could rest quietly there whenever he is here." So they built a little room on the rooftop where it was cool. They put a bed in it for Elisha, and a chair to sit on, a little table where he could read or write, and a lamp. Elisha's heart was warmed by this new evidence of love and kindness. Now he spent the night with them whenever he was in the neighborhood.

One night as he rested in his room on the rooftop, after eating supper with the man and his wife, Elisha called his servant, Gehazi. (Look carefully at Gehazi, because you are going to meet him again.) Elisha said to Gehazi, "Call the woman." The woman came, and Elisha said to her, "Is there something you would like to have? Would you like me to speak to the king about it?" The woman answered, "No, I am quite content." She did not say that she wanted a child, perhaps because she knew well enough the king could not give her a child. But Gehazi had observant eyes. "She has no son," he said to Elisha, "and her husband is getting old." Elisha said to the woman, "By this time next year you shall hold a baby son in your arms." The woman stared at him with wide-open eyes. "Do not tease me with cruel lies," she said. "You are a man of God."

So that is how the little boy was born. He was a miracle baby from the very start, an extra special gift from God, who had surely heard the prayers of the man and his wife, and had been preparing this wonderful answer for them.

Now this was really a happy home! Elisha stopped often, as he came and went.

One day the boy begged his mother, "Let me go to the field to watch my father reap the grain." His mother said, "Go, then." So he danced off, down the village street, down the mountain slope, till he came at last to the field where his father and the family servants were cutting the ripe grain. It was a hot day, too hot for a little boy to stand in the sun. Suddenly he cried out to his father, "My head hurts! My head hurts!" His father said to one of the servants, "Carry him home to his mother." His mother held him on her lap. She put cool, wet cloths on his head. She talked softly to him. But nothing she could do was any good. About noon the little boy died.

The woman carried her dead son up to Elisha's room, and laid him on the bed. Then she sent a servant for a donkey, and she rode like a woman possessed of just one idea till she came at last to Mt. Carmel. She rode up to Elisha, and threw herself on the ground at his feet, catching hold of him. "Did I ask for a son?" she cried out pitifully.

Elisha went back with her to Shunem. He went into the room on the roof and closed the door. There, beside the dead child, he prayed earnestly to God. Then he lay down on the dead child, till, bit by bit, the little cold body grew warm. He got up, walked around the room, prayed again. Once more he lay down on the child. The child sneezed seven times — and opened his eyes. Elisha called his mother. "Take your son," he said with a smile. She was so overcome with joy that she could not say a word.

That is how it happened. This was a miracle boy twice over. Twice over God gave him the precious gift of life. He was dead, but he became alive again at the voice of Almighty God. He never told anyone what he had seen there on the other side of the grave — perhaps because it was so wonderful no words could describe it. But some day you will see it for yourself — that is, if like the woman, and her husband, and the little boy, and Elisha, you trust your life to your blessed Saviour who died so that you might live forevermore.

102

The Witness

II Kings 5

She was only a child — perhaps eight, perhaps nine years old — and no court likes to depend on a child witness. The judge may explain ever so carefully what it means to swear to tell the truth, but can a child tell the difference between what she dreams up in her imagination and what actually happened? And certainly no mission board would send a little girl out alone to a heathen country. The very thought is laughable. Yet God chose her as his witness. He sent her out as his missionary.

This little girl's journey *to* God began long before she appears on the pages of our Bible. It must have been a quiet, happy journey, like the journey David sang about, "He leadeth me beside still waters." Perhaps I can re-create for you something of that journey.

She lived in a little village in the hill country, north and east of Samaria. She had parents who loved her, friends with whom she whispered confidences, neighbors she had known all her life. She could hardly have told you when she first heard about God. Her mother must have told her about God's love, about His ever-present care, almost before she learned to talk. Her father must have taught her to pray as soon as she could fold her hands and repeat a few simple words after him. And the little family, knit together in love and security, must often have talked about the promises God had given His people, and how wonderfully He had kept every one of these promises. For before this child was nine years old, she had given her heart to God in simple, childlike trust.

The world outside her village was torn by unrest and turmoil. Many people had turned their backs on God; they laughed if you said there was a living God who answered prayers and kept promises. Crime, and violence, and grinding poverty were common in her world, as they are in yours. And always the threat of war hung over the village. For just to the northeast were the Syrians. They were powerful, and heavily armed. And they were greedy for land and the plunder of war. Again and again roving bands of Syrian soldiers raided Israelite villages, leav-

ing behind them burning houses and weeping women. But in the middle
of this troubled world the little girl's family was a happy shelter,
encircled by the loving care of God.

And then suddenly one night this child, whose name we do not even
know, set out on a quite different journey — this time a journey *for*
God, and *with* God. She woke up to see the flare of torches, to hear the
hoarse shouts of Syrian soldiers. This time it was her own house that
was on fire. She was roughly seized and carried away in the darkness.
She became a slave girl in the Syrian city of Damascus. Naaman, the
great Syrian géneral, took her home to wait on his wife.

In one terrifying night everything familiar in this child's world was
swept away. At home she and her mother, as they went happily about
their work, had sung David's song: *If I take the wings of the morning,
and dwell in the uttermost parts of the sea, even there thy hand shall
lead me, and thy right hand shall hold me.* Here nobody sang — and
even if they had the little girl could not have understood them. Their
language was strange to her.

And certainly nobody here trusted in the leading of God. They all
went instead to the temple of the idol, Rimmon. But though she did
not feel like singing as she tried to obey the scarcely understood commands of her mistress, perhaps she still whispered David's song to herself as she lay on her lonely bed at night, her pillow wet with homesick
tears: "Even there thy hand shall lead me, and thy right hand shall hold
me." It was a promise, wasn't it? And God always kept His promises!
Yes, God always keeps His promises. His hand *was* leading that little
girl; His right hand held her fast and sure. He stood beside that lonely
bed, and laid a tender hand on that trembling child's shoulders. And
after she had prayed, a simple child's prayer, perhaps no more than
"Don't forget me, God. Hold me tight!" — after this she fell asleep. But
the unseen Presence beside her bed did not go away. He stayed with
her all night, and all day too.

And then suddenly one day her master, Naaman, discovered
strange white spots on his body. He stared at them in horror. Naaman
had leprosy, the dreadful disease which was almost like a living death.
Nobody could cure leprosy. Nobody? There was one Doctor so powerful
He could cure even leprosy, but only the little girl knew about this.
Should she tell about the great Doctor? Naaman was the bitter enemy
of her people. How many Israelites he had killed, in one battle after
another! Perhaps even her own father and mother; she could not be

sure. Should she tell? This question never even entered the little girl's mind. God had shown mercy to her, mercy she did not deserve. She would copy God, and show mercy to her master, who also did not deserve it.

"O how I wish," she said to her mistress, "that my master was with the prophet of God in Samaria! For he would cure his leprosy!" It was only the testimony of a child witness, yet the Syrian king snatched at it eagerly. He prepared an escort of horses and chariots for his favorite general, and he sent with him six thousand gold pieces, ten talents of silver, and ten complete outfits of fine clothes. For surely a doctor who could cure leprosy would expect a big fee! The Syrian king wrote a letter to the king of Israel, saying, "I am sending you my servant Naaman, that you may cure him of his leprosy."

When King Jehoram read the letter, he tore his clothes. "Am I God," he said, "to kill or to make alive, that they send me a man to be healed of leprosy?" Elisha said, "Let Naaman come to me, and he will find out that there really is a prophet of the true God here in Samaria."

And so Naaman's chariots, with their prancing war horses, drew up in front of Elisha's house. Elisha sent out his servant with this message: "Go and wash in the Jordan River seven times, and you will be healed." Naaman was furious. Was this the way to treat a famous person like himself? "I thought," he said, "he would surely come out, and call on his God, and wave his hand over my sores. Are not the rivers of Damascus much better than the muddy Jordan?" And he turned his horse's head, and galloped off for home.

After a while his servants dared to speak to him. "My father," they said, "if the prophet had asked you to do some hard thing, wouldn't you have done it? Why not try this simple remedy?" And Naaman, lost in the misery of his hopeless disease, said to himself, "Why not?" So the great general swallowed his pride. He rode to the banks of the muddy Jordan. He took off his clothes, and waded into the water. He ducked under once, twice, three times, four, five, six, seven times. And then he came out of the river. His flesh was soft, and rosy, like the skin of a newborn baby. The dreadful disease had vanished!

103
The Free Gift

*Y*ou have been very sick. But now you are better. Today, for the first time, you can sit up. Your mother helps you to a chair by the window. You look out. It is your own back yard that you have known since you can remember. Today it looks different. The green grass, the flowers in your mother's garden, the songs of the birds — all these things you hardly noticed before you were sick — all these seem brand-new, wonderful. You feel as if you have been born a second time, and are seeing a world just made, fresh from the hands of the great Creator.

Something like this is what happened to Naaman. He came up the bank of the Jordan River after he had dipped himself seven times in the muddy water, and he was a new man. He had gone into the water covered with sores and scabs. He came out with the rosy, unmarked skin of a little child. He went into the water weighed down by the guilt of all his past sins — selfishness, and cruelty, and pride, and how many others! He came out forgiven, washed clean, with a new heart. He went down the bank an idol worshiper. He came back a man who had

discovered the true God. Yes, Naaman had been born a second time. The world he looked at seemed brand-new, fresh and beautiful, just as it came from the hands of God Himself.

Naaman put on his tunic again, and his shoes, and his beautifully embroidered coat. Naaman was a man in a hurry. He had forty miles to travel yet today. Tomorrow would not do. He could not wait to tell God's prophet what had happened. Not only that his leprosy had disappeared, but also — and now this seemed even more important — about his new-found faith.

He could not even give a name to his experience. He was so young a convert that he did not know about the power of the Holy Spirit. He was so ignorant that he had never heard of the Saviour God had promised to send. In fact, Naaman had never heard of a merciful God at all. The gods he knew demanded a high price for their favors. They wanted money, so their priests said. They enjoyed seeing their worshipers cut themselves until the blood streamed down their bodies; or even asked to have little children thrown screaming into their altar fires.

But this God gave free gifts to people. You did not have to earn or deserve His favor. His love and His mercy were given to the undeserving, to those who were His enemies!

This time, when Naaman's escort drew up in front of Elisha's house, Elisha came out to meet them. And right then and there, on that dusty street in old Samaria, Naaman made a public confession of his new-found faith. "Now I know," he said, "that there is no God in all the earth but Jehovah. I beg of you, take a little present, as an expression of my gratitude to your God." But Elisha would not take a present. He had not healed the Syrian general. He would not take money for the free gifts of God.

Then Naaman said, "I pray you, let me have two mule-loads of earth to take home with me. From now on I will worship and offer sacrifices only to Jehovah. And may God forgive me this one thing, that when I go with King Ben-hadad into the temple of Rimmon, and the king, leaning on my arm, bows before the idol, may God forgive me that I must bow too." And Elisha said to him, "Go home in peace!"

So Naaman and his soldiers set out for Damascus, carrying with them the two precious mule-loads of earth from the land of the true God. Gehazi, Elisha's servant, watched them go, but his heart was filled with bitter envy. If a heathen Syrian was to receive the blessings of God — which he certainly did not deserve — he ought at least to be made to pay for it! Gehazi had caught a glimpse of the silver and gold and fine clothing in Naaman's baggage. "As sure as God lives," Gehazi said to himself, "I will run after him, and get some of that for myself!" So Gehazi hurried after Naaman. And even as he ran he thought up a good story to tell the Syrian general.

Naaman saw him coming from a distance. He got down from his chariot, and said to Gehazi, "Is all well?" And Gehazi, as soon as he could catch his breath, answered, "Yes, all is well. But just after you left two young students from the school of the prophets arrived to visit my master. My master says, 'Will you please let us have a talent of silver and two suits of clothing for them?' " Naaman answered, "Take two talents!" And the Syrian general insisted. He sent two of his servants back with Gehazi, each carrying a bag of silver and a suit of clothes.

When they came in sight of the city, Gehazi took the money and the clothing from them, and sent them back. He hid his loot. Then he hurried in to wait on Elisha.

"Where do you come from, Gehazi?" Elisha asked. Gehazi answered, "I did not go anywhere!" You can lie to Naaman, Gehazi, and to Elisha, but you cannot deceive God. Elisha said, "Did not my heart go with you, when I saw the man turn back and get out of his chariot to meet you? Is this the time to be counting money, or trying to make yourself rich? The leprosy of Naaman, therefore, will stick to you and your children forever!" Then Gehazi went out of the room a leper, white as snow.

And what happened to the little girl who was a slave in Naaman's house? Did her master set her free when he returned, so that she could go back to her own country and her people? Or did she choose of her own free will to stay and teach Naaman and his family all the things her mother and her father had taught her about the one, true God? I wish I could answer these questions for you, but I cannot. Perhaps some day the little girl will answer them for you herself. For if you trust your Saviour, as she did, some day you will surely meet her at that glorious celebration, the marriage feast of the Lamb.

104

Protected by Chariots of Fire

II Kings 6

*T*here was no man more hated and more feared by the people of God in those days than Ben-hadad, the king of Syria. His very name struck terror to their hearts. For this clever, powerful, cruel king was the bitter enemy of the Israelites. During all his long reign he fought against them in one war after another.

The truth is that little Israel was no match for the mighty armies of Syria. By themselves they would have been crushed in the first battle, as a man grinds a beetle beneath his shoe. It was only when God came to their help that they had any hope of driving out the invader. And the Israelites were so far sunk in idolatry that they never even thought to cry to God for help. And yet God had pity on them. Not because they deserved His mercy. They did not. But our God delights to show His goodness even to the undeserving. He remembered His promises to their fathers.

Twice during Ahab's reign God drove the Syrians out of Israel. But Ahab did not learn about God's power, nor about his own weakness. In another battle Ahab lost his life because he refused to listen to the warning God sent him through the prophet Micaiah. This battle was followed by an uneasy peace. The armies did not march for a time, but little gangs of Syrian soldiers still made sudden, violent raids upon God's people. They would sweep down upon some peaceful farm, trample the crops, burn the buildings, and carry helpless women and children off to slavery — much as the Indians in our own early history attacked the isolated settlements.

And then Ben-hadad came again. This time he did not plan an open battle but, instead, a series of secret ambushes that would bleed away the Israelite strength. But, strangely, every time the Syrian army plotted an ambush, the Israelite army changed its plans and went somewhere else. Once might have been an accident, but this happened over and over. Ben-hadad called his generals together. "Tell me," he said, "which one of us is a traitor? Someone is revealing my top-secret plans to the king of Israel!" "There are no traitors here," one of his officers answered.

"It is Elisha, the prophet. He tells the king of Israel the secrets you have cautiously whispered to us in your bedroom." Ben-hadad was furious. "Find him for me!" he commanded. "We will put an end to his tricks!" "He is in Dothan right now," one of the soldiers said. So Ben-hadad sent a big battalion of horses and chariots and foot soldiers. They came secretly, at night, and they surrounded the city of Dothan.

Early in the morning Elisha's servant got up and went outdoors. When he saw the Syrian soldiers all around the city, he was terrified. He hurried back into the house to call Elisha. "Alas, my master!" he cried out, "what shall we do?" "Do not be afraid," Elisha answered. "There are more on our side than on theirs." More on our side? The servant did not see one soldier to help fight the Syrian army. But Elisha saw them. He prayed, "Lord, open his eyes, so that he may see too." God heard Elisha's prayer. He opened the servant's eyes. And what did he see but the whole mountain behind them filled with flaming horses and chariots, God's horses and chariots, sent to protect God's servant! They stood in a protecting ring around Elisha and his servant.

Elisha went calmly forward to meet the Syrians. As he approached them, he prayed, "Make them blind, O God!" God made the soldiers blind. They could still see all right, but they no longer recognized where they were, or to whom they were talking. "You are in the wrong place," Elisha said to the soldiers. "Follow me, and I will bring you to the man you are looking for." Elisha led the soldiers down the road to the capital city of Samaria. When they were in the middle of the city, Elisha prayed again, "Lord, open their eyes now, so that they may see." God opened their eyes, and the Syrian soldiers saw, with sinking hearts, that they were surrounded, in the enemy capital.

Jehoram, the king of Israel, was elated. "Shall I kill them? Shall I kill them?" he asked Elisha. "No," Elisha said, "you must not kill them, for you did not capture them. Give them something to eat, and let them go." So the king of Israel prepared a dinner for his captives, and when they had had enough to eat, he sent them back to King Ben-hadad.

That day Ben-hadad learned that all of his powerful armies and all his clever schemes were useless against the prophet of God. And Jehoram, the king of Israel, learned that his only real protection lay in the God of his fathers, the only true God. And Elisha's servant learned that God protects those who trust in Him with powerful, unseen forces, forces more mighty than any enemy army.

And perhaps you and I should learn something too. Was it just

Elisha who was encircled by flaming chariots and heavenly warriors? No, it was not just Elisha. "The angel of the Lord," God tells us, "camps round about those who fear him, and delivers them." If you love and trust God, this promise is for you too. Like Elisha's servant, you cannot see this angel with your ordinary eyes. But he is there just the same. If you pray to God to give you the eyes of faith, you will be able to feel his powerful, protecting presence.

105
The Man Who Laughed at God

II Kings 6, 7

Day and night the gates of Samaria were locked and barred. Day and night the sentries stood guard on the city walls. Every morning King Jehoram himself walked along the top of the wall, to check on the sentries and to encourage his starving people. For King Ben-hadad of Syria had come back, and this time he intended to stay until he had totally crushed the Israelites. His armies circled the city like a great iron hoop. Every day he drew the hoop a little tighter. No one could leave Samaria. No one could get in.

The price of food soared. The rich paid great sums of money for scraps of half-rotten meat. The poor roamed the streets like gaunt ghosts, searching through the rubbish heaps for anything to fill their empty stomachs. Parents turned their eyes away from their starving children, children who cried at first, but at last, as they grew thinner and weaker, had no strength left even to cry. Some people, crazed with hunger and fear, ran shrieking through the streets until they were caught and confined.

King Jehoram would have surrendered long ago if it had not been for the prophet Elisha. "Call your people to prayer," Elisha advised the king. "Let them repent of their wickedness, and turn to the God of their fathers. He will hear their cries. He is far stronger than Ben-hadad's armies. Nothing is impossible for Him." Under his royal robes the king wore a shirt of rough goatskin as a sign of repentance. But he did not really pray. Nor did he call his people to prayer.

Already the siege had lasted for weeks. This morning, as the king walked along the wall, he was stopped by the desperate cry of a woman. "Help, my lord, O King!" she cried. He answered harshly, "How can I help you? My own flour bins are empty; my own wine jugs are dry." The woman said, "Yesterday my neighbor said, 'Let us boil and eat your son today, and we will eat mine tomorrow.' So we ate my son yesterday, but she has hidden her son." The king drew back in horror from these terrible words. "May God do so to me, and more also," he exclaimed, "if I leave the head of Elisha on his body this very day!"

Elisha was sitting in his house. The king himself pounded on the door. "Look!" Jehoram said angrily, "God Himself is responsible for this dreadful calamity. Why should we wait longer for Him? Plainly He does not plan to rescue us!" Elisha answered, "Listen to the word from God: 'By this time tomorrow you will be able to buy a quarter bushel of fine flour in Samaria for sixty cents, and half a bushel of barley for sixty cents.'" The captain who accompanied the king laughed scornfully. "Even if God made windows in heaven, and rained down grain upon us, this could never happen," he said. Elisha answered, "You will see it with your own eyes, but you will not eat any of it!"

Just outside the city gate, between the walls and the enemy camp, four lepers lived in a crude shack. They, too, were starving, though the hungry people of the city cared little what happened to these four outcasts. "Why do we just sit here and die?" one of them said. "Let us go to the Syrian camp. If they let us live, we will save our lives. And the worst they can do is to kill us."

And so, as it began to grow dark that night, they slipped into the Syrian camp. But what was this? The tents were standing. The horses were tethered. The fires flickered fitfully in the dark. But there were no Syrian soldiers anywhere. God had made the Syrians hear a noise of chariots and horses, the noise of a great army marching against them. The terrified soldiers had said to each other, "It is the armies of Egypt and the Hittites! The king of Israel has hired them to attack us." Panic-struck, that whole Syrian army, and King Ben-hadad himself, had run for their lives.

The hungry lepers went into the first tent they came to. They ate and drank till they could not eat any more. They carried away silver and gold and fine clothing, and went and hid them. Then they came back and went into a second tent, and hid the treasures they found there also. Then one of them said, "We are not doing what is right. This is a day of good news. If we wait till morning to tell our people, God will surely punish us. Come! Let us go and tell the king." For those lepers were more concerned about the starving people in the city than the citizens of Samaria had ever been about the lepers.

When they came to the city wall, they called out to the sentry, "We came to the Syrian camp, but there is nobody there. The horses are tied, and the tents standing, but the Syrians have disappeared!" The sentry sent for the king. King Jehoram got up in the middle of the night. He and his counselors came to the city gate. "I do not trust it," Jehoram said. "It is a trick of the Syrians. They are hiding in the fields, and as soon as we leave the safety of the city, they will attack us."

One of the king's advisers said, "Let someone take a few of the horses that are left, and go and see." So two chariots were brought and hitched up, and soldiers were sent to investigate. They were gone for several hours. The king waited anxiously just inside the gate. At last the chariots returned. "We followed the Syrians all the way to the Jordan River," they said. "The road was full of clothing and equipment they had thrown away as they ran."

By this time it was growing light. The people streamed out of the city to the Syrian camp. There was such a pushing and shoving that the king appointed his captain to keep order at the gate. But he could not keep order. The wildly celebrating people crowded through the gate in such numbers that the captain, who had laughed at God, was knocked down. The crowd rushed on, unheeding, and he was trampled to death under their feet.

106
The Terrible Judgment of God

II Kings 9

Some day — and it may be sooner than you expect — you will go through a door, and it will slam shut behind you, and nothing that you can do will ever open it again. Some day God is going to close the book of your life, and no pleading, or struggling, or praying, or weeping, will get you another chance. Neither you nor I know when. This is what makes everything we do so terribly important.

I do not want you to think that our God is impatient, quick to judge, unwilling to forgive a mistake to allow you a second chance. No, God is patient beyond anything you have ever imagined. Whatever in our frantic lives we know of patience, we have learned from God. God is slow to anger, long-suffering, abundant in loving-kindness, not willing that any man should die. But there is a time when even God's patience ends. Then He says simply, "It is enough." Then the hands reached out so long in mercy, and so often scorned, become hands of judgment instead.

Ahab, like many of you, had known about God's mercy since he was a little boy. But Ahab did not listen. He refused to learn. He scorned God's mercy. All his deeds were deeds of violence and greed and pride. Queen Jezebel had grown up in a heathen land, but she had been only a young girl when, by the mercy of God, she came as Ahab's bride to the Land of Promise. She, too, for many long years now, had heard the wonders of God, had learned His law, had seen His goodness, had trembled before His power. But she would not listen either. And if Ahab was a man of violence, Jezebel was a woman of blood. Her very hands dripped with the blood of her enemies, God's faithful servants.

And what of King Jehoram, Ahab's son, and King Ahaziah, Ahab's grandson and now king of the neighboring kingdom of Judah? They, too, grew up among God's people, heard God's law, saw His marvels, knew about His freely offered mercy. And they, too, turned their backs on God. And at last the dreadful day of God's reckoning has come.

Once again Israel is at war with its old enemy, Syria. King Jehoram has not called on God to help. Instead he has sent for his nephew, King Ahaziah of Judah, to join him in the fight. The army is camped at Ramoth-Gilead. King Jehoram has been wounded, and has gone back to his palace in Jezreel to rest and get well again. Today King Ahaziah is absent too, for he has gone to pay a visit to his wounded uncle. Captain Jehu has been left in charge of the army.

It is evening. The captain and all his officers sit in the courtyard around the fire. A strange-looking man comes in. It is one of God's prophets. "I have a message for you, O captain!" the stranger says to Jehu. Jehu gets up and follows the man into the house. The stranger takes out a little bottle of oil. He pours it over the head of the astonished Jehu. He speaks startling words: "Thus says the Lord God of Israel: 'I have anointed you king over My people. You are to execute the family of Ahab, that I may avenge the blood of My servants whom Jezebel has murdered. Every man-child of Ahab shall die, and the dogs shall eat Jezebel, and there shall be no one even to bury her!'"

Shaken, hardly believing his ears, Jehu goes back to the courtyard. "What did that crazy fellow want?" the others ask him. Jehu is almost afraid to tell them, but at last he admits, "He said, 'Thus says the Lord, "I have anointed you king over My people Israel."'" The army officers get up at once. Each one of them kneels down right there on the steps and swears allegiance to Jehu. Then they blow the trumpet and announce, "Jehu is king!" "Do not let anyone escape from the city, to carry a warning to Jezreel," Jehu commands. And so Jehu and his soldiers set out for Jezreel.

The watchman on the tower at Jezreel sees them coming a long way off. "I see a company of men," he reports to King Jehoram. "Send out a horseman," Jehoram says. "Find out whether they come in peace." The horseman rides out, and he says to Jehu, "The king wants to know if you come in peace." Jehu answers, "What have you to do with peace? Fall in behind me!"

The watchman reports, "The rider is not returning." A second rider is sent out, but he does not come back either. Now the watchman can see well enough to identify the men. "The driving," he says, "is like that of Jehu, for he drives furiously."

Wounded as he is, King Jehoram gets at once into his chariot. He and King Ahaziah ride out to meet Jehu. "Is it peace, Jehu?" they ask. And Jehu answers, "How can there be peace as long as your wicked mother Jezebel lives?"

"This is treachery, O Ahaziah!" Jehoram cries out, even as both kings turn to flee. Jehu draws his bow back to its full length, and he shoots Jehoram through the heart so that he dies. The soldiers pursue after Ahaziah, and kill him too.

The new king, Jehu, drives into Jezreel. Queen Jezebel is waiting for him. She has painted her face, arranged her hair, put on her best robe. She sits at her window, and calls down to Jehu mockingly, "Is it peace, you murderer of your master?" Jehu looks up to the palace windows. Then he calls out, "Who is on my side? Who?" Two or three servants look out of the window. "Throw her down!" Jehu says. The servants throw Jezebel down through the window. The chariot of Jehu drives over her dead body, and her blood spatters on the palace walls.

That is the way she dies, this wicked woman who thought she was stronger than God!

107
The Man Who
Ran Away From God

Jonah 1, 2

*t*he giant sugar maple stood in the corner of the pasture lot. Long ago — when all this farm land was still forest, and only Indians camped beside the tree overnight, on their way up and down the river — one branch had been struck by lightning. Now a pair of woodpeckers had pecked out a hole in the dead branch, and were raising their family there. On hot days the cows lay down gratefully in the shade to chew their cud. And every spring the farmer — as the Indians had done before him — put a wooden spout into the side of the tree and took a little of its sweet sap to make maple sugar.

Under the ground the roots spread far and wide, finally fanning out into feathery rootlets which sucked up the rain and the minerals in the ground, and fed them to the trunk. The trunk distributed them to the leaves, and the flowers, and the seeds, with plenty of the sweet sap left over for the farmer.

One day the trunk said to itself, "Why should I be nothing more than a channel for the sweet sap? The leaves, flowers, seeds, and the farmer, get all the benefit. This is foolish. They have done nothing to deserve the sap. From now on I will keep all the sap for myself." After a while the leaves dried up and dropped to the ground. The next spring there were no leaves — no sweet-tasting sap either. The farmer said, "I wonder what happened?" Sadly he fetched his axe. He chopped down the tree and cut it into firewood.

Once there was a man who did not wish to be a channel to share God's blessings with others. He wanted to hoard them all up for himself and for his own people, the Israelites. He was a prophet. His name was Jonah. At first Jonah was a faithful and a happy prophet. For the messages God gave him to deliver were happy messages. The people of Israel were wicked; their king, Jeroboam II, was even more wicked. Certainly they did not deserve God's help. But God saw how they suffered, and He pitied them. He sent Jonah to tell them that He would drive out their enemies and restore their own land to them. It was wonderful to bring a message like this. It was even more wonderful when God made it all come true.

Then one day God said to Jonah, "Get up! Go to Nineveh, that great capital city of the Assyrians, and warn them to change their ways. For their wickedness has come up before Me." Jonah was indignant. Nineveh was the most powerful city in the world at that time. It was perhaps the wickedest city, too. Certainly it was the city most hated and feared by the Israelites. For the people of Nineveh had burned Israelite cities, tortured Israelite captives, and murdered helpless Israelite children.

It was not that Jonah was afraid the Assyrians might throw him into prison. It was not even that Jonah thought it was hopeless to raise his lonely voice in the middle of all that wickedness. It was just that Jonah hated the people of Nineveh. "No, I will not go," he said to himself. "God's love and God's mercy belong to His chosen people, the Israelites. No one else has a right to share in them. I will not warn the people of Nineveh. For if they listen, and repent, then

God will surely have mercy on them. They do not deserve His mercy!"

So Jonah turned his back on Nineveh, and ran in the opposite direction. When he came to the seaport of Joppa, he found a ship there going to Tarshish, a remote city on the farthest edge of the Great Sea. He paid his fare, sank exhausted on the deck, and fell asleep.

"Whither shall I flee from thy presence?" David had said long before this. "If I take the wings of the morning, and dwell in the uttermost parts of the sea, even there shall thy hand lead me." Jonah, too, found it was not easy to escape from God. God's hand was still leading him even while he was breathlessly running away. The boat put out to sea. Then God sent a fearful storm. The wind blew so hard and the waves piled up into such mountains that the boat was almost broken in pieces. The terrified sailors threw the cargo into the water. Each of them frantically called on his own god. "Someone on board," they said to each other, "must have committed a great crime. That is why this storm pursues us!" They cast lots to discover the guilty man. The lot singled out Jonah. "Tell us!" they cried, "What have you done to deserve this storm?"

Jonah did not try to lie. "The storm is my fault," he admitted. "I am running away from God. Throw me into the sea, and the storm will stop." The sailors were reluctant to do this. They rowed desperately to try to reach the shore. But the storm became so violent they could not make any headway. They prayed, "O Lord, do not let us all die because of this man's sin! And do not lay his death to our account!" Then they threw Jonah overboard. Immediately the storm stopped.

Jonah sank down to the bottom of the sea. The waves closed over his head. But even in that watery grave God's hand still led and held him. God sent a great fish to swallow Jonah. Jonah spent three days and three nights in the stomach of the fish. What did he think about there in the darkness? What did he do all that time? He did what everyone should do in time of trouble, no matter what the trouble is. He prayed to God. He cried out desperately for God's mercy. It seemed as if the gates of life had clanged shut on him forever, but still he prayed.

God heard Jonah's prayer from inside his living tomb. He spoke to the fish. The fish vomited Jonah back up on dry ground.

108

Who Is My Neighbor?

Jonah 3, 4

*T*he great fish swam away. The man lay on the beach, motionless, like some scrap of wreckage discarded by the drifting waves. After a long time he opened his eyes, and then sat up stiffly. Nothing seemed familiar. It was as if he had been suddenly snatched from another world and dropped here on this lonely strip of sand. Where was he? Had he dreamed all that about the boat, and the storm, and the terrible darkness of the bottom of the sea, and the still more terrifying darkness of the inside of the fish? Or had it all happened, and was this desolate spot the land of the dead?

Gradually his mind cleared. *No, he had not dreamed it!* It had really happened. And then at last he understood. He was not dead either. He was alive! He had prayed frantically inside the fish. Now he prayed another kind of prayer, a song of amazed thanks to God:

I cried to God, and He answered me.
I cried out of the belly of death, and You heard my voice!
You threw me into the heart of the sea.
All Your waves passed over me.
The weeds wrapped around my head.
I went down to the bottom of the mountains.
Yet You have brought my life back from the pit, O my God!
I will bring You the sacrifice of thanks.
For God is the One who saves!

And God, who had followed the man even into the belly of the fish, who was still holding him with His strong right hand, said, "Go to Nineveh, and give them My message!" Jonah got up. He shook the sand out of his clothes. He set out for Nineveh.

The city of Nineveh was very large. Nearly half a million people lived inside its heavily fortified, double walls. It took three days to walk from one end of the city to the other. There were no newspapers or radios in Nineveh, of course, but they had their own way of finding out the news. When the king wished to tell his people something,

he sent heralds to call it out as they went from street to street. As soon as the people heard the herald's voice, they dropped whatever they were doing, and came running to hear the news.

That is the way Jonah delivered God's message. He went from street to street, calling out as he went, "Yet forty days and Nineveh shall be destroyed! Yet forty days and Nineveh shall be destroyed!" The people of Nineveh did not laugh when they heard Jonah's message. They trembled instead. For inside each one of them was a voice that whispered, "This is exactly what you deserve." Not one of them had ever heard God's Ten Commandments. But they knew in their hearts that it is wrong to lie, and steal, and kill; to be cruel, and selfish, and greedy.

They did not go back to finish the work they had dropped when they heard the herald's voice. No, they took off their fine clothes, and dressed themselves instead in coarse, scratchy burlap, to show they knew their hearts were wicked. They put away the delicious food they had been preparing for supper, and went hungry instead, to show they were sorry for their wickedness. Even the king got down from his royal throne, and took off his purple robe, and sat down on the ash heap. He sent his heralds all through the city to proclaim:

"No man, no animal even, is to eat anything, or drink anything! Everyone must turn from his wicked ways, and everyone must cry mightily to God! Who knows? Perhaps God will forgive us, so that we do not die."

God in heaven saw what was happening. Not just that the people of Nineveh wore sackcloth, and fasted, and sat in the ashes. These were just outward signs, of no importance by themselves. God saw that the people were truly sorry for their wickedness, that they had turned away from their violent ways, that the prayers they prayed to Him came from the heart. God forgave them! He did not destroy the city of Nineveh.

When Jonah realized that the people had repented, and that God had forgiven them, he was very angry. "This is just what I was afraid would happen," he said to God. "That is why I ran away. And now that You have been merciful to the people of Nineveh, I wish that I were dead!" Jonah, Jonah, if God had given you what you deserved, you would have been dead long ago! Have you already forgotten how little you deserved, and how much God did for you just a few days ago?

Jonah went outside the city. He sat down to wait and see what happened. Perhaps he hoped God would change His mind again, and would still destroy the wicked people Jonah hated so much. It was very hot. The sun blazed down upon his head. And God, looking down in mercy on this undeserving servant of His, made a plant grow up beside where Jonah sat sulking. By His marvelous power He made it grow tall in one night. The next morning Jonah could sit comfortably beneath its great leaves. He was glad to have its cool shade.

The next day God sent a worm to gnaw away the root of the plant, and it withered. Then God sent a hot east wind to blow on Jonah, and the sun beat down so fiercely upon his head that he was in danger of fainting. Again Jonah said, "I wish that I were dead!"

"Have you any right to be angry just because the plant is dead?" God asked Jonah. "You did not make the plant grow, nor did you do anything to take care of it. It grew up in one night, and died the next night. Yet you were sorry to see it die. Ought I not to care for the great city of Nineveh, where there are a hundred and twenty thousand little children too small to tell the difference between their right and their left hand, and many innocent animals, besides?"

What did Jonah answer to this? The Bible does not tell us. It does not really matter either. What does matter is whether you and I have learned the lesson God taught Jonah so long ago. God has forgiven our sins. We know all too well how little we deserved this. But are we ready to carry God's message of forgiving mercy to other undeserving sinners? Do we pray for them? Reach out our hands to them in kindness? Hurry to tell them the Good News that has changed our lives? Or are we, like Jonah, hugging the blessings of God to ourselves, and only too willing to see the judgment of God fall on everyone else?

109
The God Who Answers Prayer

II Kings 18, 19

hezekiah was a man who believed in prayer. Even when everything looked hopeless, he hoped in God. And when the vast Assyrian army appeared before the gates of Jerusalem, Hezekiah spoke quietly to his frightened people. "Do not be frightened," he said, "by the size of Sennacherib's army. For there is Someone with us greater than all those with him. He has only the arm of flesh. But the Lord our God is with us, to fight our battles."

Not that King Hezekiah expected God to work a miracle to save his city while he sat idly by with folded hands. Hezekiah had been expecting the Assyrian army for eight years. For it was eight years ago that these same Assyrians had destroyed the nation of Israel, just to the north. They had burned the city of Samaria to the ground. And the people of Samaria had been driven eastward in a dreadful death march. What had happened to them? No one knew. They were never heard from again. They became the ten lost tribes of Israel. They were a dreadful lesson of what happens to a nation that forgets God.

Yes, Hezekiah had known for eight years that his city would be the next one attacked by Sennacherib. And while he waited for the battle he knew was coming, he built up the walls of his city. He strengthened its fortifications. He collected large quantities of arms — shields, and swords, and spears. He even dug a deep tunnel underneath the city walls so that the springs of water outside the walls fed into a pool inside the city. "Why," he said, "should the king of Assyria find an abundance of water when he comes to fight against us?" If some day you visit Jerusalem, you can see for yourself the tunnel Hezekiah dug through the rock to protect his city from the Assyrian invaders.

But Hezekiah did not trust in his city walls, or his swords and spears, or his water tunnel. He trusted in God.

The Assyrian general stood outside the wall of the city of Jerusalem, and shouted to the people in the city: "How can you be such fools as to try to fight against the great king of Assyria? If I should give you two thousand horses, you would not even be able to find riders to put on them! Why, you could never capture even the least of my king's soldiers!"

"Don't speak in our Jewish language," Hezekiah's officers said, "for then the common people on the wall will understand what you say. Speak in Syrian, for we officers know Syrian!" The Assyrian general laughed scornfully. "Do you think the king of Assyria sent this message just to you who are officers? No, he sent it to the common people, those who will suffer all the horrors of the siege unless they surrender to us at once." Then he shouted even more loudly, "Do not let King Hezekiah fool you, saying, 'God will deliver us'! Has any of the gods of the other nations been able to save his people from Assyrian armies? Where are the gods of Arpad, and of Samaria? Haven't you heard how we utterly destroyed all those cities? Make peace with us now, while you are still alive to do so!" Then the Assyrian general handed up to the officers on the wall a letter to King Hezekiah, demanding his immediate surrender.

Did Hezekiah call a staff meeting of all his officers to consider this demand? No, he took the letter to God's temple. He spread out before God the impudent letter of the king of Assyria. Then he prayed: "O Lord of hosts, the God of Israel, You who sit above the cherubim, You are the only God of all the kingdoms of the earth. For You made the heaven and the earth. Bend down Your ear, O

God, and hear; open Your eyes, and see how Sennacherib has defied the living God. It is true that the kings of Assyria have laid waste all the other countries, and have thrown their gods into the fire. For these were not real gods, but only the work of men's hands, gods of wood and stone. Save us from his hand, I pray You, our God, so that all the people of the earth may know that You are God, and You alone!"

Scarcely had Hezekiah left the temple when the prophet Isaiah sent him God's answer to his prayer: "Thus says the Lord, 'I have heard your prayer. Now I have a message for the king of Assyria. This is the message: "Jerusalem laughs at you in scorn. Whom do you think you have defied? You have dared to speak against the Holy One of Israel. I know your going out and your coming in, and your raging against Me. Therefore I will put My hook in your nose, and My bridle in your mouth. I will turn you back by the way you came. You shall not shoot one arrow against this city. For I Myself will defend this city." ' "

That very night the angel of God went through the camp of the Assyrians, and when morning came one hundred and eighty-five thousand of the Assyrian soldiers were all dead bodies. Sennacherib had to turn back home in humiliating defeat.

Hezekiah had prayed for himself and for his people. But he also prayed for you and for me: "that all the people of the earth may know that You are God, and You alone." Now it is true that our God does not work a miracle like that every day. But the miracles He does work are signs intended for you, for me, for "all the people of the earth." They are signs which carry a message. Have you read those signs? Our God *is* God of all the earth. He grants power, and He takes it away. He gives life, and He takes it away. He chooses the day of your birth, and the day of your death. He *rules*. And he answers prayer.

110

Josiah Discovers a Great Treasure

II Kings 22, 23

I was only six years old when my grandfather died, and my father became king of Judah, so now I lived in the royal palace, but I didn't really understand what people meant when they said I was next in line for the throne. I was too young. I didn't have time to get used to it either, for only two short years later my father died also. Now I found myself sitting all alone on the great throne, while the trumpets all around me blew loudly, and the people shouted, "Long live King Josiah!" It was exciting to sit there while all the captains and the princes bowed low before me, but it was frightening too. Even though I was only a little boy, I realized I needed help to be a good king.

The next thing that stands out in my memory is when I was sixteen. I was old enough now to have some say about how things were done, to be a real king instead of just a king in name. But there is something else, something I remember better than just seeing my servants jump whenever I spoke a command. It was this: my capital city, Jerusalem, was filled with the statues and altars of many different gods. My grandfather had built many of these, and my father had added others. There was one God that interested me especially. This was Jehovah, the ancient God of our people. When I was still a child I had heard many stories of the wonderful deeds He had done for our people, how He had led us in the desert, even lived among us in a tent, and still lived in the golden temple in Jerusalem. I felt myself more and more drawn to this God. I tried to find out all I could about Him. "There was a book once," some of the priests told me, "but it has been lost for many years." Still I often spoke to this God in prayer. And I seemed to hear Him speaking to me in my heart. And the more I learned about Him and the more often I talked to Him, the more I loved Him. This love for God which seemed to grow in my heart was the most important thing that ever happened to me. It changed my whole life.

I realized now that Jehovah was the only true God. The idols

my father and grandfather had set up were just statues made of wood
and stone. They had no right to be here in Jerusalem, which was
God's city, and certainly not in the temple, which was God's house.
I gave orders to have all these false gods torn down and destroyed.
We ground these idols up into dust, and scattered the dust on the
graves of the false priests who had worshiped them. After I had gotten
rid of all the idols in Jerusalem, we went out into the countryside and
destroyed the idols and their altars there too.

Then I noticed the shabby condition of God's house. It was
hundreds of years since anyone had bothered to repair the great
temple Solomon had built for our God. In many places it was broken,
and rubbish was piled high in odd corners. Because I wanted all my
people to have a share in restoring God's house, I put boxes in the
entrances where they could bring gifts for this work. I hired workmen
to clean the temple and to repair it.

While all this was going on, one of the workmen came to me in
great excitement. "We found a book in the temple!" he said. "Look!
It seems to be important." "Read some of it to me," I told him. So
he read to me out of the book. And as I listened I realized that this
book must be the lost law of our God. It was just what I had most
longed to discover. But when I heard what it said, my heart sank.
There were wonderful promises in the book for those who loved and
trusted God. But there were dreadful punishments too, for those who
put their trust in idols. Jerusalem had been filled with idols when I
became king. Would these dreadful punishments fall on me and my
people? I was so troubled that I tore my clothes, and wept bitter tears.

"Go and ask God's prophet about this," I told my men. So they
went to Huldah, the prophetess. And this is the message Huldah sent
me: "Those who put their trust in idols will be punished. But tell
Josiah that God has seen his tears. Because he has sought God, and
is truly sorry for those sins, the punishment will not come while
he is king."

So that is how we found the book. Now we could really learn
about our God. We could read how He had led our fathers, how
He had blessed and cared for them, all the wonders He had performed.
We could know all the promises He had given to those who trust
in Him. And — this was important too — we could know the punishments sent to those who turn away from God to trust in idols.

This book was a great treasure. But it did not belong just to me, the king, and to God's priests. It belonged to all the people, the poor just as much as the rich, the young as well as the old, yes, to the children too. I called all the people together. We gathered in the temple of God. And there every day I read to them the Word of our God. They all listened with eager ears and hearts.

Then I stood up by the pillar of the house of God. There I renewed my covenant with Him. I promised to try to keep His commandments, and to trust Him alone. All the people made the same promise. They would worship only the living God of their fathers. They would obey Him and trust Him. They would be His people, as He had promised to be their God.

So this is what I hope you who come after me will learn from my experience. Guard carefully the Word of our God. Do not let it be lost or forgotten. Read it often. Learn it well. Tell over to yourselves, and to your children, what God has done for you. Obey His commands. And trust always, for everything you need, in Jehovah, the one living, all-powerful God.

111
The King Who Burned His Bible

Jeremiah 36

It is report-card day, and yours is not good. And, even worse, your conduct mark is at the very bottom. You hate to show it to Dad and Mom. Your feet drag as you walk home. You pass a brightly burning fire. The devil whispers in your ear, "Why take it home? Drop it in the fire. No one will be the wiser!" You look longingly at the fire. And then your conscience reminds you, "They would find out sooner or later. You would just get in deeper. Besides, you know those marks are your own fault. Go home. Admit you did wrong. Promise to try harder the next time."

You have heard of the ostrich, I am sure. When danger approaches, the ostrich buries his head in the sand. He is sure that if he does not look at what he is afraid of, it will go away. Once there was a king in Jerusalem who tried out the ostrich's method. He closed his eyes when he saw danger approaching. He closed his ears when he heard God's warnings. "I will burn up God's Word," he said, "and then I will no longer have to listen to His threatenings."

He was a wicked king, and the Jerusalem he lived in was a wicked city. It is true that King Jehoiakim and all his subjects were faithful "church" members. They went to the temple regularly. They offered all the sacrifices God commanded. They put their gifts in the offering plate, and when there was a day of fasting, they made a great show of going hungry. But it was all only an outward show.

Jehoiakim thought that God should be satisfied with this. He should not interfere with the private lives of His people. But when God looked down from heaven, He did not even see the sacrifices and the gifts, and all the fasting. He saw the streets of Jerusalem running with blood. Murder, and robbery, and lies, and cruelty, and greed — these were what God saw. Brother sold his own brother into slavery. Every man hurried to snatch the tiny inheritance of the widow or the orphan. Even God's holy temple was filled with idols. False priests stood beside the priests of Jehovah, offering sacrifices to their false gods. And outside the city burned the cruel fires of Baal. Here the king himself set his subjects an example by throwing his first-born son into the flames.

God had reason to be angry. And yet God waited in patience. He sent His prophet Jeremiah to give His people one last warning, to see whether He could not still save them from destruction. "Listen to My voice," God said, "and I will be your God. Walk in My way, and it will be well with you." The king and the people shrugged their shoulders. "Look how faithfully we go to the temple," they answered. "We are God's chosen people. He will never forsake us. He has made a solemn covenant with us." And they turned away laughing, and went back to their wickedness.

Our God, how patient are His ways! He spoke to Jeremiah: "Write down all the warnings I have sent you to tell My people. Perhaps when they hear them again, the people will repent, will still turn from their wicked ways, and then I will forgive them." So Jeremiah and the scribe, Baruch, sat down together. Jeremiah dictated to Baruch all the messages God had sent in all the years Jeremiah had been God's messenger. What Jeremiah could not remember, the Holy Spirit helped him with.

"Take the book," Jeremiah said to Baruch, "to God's temple on the next fast day. Read it when all the people are there. Perhaps they will still turn back from their evil ways. For God's anger against this wicked people is great!"

Baruch took the book to the temple. A great crowd had assembled for the fast day. Baruch read the book out loud so that everyone could hear. Someone ran to the palace to tell the king what had happened. He came into the room where all the royal princes sat talking together. "Baruch has read to the people a book from God," the messenger said. The princes sent for Baruch, and Baruch read God's warning message to them too. The book frightened the princes. "We will surely tell the king about this," they said to Baruch. "Tell us, where did you find out all this that you have written down here?"

"Jeremiah told it to me," Baruch answered, "and I wrote down with ink every word he spoke." The princes said, "Go and hide, you and Jeremiah both! Do not let anyone know where you are." Then the princes went in to see the king. King Jehoiakim was sitting in his winter palace. It was a chilly day. A bright fire burned in the fireplace, and the king warmed his hands at the flame. The princes told the king what had happened.

"Get the book!" King Jehoiakim commanded. "Let us see what all this is about." A servant brought the book. He began to read it. The royal princes stood behind the king's chair. The servant read three or four pages. "Bring that book here," the king said. Jehoiakim took his knife and cut the precious pages of God's Word into little bits. He threw the fragments into the fire, and watched while the flames destroyed the life-saving warnings. "Do not burn it all," the princes begged. The king shrugged his shoulders and turned away. "I am not afraid of God's threats," he said. Then he called a soldier. "Take Jeremiah and Baruch and throw them into prison," he said. But Jeremiah and Baruch were nowhere to be found. God Himself had hidden His faithful servants.

So the king who acted like an ostrich pulled his head back up out of the sand and looked around him. He didn't hear anything frightening; the voice of warning had been silenced. He didn't see anything dangerous; the book of warning had been burned to white ashes. The king flapped his evil wings proudly, and charged forward — straight into the mouth of destruction.

112
The Weeping Preacher

Jeremiah 38

he is best remembered as the preacher who wept.

He never really wanted to be a preacher at all. He would have liked to live in some peaceful time of history, in a little town where he knew everyone by name, with a family of boys and girls growing up in his house. But it is God who chooses where we shall live, and when. When God first called Jeremiah to be a prophet, he shrank back. "O Lord God," he begged, "I don't know how to preach! I am only a child." "Don't talk like that," God said. "I chose you as My spokesman even before you were born. You are to go wherever I send you, and to say whatever I tell you to say. But do not be afraid. I will always be with you to take care of you." Then God reached out His mighty hand and touched Jeremiah's mouth. "See!" He said. "I have put My words in your mouth."

It was a lonely life, being God's preacher. He never was able to have a family of his own, not even any friends. Some of the people laughed at him; most of them just hated him. For the word which he brought from God was the truth, and nothing is so bitter to a people sunk deep in sin as God's truth. Many times it seemed to him that this kind of life was harder than he could bear. And then he would cry out, "I will not preach any longer! I will not ever mention God's name again! I am only a laughingstock to my people." But in the end God always had His way. "You, Lord, have persuaded me," he would say, "and I was persuaded. You are stronger than I am. When I said, 'I will not speak any longer,' Your word was like a burning fire shut up inside of me, and I had to let it out!"

But it was not for himself and his lonely life that he wept. He wept for his people. They may have laughed at him. Surely they hated him. But he loved them just the same. And as he looked into the future, and saw the dreadful judgments of God that were surely coming to this mocking, careless, wicked people, he wept. But all through his tears he kept on preaching. For his voice was God's mercy, sent to call back a people who did not wish to change.

"Change your ways," he said over, and over, and over again. "If you treat men justly, and do not take advantage of the helpless widow and orphan, and stop killing and lying and stealing, and trust only in the true God, instead of in idols made of wood and stone, then God will still forgive and have mercy on you. But do not ever think you can go on living these lawless lives, and that God will take no notice of what you are doing."

But the people would not listen. "Look!" they said to Jeremiah. "We are God's covenant people. Don't you see, we have the temple of the Lord right here in Jerusalem, His very house, where He lives among His chosen people. What is this ridiculous talk of judgment you keep repeating?" And they went on lying and killing and stealing and sacrificing their little children to idols.

He preached through the reign of good King Josiah, and through the reign of Josiah's wicked son, Jehoahaz, who was carried off in chains to Egypt only three months after he became king. He preached through the reign of Josiah's second son, Jehoiakim, another wicked king, and the reign of Jehoiachin, Josiah's grandson, also very wicked, who was carried off to Babylon in chains three months after he ascended the throne. He was still desperately preaching in the reign of Zedekiah, Josiah's third wicked son. "Repent!" he cried out, "and God will still have mercy! Repent! Repent!" And the tears streamed down his face as he begged them to listen.

"Traitor" is a dirty word in any language. And "Traitor" is just the name they hurled at Jeremiah at last. When his dreadful prophecies began to come true, and the Babylonian king arrived at the gates of Jerusalem, Jeremiah had a final word from God: "If you stay in the city, you shall all die. But if you surrender, you shall at least save your lives." The princes said to Zedekiah, "This man is a traitor! He must die before he weakens the will of the people to fight." Zedekiah shrugged his shoulders. "Do whatever you like with him," he said. So the princes dragged Jeremiah to the dungeon deep beneath the palace. They opened the trap door and threw him into the deep, dark pit. The floor of the dungeon was deep in mud. Jeremiah sank into the mud. There was no light here, and no food.

But God had not forgotten His promise to care for His messenger. In the king's court there was a Negro servant who had more pity in his heart than all the great princes of the kingdom. "This is a wicked thing they have done to Jeremiah," he said boldly to the king. "They have thrown him into the dungeon where he will starve to death." Zedekiah felt a moment's remorse. "Take men, and get him out, if you can, before he dies," he said. The Negro servant took thirty men to help him. They threw down ropes to Jeremiah, and old rags too. "Put the ropes under your arms," they called down to him, their voices echoing weirdly in the dark dungeon, "and put the rags under the ropes." Jeremiah did so. Then all thirty of the men pulled hard, and so they dragged Jeremiah back out of the dungeon into the blessed light of God's day. After this, Jeremiah sat in the king's courtyard. He was still a prisoner, but every day, as long as there was a mouthful of bread to be found, the king commanded Jeremiah should be given a piece of bread. And still he preached, and still he wept for the terror that he knew was coming.

113
The Death of the City

II Kings 25; Lamentations 4

It is better, Jeremiah said, to die by the sword than to die of hunger. And if a whole city dies of hunger, that is a thing so terrible that I can hardly find words to describe it to you.

The city was overcrowded to begin with. For as the armies of Nebuchadnezzar swept across the land, looting and burning and killing, every person who could, fled to the protection of the city walls. Those who had a little money, or close relatives, found shelter in somebody's house. The poor and the friendless had to make do as best they could on the city streets, squatting down in the market place, or in the shadow of some building. Not one of them dreamed it would be eighteen months before they saw the countryside again — if, indeed, they lived to see it at all.

At first, though, no one was too much concerned about the siege. The unusual crowds in the streets gave the city an air of excitement, almost of a holiday. And though Nebuchadnezzar had encircled the city with his army as with a hoop of iron — anyone who stepped up on the city walls could see this for himself — the city was supposed to be unconquerable. Who could scale the steep slope on which Jerusalem was built? Who could breach its double walls, guarded by so many towers? Besides, there was plenty of food stored up inside the city walls, and there was water too. It was for just such an emergency as this that King Hezekiah had built his cunning tunnel beneath the solid rock of the city, bringing inside the walls the water from the fountain outside.

Long before the food ran out they expected that their ally, the king of Egypt, would march to their relief. And even if all else failed, there was always the sure covenant of God. For this was the city where God had chosen to live; they were the people He called His own. He would never allow His holy temple to fall into heathen hands!

O blind people, who have eyes but cannot see, who have ears, but choose not to hear! Those armies camped outside your gates are God's armies, the special instruments of His terrifying judgments. You have no claim on God, for you deserted Him long ago.

Days pass, weeks, months. Nebuchadnezzar camps relentlessly outside the city walls. Bit by bit the supply of food grows less.

And then suddenly there is fresh hope. A runner manages to slip through the Babylonian camp into the city. He has wonderful news. The Egyptian king is coming to their help. You hear laughter in the streets again, boasting too. Nebuchadnezzar has heard the rumor also. He breaks camp, and hurries to meet this new enemy.

He is not gone long. Pharaoh has turned back again. No one knows just what has happened. Was the Egyptian king bought off? Or was he just frightened when he saw the Babylonian army? Whatever the reason, he has gone back home to Egypt.

The Babylonian army surrounds the city again. Now Nebuchad-nezzar brings up his siege engines. These are great towers, almost as high as the city walls. They are shielded by metal armor. The lower part of the tower houses a battering ram, to smash down the city gates. In the upper half there is a platform from which the soldiers can shoot over the walls.

Now day and night the crashing of the battering ram reminds the people of their danger. Food grows more and more scarce. The people walk the streets with glazed eyes — if they have the strength left to walk at all. All of life has been reduced to a desperate search for a few crumbs of bread to keep body and soul together. Disease breaks out, as it always does among starving people. The street echoes with the cry of "Unclean! Unclean!" as the sick creep from place to place. There is no place to bury the dead, and no man strong enough to dig them a grave. And then the last final horror begins. Mothers look with hungry eyes at their own children. At first they recoil from the dreadful thought, but it returns. They kill their little ones, boiling them in the family pot, and eating them with famished mouths.

The defenders on the walls can no longer see straight to shoot an arrow. The walls, weakened by the terrible pounding of the battering ram, break at last. The wild Babylonian soldiers pour into the city, killing, mutilating, burning, as they go from street to street. King Zedekiah and his court try to escape through a secret little back gate in the king's garden. But they are quickly captured and dragged back. Nebuchadnezzar murders the king's little sons before their father's eyes; then he blinds the king, so that this awful sight shall be his last. Zedekiah is chained hand and foot, and led off to Babylon.

Those people who survive are carried away too. Some in chains, some with a ring through their nose as if they were wild animals, some pushing crude carts which carry little children or aged parents. It is a long way to Babylon; many die along the road. The soldiers go through the city. They pack up all the treasures of God's temple, the gold, the silver, the beautifully embroidered curtains. All these will decorate the temples of their Babylonian idols. They knock down the temple walls. They burn the palace, and all the houses. Nothing is now left of the proud Jerusalem but a heap of smoking ashes.

Yet among the pitiful column of broken men and women who stumble mile after mile beneath the blazing sun, driven by the whips of their new masters, or falling by the roadside never to rise again, there are still children of God, people whom He loves. In their terrible trouble He has not forsaken them. He goes with them, even into exile and slavery. In their bitter grief they will learn the lesson of trust, as they never learned it in happier days. And after they have learned, God will bring them back again to their own land.

114

The Strange Leading of God

Daniel 1

All this happened to me a long time ago. I was just a boy then, perhaps thirteen years old, perhaps fourteen. Jerusalem still stood on its hilltop, shining and beautiful, and King Jehoiakim was still alive.

I will never forget that day! The hated Babylonian soldiers stood drawn up, rank on rank, in our city streets, at the very entrance of God's holy temple. Nebuchadnezzar was there too, though he was not emperor yet, for his father was still alive. The streets were crowded with our people, grim-faced, sullen, afraid. My parents were there with the others, and I, as boys will, had pushed forward to the front row.

It was a shameful sight! King Jehoiakim was on his knees before the Babylonian general. "As Jehovah lives," he said solemnly, "I swear I will serve you faithfully." It was the strongest oath an Israelite could make, but Nebuchadnezzar greeted it with a sneer. And then the priests came down the temple steps. They carried the beautiful golden dishes that belonged to God. They laid them in a pile before the Babylonian general. Still Nebuchadnezzar was not satisfied. "I will also take hostages of the royal family," he said to King Jehoiakim, who was still kneeling before him, "to make sure what you do backs up these fine words of yours." His cruel eyes circled the crowd. He pointed at one of the princes. "Seize him," he said to a soldier. He pointed to a second, a third. I tried to make myself as small as possible, but it was no use. He pointed at me!

A soldier stepped forward and took me roughly by the arm. My hands were bound behind me. I was roped to the other boys. And so, as if we were a herd of cattle, we were driven out of the city. "God, help me now!" I prayed, as I lifted my eyes for one last time to the holy temple where our faithful, covenant God lived among His people. I did not dream that before many years had passed the lovely city on the hilltop would be only a heap of smoking ashes. That God's temple would be leveled to the ground. That nearly all the people in that crowd would be dead. God, in His mercy, spared me that vision.

Can you imagine, my friends, what it is like to be at one moment rich and young and free, and at the next moment a chained slave carried off by force to a strange country where they speak words you cannot understand, and bow before an idol made of brass? Can you see that little column of lonely, frightened boys, stumbling endlessly on beneath the broiling sun? Can you hear the coarse jokes of the soldiers as they drive them forward? Look closer, then. For there is something else I want you to see, something harder to discover, but more important than the chains and the whips and the Babylonian soldiers.

There is Someone who walks beside those boys, leading them, even helping them up when they fall. The boys themselves, numb with grief, are scarcely aware of Him yet. But He is there just the same. For our God never deserts those who love Him. And often it happens that the darkest moments of our lives are but a door, His door, to some special service He has planned for you to do. I have found this out for myself in my own life, and this is what I want to share with you.

We came at last to Babylon. Not one of us knew what was going to happen to us. But we had every reason to fear the worst. Would we be thrown into some dark dungeon, to starve and rot to death? Or perhaps tortured to amuse a Babylonian holiday crowd? Or perhaps — this was the best we dared to hope for — become slaves in some rich man's house? It was not knowing that was so hard to bear. But when you do not know what is going to happen to you, but know all too well there is nothing, not one single thing, you can do to help yourself, that is when you pray to God with new earnestness. My friends and I cried to Him both day and night. We prayed to be protected, to be kept alive; we also prayed that, whatever happened, He would keep us faithful.

One day the man in charge of the prisoners called me and three of my friends aside. "You four have been chosen," he said, "to go to school, to learn all the wisdom of the Babylonians. You are to study for three years, and after that you will stand before the king in his royal court. Meanwhile you will be served the very same food he eats, as it comes from his own table."

We had been half starved ever since we had been snatched from home. And now they spread before us a dazzling array of meat and wine and delicious pastries! But even as we reached out our hands to take the food, something, Someone, spoke to us within our hearts: "That food has been sacrificed to idols. It would be wrong for you to touch it!" Trembling we set it back upon the table. That night we went to bed more hungry than before. Again we prayed. We prayed desperately that God would give us strength to do what was right.

The next day I spoke to the steward. "Our God," I told him, "does not allow us to eat that food." He was a kind man; God Himself had worked that kindness in his heart. "But if you do not eat it," he said, "I will get in trouble, because you will not look as handsome and healthy as the other boys." I said, "Try it out, for ten days, I beg you. Give us only bread and vegetables to eat, and see if we do not do as well as the other boys." He agreed, and for ten days we ate bread and vegetables, while all the other boys ate the food from the king's table. At the end of the test it was plain to see we were even healthier than the others. Not from the bread and vegetables, you understand, but by the power of our faithful God, who answers the prayers of His children.

For three years we studied the learning of the Babylonians. Then we were brought before King Nebuchadnezzar. He talked to each of us in turn. He appointed me and my three friends to stand beside his throne and advise him. Sometimes at night, when we prayed together, we wondered. What were we doing here in this foreign land? What did God have planned for our lives? Where was He leading us? We did not know. We had to wait patiently for God to show us what He wanted us to do.

115

The Lost Dream

Daniel 2

*T*he king awoke from his dream with a start. He looked around him fearfully. The room was his own room, but he felt as if a mysterious weight was pressing down on his chest. Hastily he got up from his bed. "I will send for my magicians," he said to himself. "They can explain my dream." And then he stopped dead. "But I don't remember what it was I dreamed!" he said unbelievingly. The feeling of terror remained, but the dream itself was gone. Nebuchadnezzar hesitated only for a moment. "If they are really magicians," he said, "they will be able to tell me what it was I dreamed."

And so early that morning the wise men of Babylon gathered before the great throne. Nebuchadnezzar said to them, "I have dreamed a dream, and it troubles me. I want to know what it means." The magicians answered, "O King, live forever! Tell your servants the dream, and we will show you what it means." Nebuchadnezzar said, "The thing is gone from me. That is just why I sent for you. Tell me what I dreamed, and what the dream means. If you do this, you shall receive gifts and honor. But if you don't do it, you shall be cut up into little pieces, and your houses made a heap of rubbish."

"Tell us your dream, and we will explain it," the magicians said again. Nebuchadnezzar was angry. "I told you I had forgotten it," he said. "You claim to know things that are secret. Then surely you can tell me what I dreamed. Or have you been lying to me all these years? If you can tell me what I dreamed, then I will know that what you claim is its meaning is true." The magicians looked at one another helplessly. "There is not a man on earth," one of them said at last, "who can do what the king asks. Neither has any king ever made such a demand of any wise man or magician. What the king asks is a rare thing. Only the gods, whose dwelling is not on earth, could tell the king what he has dreamed."

Nebuchadnezzar flew into a rage. "Kill them, every one of them," he shouted to the captain of the guard. And so Arioch, the captain of the guard, arrested all the wise men who were there, and he went from street to street and house to house to round up any wise men who had not been at court that morning. "Why is the king in such a hurry to kill off all his wise men?" Daniel asked when Arioch knocked on his door. Arioch explained what had happened. "Let me speak to him first," Daniel begged. So Daniel hurried to the palace. "Give me a little time," he said to the king, "and I will tell you your dream, and also what it means."

Daniel called the three other boys who had come with him from Jerusalem as captives, and who, like him, had been trained in all the wisdom of Babylon. "Shadrach, Meshach, and Abed-nego," he said to his friends, "let us all pray hard to the God of heaven, that He have mercy on us, and tell us this secret, so that we do not die along with the other wise men." And there in that upstairs room these four young men, who had been snatched away from Jerusalem while they were still only children, prayed to the God who knows all secrets. And God answered their prayers. He revealed the king's dream to Daniel in a vision. Then Daniel said, "I thank and praise You, O God, that You have answered our prayer. For our God is the one who removes, and who sets up kings; He knows what is hidden in darkness, and reveals secret things."

The next morning Daniel bowed low before Nebuchadnezzar. "Are you able to tell me what I dreamed, and what it means?" the king asked. Daniel answered, "There is no magician on earth who can do what the king asks. But there is a God in heaven who reveals secrets. He is the one who sent the dream to the king, so that the king should know ahead of time what is going to happen. This, O King, is your dream:

"You saw an enormous statue, gleaming brightly, frightful to look at. Its head was made of fine gold, its chest and arms of silver, its stomach and upper legs of brass, its lower legs of iron, its feet part iron and part clay. Then a great stone struck the statue, and it broke into tiny pieces, like dust, and the wind blew them away. After this the stone which destroyed the statue grew into a great mountain that filled all the earth.

"You, O King, are king of kings. But it is God who gave you power, and strength, and glory, so that even the animals in the fields and the birds in heaven submit to your rule. You are the head of gold. After you shall come another kingdom, not as great, made of silver. And after that, another, made of brass, and after that, still another, made of iron. But after all these empires have been destroyed and forgotten, then the

God of heaven shall set up a kingdom that shall never be destroyed, but shall stand forever, and shall grow to fill the whole earth."

Then Nebuchadnezzar got down from his throne and bowed before Daniel. "Truly," he said, "your God is the God of gods, and the Lord of kings, and the revealer of secrets." He gave Daniel many gifts, and made him ruler of the province of Babylon.

Yes, our God is the one who sets up and who removes kings, and reveals to His children His secret plans about what will happen in the future. Do you know His great secret? It is the secret of the stone that grows to fill the whole world, and that becomes a kingdom that lasts *forever*. That stone is our Lord Jesus Christ. Proud Nebuchadnezzar, and even trusting Daniel, saw Him only faintly and far off, in a dream and in a vision. But you and I, by God's grace, have heard the joyful news of His birth, and His perfect life, and His death for our sakes on the cross, and His victory over death on Easter day. His kingdom shall fill the whole earth, and shall last forever. May God in His mercy grant that you and I may be willing subjects of that great King!

116
Seven Times Hotter

Daniel 3

He called himself the king of kings, and everything he did was done large. Other cities had walls; Babylon had a wall so massive that a chariot could be driven along its top. Other cities had palaces and gardens; Babylon had the world-famous hanging gardens, built high up in the air on pillars, planted with rare and exotic trees and flowers. And so when Nebuchadnezzar decided to build an idol, it is not surprising that he built this large also. The idol stood as high as a ten-story building, and it was completely covered with overlapping plates of pure gold. There was no place inside the city where such a colossal image could be properly seen and worshiped, so the king of kings, as he called himself, set it up in the open plain outside the city gates. Here there was room for a vast throng of worshipers to assemble all at once.

When the idol was finished, and had been set up in its place, and an orchestra had been collected to honor the god with music, Nebuchadnezzar sent out a decree through all the towns and villages of his kingdom: *All the governors and mayors and councilmen and supervisors and judges and sheriffs, every family and tribe and nation, all people everywhere in my realm must now assemble in the great plain where I have set up the golden image. And when they hear the orchestra play, at the sound of the cornet, flute, harp, sackbut, psaltery, and dulcimer, then every man must bow himself to the ground and worship the golden idol I have set up. If any person dares to disobey this command, he shall be burned to death in the fiery furnace.*

In those days the king's word was law, and no man dared defy him. And so they all assembled — the mayors and governors and councilmen and supervisors and judges and sheriffs, every family and tribe and nation — on the great plain where the golden image stood. Among them were Daniel's three friends, Shadrach, Meshach, and Abed-nego, for the king had made these three men governors, for the sake of Daniel.

When everyone had come at last, and that whole crowd stood silent and afraid, the orchestra began to play. And at the sound of the cornet, flute, harp, sackbut, psaltery, and dulcimer, every single person in that whole sea of people bowed himself to the ground and worshiped the golden idol Nebuchadnezzar had set up. Every single person except three brave men — Shadrach, Meshach, and Abed-nego. Perhaps no one would have noticed this if these three man had not had bitter enemies present. For there were many men born in Babylon who envied the high offices Nebuchadnezzar had given to the captive Jews. These jealous men hurried to inform on Shadrach, Meshach, and Abed-nego. "O King, live forever!" they said to Nebuchadnezzar. "There are certain men from the Jewish nation who do not obey your laws, nor worship your gods. These men did not bow down and worship the golden image!"

Nebuchadnezzar sent immediately for Shadrach, Meshach, and Abed-nego. "I have been told," he said to them, "that you did not obey my command, to worship the golden image when you heard the orchestra play. Now then, I will give you one more chance. If you bow down and worship when you hear the music, it is well. But if not, you shall be thrown into the fiery furnace."

Were Shadrach, Meshach, and Abed-nego afraid? Yes, I think they were afraid. The brave man is not the man who is never afraid. He is the man who does what is right even when he is afraid. And so these brave men answered, "Our God is able to save us from the fiery furnace. But even if it is not His will to save us, O Nebuchadnezzar, even then we will not bow down and worship the golden image."

Nebuchadnezzar was very angry. His face grew dark with rage. "Heat the furnace seven times hotter!" he commanded. And then he called his strongest soldiers. "Bind these men," he said, "and throw them into the furnace." So Shadrach, Meshach, and Abed-nego were bound hand and foot, and thrown into the furnace. The fire was so hot that the men who threw them in were killed by the heat of the flames.

Then Nebuchadnezzar came a little nearer to the furnace. He looked into the flames, and he was afraid. "Did we not," he asked his servants, "throw three men, bound hand and foot, into the fire?" And they answered, "Even as you commanded, O King." Nebuchadnezzar said in terror, "But I see four men, and they walk freely in the middle of the flames, and the face of the fourth one resembles the face of a god!" You have reason to tremble, O Nebuchadnezzar. For what you see is indeed a message to you from God Himself, the one who is able to deliver His servants, and who goes with them even into the flames of the fiery furnace.

Nebuchadnezzar stepped still a little closer to the raging flames. "Shadrach, Meshach, and Abed-nego!" he shouted, "servants of the Most High God, come out, and come here!" Then Shadrach, Meshach, and Abed-nego came out of the furnace, out of the middle of the fierce fire. And all the king's counselors stared at them in astonishment. For the fire had not so much as touched them. Not one hair of their heads was singed, nor had their clothes been burned, no, not even the smell of the fire was on them. Only the ropes had burned.

Then Nebuchadnezzar said, "Blessed be the God of Shadrach, Meshach, and Abed-nego, who has delivered His servants who trusted in Him! There is no other God who is able to deliver in this way!" After this Nebuchadnezzar promoted Shadrach, Meshach, and Abed-nego to even more important positions than they held before.

117

The King Who Ate Grass

Daniel 4

*N*ebuchadnezzar, king of Babylon, king of kings, ruler of all men everywhere, and even of the beasts in the field and the birds in the air, to all people and nations and languages that live anywhere on the earth: May peace be multiplied to you! It seems good to me to tell you about the signs and wonders the Most High God has done in my life. His signs are great! His wonders are mighty! His kingdom is an everlasting kingdom, and He rules over all men, in whatever country they live, or in whatever time their life is set.

I, Nebuchadnezzar, was enjoying myself in my palace in Babylon. But then I had a dream which troubled me. Not all the wise men of Babylon could explain to me what my dream meant. Last of all, Daniel came in before me, a man in whom is the wisdom of the gods themselves. I told him my dream. "O Daniel, master of all magicians, from whom no secrets are hid," I said to him, "tell me the meaning of my dream. I dreamed I saw a tree. It grew straight and tall until it reached up to heaven itself. Its leaves gave shade to all the animals of the earth; all the birds of the sky nested in its branches; and its fruit fed people everywhere.

"I was lying on my bed and, as I looked at the tree, a holy watcher came down from heaven. He cried out, 'Cut down the tree, and chop off its branches, and shake off its leaves, and scatter its fruit. Let the animals and the birds find shelter somewhere else. Leave only the stump and the roots in the ground. Let him be wet with the dew of heaven, and live among the animals who eat grass. Let his heart be changed from a man's heart, and let a beast's heart be given him, until seven years have passed over him. This is the decree of the holy ones, so that all people living may know that the Most High rules in the kingdoms of men. He gives power to whomever He will!'

"This, O Daniel, is my dream. Not all the wise men in my kingdom can explain this dream. But I know that you are able to, for the spirit of the holy gods is in you."

Then Daniel seemed struck dumb as he stood before me. His face grew sad, and I could see that his thoughts troubled him. I said to him, "Do not let the dream or its explanation trouble you, O Daniel!" And he answered, "My lord, may the dream happen to those who hate you, and its explanation to your enemies! The tree which you saw, which reached up to heaven, providing food for all people, in whose shelter the beasts of the earth and the birds of the sky lived, that tree, O King, is you! You have grown mighty, so that your power reaches to the ends of the earth. As for the holy watcher you saw come down from heaven, saying, 'Cut down the tree!', this is what it means: The decree of the Most High is that you shall be driven from among men, to live with the animals in the fields, to eat grass as an ox does, and to be wet every night with the dew of heaven, till seven years have passed; until you know that it is the Most High who rules in the kingdoms of men, and that He gives power to whomever He wishes. But the command to leave the stump and the roots in the ground means that your kingdom shall be restored to you after you have learned that it is God, not man, who rules. And now, O King, I beg of you, break off your sins. Show mercy to the poor. It may be that God will still have mercy on you, and lengthen your years of peace."

These words of Daniel were wise, but I, Nebuchadnezzar, was not yet ready to listen to them. My kingdom seemed strong and sure, and his prophecy of evil days coming seemed a child's fable. And, indeed, for a whole year I continued to live in peace. I forgot my dream, and Daniel's explanation of it. One day I was walking in my royal palace, looking down at the city around me. I said to myself, "Is not this the great Babylon, which I have built, by the might of my power and for the glory of my majesty?" Scarcely were the words out of my mouth when there came a voice from heaven, saying, "O King Nebuchadnezzar, your kingdom is departed from you! You shall be driven from men, to live with the beasts of the field, to eat grass like an ox, till seven years have passed." And that very hour it happened, just as the Most High God had commanded. I no longer thought of myself as a man. I thought I was a beast of the fields. I was driven away from my palace. I ate grass like the oxen, and was wet every night with the dew from heaven. My hair grew as long as eagles' feathers, and my nails became like birds' claws.

For seven years I lived in this dreadful condition. And then, as suddenly as God had punished, so suddenly did He have mercy. I looked up to heaven, and my understanding returned. I blessed the Most High, and praised and honored Him. He lives forever. His kingdom never ends. All the people of the earth do His will. No man can stay His hand, or say to Him, "What doest Thou?"

Once again my counselors and lords bowed before me. Once again I was established in my kingdom, with even greater power than I had before. But now I no longer boast of what I have done. Instead I praise and extol and honor the King of heaven. All His words are truth. All His ways are just. And those who walk in self-pride, He is able to abase.

So this is the message I would leave with you. I do not know whether you are rich or poor, powerful or humble, experienced in years or mere children. I care not where you live, or when. You have no power of your own. You could not draw one breath or take one step without God's help. I could have saved myself seven years of misery, if I had only been willing to listen to the gracious warning of the Most High. Do not be stupid, like the ox, who must be led about with a ring in his nose. Give honor to God! Seek always to do His will in your life! Otherwise you, too, may have to learn, as I did, by bitter experience.

118
The Scales of God

Daniel 5

Once upon a time, far away and long ago, there was a beautiful city, and in the city there was a beautiful garden, and in the garden there was a beautiful palace, and in the palace lived King Belshazzar.

Belshazzar did not build the city, nor the garden, nor the palace. It was his grandfather, Nebuchadnezzar, who had built them all. People came from far away to look at the city and the palace. But most of all they came to look at the garden. For Nebuchadnezzar had made the garden to please his wife, who was homesick for the mountains of the country where she grew up.

They called them hanging gardens, but sky gardens would be a better name. For they were built high up on pillars, something like the "sky roads" you may have seen if you have visited a big city. Terrace on top of terrace, they seemed to reach almost to the sky. There were flowers here, and trees, from all over the world. There were fountains to cool the air when it was hot, and brooks and waterfalls running down from terrace to terrace to water the gardens.

King Nebuchadnezzar had died long ago, but the beautiful queen for whom the gardens had been built still lived in the palace where her grandson now reigned.

For days now the palace had been buzzing with preparations. King Belshazzar was giving a feast. He had invited a thousand guests. There were oxen and sheep to be roasted whole, great trays of sweetmeats to be baked, and jar after jar of wine to be brought up from the cellars and opened and tasted. The great banquet hall was lighted by hundreds of candles. King Belshazzar sat alone — as was proper for a great king — on a platform at one end. The guests — all the rich and power-ful and famous from his kingdom, and Belshazzar's wives (for he had many) — sat before him. Belshazzar's grandmother, the queen for whom the gardens had been made, was not there. I do not know whether she was not invited, or whether, perhaps, she felt too old and too tired for such a grand party. Hundreds of slaves hurried back and forth, waiting on the king and on his guests.

It was a great feast, but, so the king thought, not quite great enough. What more could he do to impress on everyone how powerful he was? He called one of his slaves. "Bring the golden dishes from the temple of the God of the Israelites," he said, "the ones Nebuchadnezzar brought to Babylon when he carried the people of Israel here as captives." The slave brought the golden dishes that belonged to God, and King Belshazzar and his guests and all his wives drank wine out of them. And as they drank, they boasted loudly that their gods, made of gold and wood and stone, were more powerful than Jehovah, the God of Israel.

In His heaven, far above, God heard the wicked boasts of King Belshazzar. It was true that the Babylonians had carried God's people into captivity. But *not* because they were more powerful than Jehovah. Oh, no! They were *allowed* by God to capture the Israelites, to teach God's people that they must serve and trust only in the one true God.

Suddenly, in the middle of all the merrymaking, a deathly hush spread over the banquet hall. For on the wall opposite King Belshazzar a hand appeared, a real hand with fingers, but no arm or man behind it. The hand wrote letters on the wall. The king grew pale with terror; his knees knocked against each other. He spoke, hardly louder than a whisper: "Bring the magicians, to read this writing for me." The magicians came, but not one of them could read the writing, or tell the king what it meant. Then the old queen appeared in the doorway. "There is a man called Daniel," she said, "one of the captured Israelites. He was able to tell your grandfather the meaning of his dreams. Send for him."

So Daniel was brought, and this is what he told the king: "It was the Most High God who gave your grandfather Nebuchadnezzar power and glory. But he forgot that these things were gifts from God. He grew proud, and therefore God punished him. For seven years he ate grass like the beasts in the fields, until he learned that the Most High God rules in all the kingdoms of men, and sets up over them whomever He wishes. All this, O Belshazzar, you knew. But you, too, have boasted of your own greatness, and have dared to drink your wine from the golden cups which belong to God. That is why God has sent this hand, and this writing.

"The meaning of the writing is this: MENE — God has counted the days of your rule, and has ended them. TEKEL — God has weighed you on His scales, and you are found short. PERES — your kingdom is divided and given to the Medes and Persians."

That very night the armies of the Persian general Darius attacked the city of Babylon, and Belshazzar was killed!

All of this was far away and long ago. But perhaps not so far away as you might think. For the day is surely coming, and it may be soon, when God is going to count and to end my days, and yours; when God is going to weigh my life, and yours, on His scales. Do not think for a moment that when that dreadful day arrives, and you stand before the judgment seat of God, that you will come out better than King Belshazzar. For the only ones who will balance God's scales will be the ones who have taken refuge in Jesus. If you trust in Jesus as your Saviour, God will add to your side of the scales the good deeds and the saving death of His precious Son. Even now, as you hear this story, He is speaking to you in your heart. "Come unto me," He says; and "He that cometh to me, I will never cast out!"

119
"Who Stopped the Mouths of Lions"

Daniel 6

He was only a boy when he saw it for the last time, and now he was an old man. But he had not forgotten. Every morning, and noon, and night, before he knelt down to thank God, he opened his window to the west, and, looking out, he remembered the shining city set on the top of the hill.

Not that he could see Jerusalem from his window. It was hundreds of miles away, and between lay the terrible desert which no man could travel through. And, for that matter, all that was left now of the shining city was a heap of broken stones and dead ashes. But Jerusalem lived forever in his heart, and before he prayed it helped him to remember the wonderful temple where God Himself had lived among His people.

God was just as near to him in Babylon as in Jerusalem. No one had better reason to know that than Daniel. For nearly seventy years now God had walked beside him in this heathen land, protecting him in every danger, giving him the wisdom to solve every problem in his life, and even moving the hearts of mighty kings to be kind to him. He had come here as a captive boy in chains; today he was second in power only to the emperor, Darius, himself.

There was good reason for Darius to value his services. There was no other man in his whole realm so wise or skillful in affairs of state as Daniel was. But the others, those who had to serve under him — they hated him just because of his many honors. Day in and day out these men spied on Daniel, hoping to discover some little error in judgment, some special favor given to his own people, anything suspicious they could report to the emperor, and thus discredit this hated Jew.

"We shall never get rid of him," they said at last, "unless, perhaps, we could persuade the emperor that his religion is a sign of disloyalty?" The others were delighted with this idea. "Of course! Why didn't we think of that before? You know the conceit of the emperor. It will be easy to persuade him that he is a god himself, and that anyone who prays to another god is a traitor."

The next morning the conspirators appeared at court. "O King

Darius, live forever!" they said. "All the presidents and counselors and governors of your realm have decided that you should issue a decree that, for the next thirty days, any man who prays to any other god except your royal self shall be thrown into the den of lions. Now, O King, sign the decree, so that it may become one of the laws of the Medes and Persians, which cannot be changed."

King Darius was flattered — who would not be? He forgot that he was only a man, ruling by the grace of God. He signed the decree.

Daniel knew that the decree had been signed. But that did not stop him. For he knew also who it is that holds the keys of life and of death. It was not King Darius. That evening, as he usually did, he opened his window to the west, and, looking out, he thought about Jerusalem, and the temple of the God of heaven and earth, the only true God. He remembered the wonderful promises of his faithful God. Then he got down on his knees and prayed. He thanked God for all His past mercies, and prayed that God would strengthen and guide him in this new trial.

The conspirators looked through the open window. They saw Daniel on his knees. They gloated over this expected victory. Then they hurried to the palace. "Did you not, O King," they asked craftily, "pass a law that whoever prayed to any god except your most honored self should be thrown into the lions' den?" Darius answered unsuspectingly, "I did." The conspirators could hardly conceal their delight. "That Daniel," they said, "who come here as a captive from Jerusalem, has defied your law. He prays to his own God three times a day!"

Darius was stricken to the heart, for Daniel was his favorite, his most highly valued counselor. All that night he sat up, his thoughts in turmoil, trying to think of some way to save Daniel. But the next morning the relentless conspirators were there again. "You know, O King," they said, "the law of the Medes and Persians. Once a decree has been signed, no one, not even the king himself, can change it."

So the king ordered Daniel to be brought. He said to Daniel, "Your God, whom you serve continually, will be able to save you." Then Daniel was thrown into the den of the hungry lions, and a great stone was rolled in front of the entrance, and it was sealed with the king's own seal.

That night Darius could not sleep. He could not eat. Even the music, which usually soothed him when his spirit was troubled, now only troubled him the more. Very early the next morning he got up. He hurried to the lions' den. "O Daniel!" he cried out in anguish, "servant of the living God, is your God able to save you from the lions?" And then, to his unutterable joy, he heard the voice of Daniel, strong and alive: "O King, live forever! My God sent His angel to shut the lions' mouths, and they have not hurt me."

Then the king was exceedingly glad, and ordered that Daniel should be taken out of the lions' den. The wicked conspirators were brought, and they were thrown to the lions, who devoured them almost before they fell to the bottom of the den.

120

"If I Perish, I Perish"

Esther 1-4

My name is Ahasuerus. I am king of the great empire of Persia — all twenty-one provinces! From the Euphrates River in the east all the way to the Nile in the west, no man dares to disobey my commands. My word is law! Never before has there been a king so powerful or so rich as I am.

But what is the good of power and money unless people know you have them? And so I summoned to my palace in Shushan all the nobles and princes of my kingdom. For a hundred and eighty days I entertained them with feasting and drinking. I showed them my gardens, the pools of water, the embroidered curtains hanging from silver rings, the marble pillars, each topped by a pair of bulls supporting the ceiling of my throne room, the gold and silver sofas set everywhere for guests to sit on, and the glittering mosaic floors. My slaves offered them wine in golden cups, each cup carved in the shape of a strange animal, and each cup different from every other.

Oh, they were stunned by my magnificence! But still I was not content. What more could I show them? I called a slave. "Command the queen to come out here," I ordered, "with the crown on her head, so that everyone can see that besides all these other wonders I also have the most beautiful woman in all Persia as my queen!" After a while the slave came back. "The queen," he said, "refuses to come." For a moment everything went black before my eyes. But I controlled myself. I asked my advisers, "How shall we punish this queen who has dared to disobey me?" They said, "Take away her crown. Give it to someone else. The queen's disobedience is an insult not only to you but to every man in your kingdom. Other women, too, now will dare to disobey their husbands." Quickly a scribe was called. "Write a decree," I ordered, "that Vashti shall no longer be queen, because she refused to obey my command." I signed and sealed the order with my own ring, and it was sent to all the provinces of my kingdom.

After some days I asked my advisers, "Who shall be the new queen of Persia?" They had an answer ready. "We will collect from all parts of your kingdom the most beautiful young girls we can find. You can choose from among them the one you wish to be your queen."

My name is Haman. I am a lucky man — perhaps the luckiest in the whole Persian empire. I am the king's favorite counselor. He has heaped me with honors, and if there is anything I wish, I have only to ask and it is done. All the king's servants know how important I am. For as I come in and out of the palace, they bow low before me, almost as if I were a god! My heart swells with pride when I see every head touch the ground because I am passing by.

I would be completely happy except for one man. This man, Mordecai, refuses to bow when I go into the palace. He is a Jew, one of the people brought here as captives by Nebuchadnezzar. My anger burns hot within me when I see how he dares to stand upright and stare me in the face as I walk by. He shall pay for this! And not himself alone! I shall ask the king to order the death of every Jew in the kingdom. But first I must find out my lucky day. I order the magicians to cast lots. They cast lots every day for a whole year. At last there comes a day that is lucky for me. I go to see the king. "There is a troublesome people in your kingdom," I tell him, "who do not obey your laws. Let me get rid of them for you. I will pay a handsome sum into your treasury out of the loot we get."

"Arrange it however you like," the king said, and he handed me the royal ring. It *was* my lucky day! I wrote a decree that on the thirteenth day of the first month all people everywhere should kill any Jews living among them. I signed it with the king's own ring, and sent it out to every province. But as I was leaving the palace, Mordecai stared at me insolently. "Soon," I thought, "you will bow low indeed!" Today I was truly happy.

My name is Esther. I am the new queen of Persia, chosen from all the girls brought to the palace because the king loved me. Before I became queen, I lived with my cousin Mordecai, for my father and my mother were both dead. Now that I lived in the palace, Mordecai came to the gate every day to inquire about me, and sometimes he sent me messages. One day there was a special message. Mordecai had overheard a plot to assassinate the king. I told the king about this plot. The guilty conspirators were caught and executed.

And then one day Mordecai was not wearing his usual clothes when he came. He was dressed in sackcloth, with ashes sprinkled on his head. I was distressed. I sent a servant out with a new suit of clothes. But the servant came back. "He refuses to put them on," he said. "Find out what is troubling him, immediately!" I commanded.

The servant returned. He brought a copy of a decree, signed by the king, ordering the murder of every Jew in the kingdom. "Mordecai says," the servant told me, "that you must beg the king to stop this decree. Perhaps this is the very reason God raised you to the throne, so that you could save God's people!"

I was terribly frightened. For the Persian law is that anyone who enters the king's presence without being sent for will die. Unless, that is, the king holds out his golden scepter. I had not been sent for, for thirty days. But I knew I must try to save God's people, even if it cost me my life. I sent a message back to my cousin: "You and all the Jews in Shushan must fast and pray to God for me for three days. I and my women will do the same. And then I will go in to the king, even though I have not been sent for. And if I die, I die!"

121
The Sure Promise of God

Esther 5-8

*E*sther had eaten nothing for three days. But it was not hunger that gave her this sinking feeling. It was fear. "This may be my last day on earth," she thought to herself as she crossed over from the women's apartments to the king's part of the palace. But, frightened as she was, she did not turn back. For she knew that the lives of thousands of God's people depended on what she did this morning. She was just a young girl. She had never dreamed she would some day be called on to act the part of a hero. "God of my fathers, help me!" she prayed under her breath as she entered the great throne room.

Ahasuerus, dressed in all his royal robes, sat on his beautiful throne at the further end of the hall. Esther took a few faltering steps forward. Then she stopped dead still. The king had seen her! Esther's heart was in her mouth. And then suddenly Ahasuerus smiled. (Surely it was God Himself that prompted that smile!) The king reached out his golden scepter. Esther came slowly forward. "What do you wish, Queen Esther?" the king asked. "Whatever it is, I will give it to you, even to the half of my kingdom." She answered, "If it please the king, let the king and Haman come tonight to the banquet I have prepared." The king called a messenger. "Hurry!" he said. "Tell Haman to get ready. He is invited to Queen Esther's banquet."

That night, after the king and Haman had feasted and drunk, Ahasuerus asked again, "What do you wish, Queen Esther? Whatever it is, I will give it to you." She said only, "If I have found favor in your sight, let the king and Haman come again tomorrow to the banquet I will prepare. Tomorrow I will tell you what it is I wish."

Haman went home. He called for his wife. He called in all his friends. He told them how rich he was, and how many children he had, and how the king had honored him. "Moreover," he said, "Esther the queen invited nobody else to the banquet she had prepared for the king but me. And she has invited me to come tomorrow again. But all this means nothing to me, for, as I left the palace, I saw Mordecai the Jew sitting at the gate, and he did not bow down to me!" Then Haman's wife said, "Build a gallows in our yard. Build it seventy-five feet high. In the morning get the king's permission to hang Mordecai on the gallows. Then you can go merrily to the banquet." This idea pleased Haman. He had the gallows built.

That night, by the grace of God, Ahasuerus could not sleep. He asked a servant to read the records of his kingdom to him. There he read that Mordecai had informed the king of a conspiracy against his life. "What reward was given to Mordecai for this information?" Ahasuerus asked. "No reward," the servant answered. By this time it was very early morning. "Who is in the courtyard?" the king asked. "Haman is waiting there," the servant said. "Bring him in," the king commanded. When Haman came in, the king asked, "What shall be done to the man whom the king delights to honor?" Haman thought to himself, "Whom would the king delight to honor more than myself?" So he said, "Let the royal robes be brought, and the king's own crown, and the king's own horse. Let one of the noble princes dress that man in the robes and the crown, and set him on the horse, and lead him through the streets, crying out to all the people, 'Thus shall it be done to the man whom the king delights to honor!' "

"Hurry!" the king said, "and do everything you have suggested to Mordecai!" Haman's heart almost stood still; but he had to obey. So Haman dressed Mordecai in the king's royal robes, set on his head the king's crown, mounted him on the king's own horse. He led him through the streets, calling out, "Thus shall it be done to the man whom the king delights to honor!"

Then he rushed home, burning with anger and humiliation, and told his wife and his friends what a dreadful thing had happened. While he was still talking to them, a messenger arrived to remind him of the banquet with Queen Esther. Again Haman and the king feasted and drank — though Haman could hardly choke the food down. Then Ahasuerus said to Esther, "What do you wish, Queen Esther? Whatever it is, I promise to give it to you." Esther kneeled down at the king's feet. "I beg you," she said, "save my life, and the life of my people. For we have been sold to be killed." "Who," Ahasuerus asked, "has dared to do such a thing?" Esther answered, "It is this wicked Haman here." The king was so angry he could not speak. He went into the garden to compose his thoughts. While he was gone, Haman fell at Esther's feet. He begged her to save his life. Just then the king came back. He saw Haman clutching Esther's feet. "What!" said the king. "Will he dare to attack the queen in my own house?" One of the servants said, "There is this gallows, seventy-five feet high, which Haman built in his yard, to hang Mordecai on." The king commanded, "Hang Haman himself on it at once!"

Then Ahasuerus gave Mordecai all the offices and honors which had belonged to Haman. "I cannot alter the decree Haman sent out," he said, "for the laws of the Persians cannot be changed. But send out another decree, to tell the Jews everywhere to prepare to defend themselves against their enemies." So Mordecai sent out the decree, sealed with the king's own ring.

That day on which the Jews defended themselves against their enemies is called the Feast of the Casting of Lots, or *Purim* in the Persian language, because Haman had cast lots to discover his lucky day. The Jews celebrate it every year. But what you and I remember most of all about it is that God, who had promised that a son of David should some day establish a kingdom that would never end, kept that promise. He did not allow His people to be all killed off.

122

The Great Shout of Laughter

Ezra 1-6

*t*he long procession wound slowly north along the ancient caravan trail. They could make only a few miles a day. Some of them were old, and some, small children. Most of them had to walk. They had some horses and donkeys, and even a few camels, but these animals were needed to carry what little provisions they had been able to bring along, and also the precious gold and silver dishes which belonged to God.

A very few of the older people had traveled this trail before. They had been in that terrible march in the opposite direction, when they had gone to Babylon, bound and captive, driven like cattle by their ruthless conquerors. But most of the great crowd of almost forty thousand people had been born and had grown up in slavery in a foreign land. They had never seen their own country.

Though the sun was hot, and the miles seemed to stretch endlessly on and on, and their feet were sore from the unaccustomed walking, still there was a festive air about the crowd. When they made a rest stop from time to time, to allow the stragglers to catch up, there was much excited talk. "I never thought I would live to see a Persian king actually commanding us to return to our own country, and to rebuild God's holy temple," one of them said. And another added, "Yes, and taking out of his idol's temple the gold and silver dishes Nebuchadnezzar stole from God's house in Jerusalem! Imagine that!" Someone else said, "We should not have been surprised. Isn't that exactly what God promised in the letter Jeremiah wrote us?" One of the men quoted the letter, which had been read so often that most of them knew it by heart: "After seventy years I will cause you to return to Jerusalem. For the thoughts I think towards you are not thoughts of evil, but thoughts of peace. You shall seek Me, and find Me, when you search for Me with all your heart. I will bring you again to this city."

One of the children asked, "Did Abraham travel this same road, Father? Did he stop to rest right here?" "Yes, this is the road he traveled," his father answered. "Perhaps, who knows, he did rest right here." "But he was almost alone," someone else added. "And he did not know where he was going. And there was no city when he did get there, only strangers living in the land." "There will be no city for us either," someone else answered, "only strangers living in *our* land." They were all quiet, thinking about this sobering fact. Few of them had ever seen the city, but they had heard so much about it, it seemed quite impossible to believe Jerusalem was now only a heap of rubble. "Get moving!" someone down the line shouted. "The rest stop is over." Slowly they stood up and started again on their long march. Jerusalem might be only a pile of rubble, but in their mind's eye they still saw the beautiful city gleaming on the hill, and, above it all, the temple of God.

When they finally reached their destination, they stood numb with shock, staring at what had been Jerusalem. They stumbled about among the rocks, trying to find where the temple had stood. And the streets of the city, where had they been? And the gates in the crumbled walls? Finally, in despair, they turned away. First of all each family must find its own inherited plot of ground, and build some sort of shelter.

Later they began to clear away the rubble where Solomon's temple had stood. Then they set up an altar where they could offer sacrifices to God. It was nothing like King Solomon's great brass altar, but they had built it themselves, out of hearts grateful to God. From then on the priests offered sacrifices every morning. For God *had* remembered His promise. He *had* brought them back to their own land!

Next they laid the foundation of the new temple. They celebrated that day. The priests blew trumpets, the cymbals rang out, and the people sang praises to God. A great shout of joy went up when the last stone was fitted into the foundation. But the older folk wept instead. For they could remember how much grander and more beautiful Solomon's temple had been. And so there was a great noise which could be heard far away; but you could not tell which was louder, the shouts of joy, or the bitter weeping of those who had seen that other temple.

It took them more than four years to rebuild the temple. But at last it was finished. It was much smaller than the first temple, and not nearly as elaborate. And there was something else. The innermost room, the holy of holies, was empty! There was no ark to place there, no mercy seat, sheltered by the outstretched wings of the golden cherubim. And no dazzling cloud to show the presence of God, whose house this was! The ark had been lost when Nebuchadnezzar's soldiers burned the city. Some said that Jeremiah had hidden it in a cave in one of the mountains. However that may be, it was gone forever. The holiest part of the house of God stood empty! It was not empty because God no longer lived among His people. No, it was empty because the time had come for God's people to expect from God something more, not something less. They must fix their eyes not on a building made of wood and stone, but on that living building, that never-ending house God had promised to David so long ago.

After the temple was finished, the Israelites held a great feast of dedication. Each family brought a lamb, and once again they celebrated the Passover feast, for now, a second time, God had rescued them from slavery, and brought them to their own land in peace. In Babylon they had said sadly, "How can we sing the Lord's songs in a foreign land?" But now they had a new, a joyful song to sing:

> *When Jehovah brought back those that returned to Zion,*
> *We were like unto them that dream.*
> *Then was our mouth filled with laughter,*
> *And our tongue with singing:*
> *Then said they among the nations,*
> *Jehovah hath done great things for them.*
> *Jehovah hath done great things for us,*
> *Whereof we are glad.*

(Psalm 126)

123

The Living Tent

Sometimes when you are traveling, you come to a sign which says, "Road ends 500 feet." And then a minute later your road does come to a dead end. You find yourself on a roadless desert which stretches before you unmarked, impassable.

Perhaps it seems to you that we have come to such a dead end on our journey. Four hundred years stretch ahead of us, a desert, with no paths marked, no voice from God, no prophet.

And yet this is not a dead end. It is only a pause, a rest stop, a chance to think over what God has done — and a lesson in waiting for God. God always leads His people in this way. Periods of great activity are followed by days, even years when God is silent. You remember that the Israelites spent nearly four hundred years as slaves in Egypt. Many despaired. Some even thought God was dead. But these years of testing were followed by the tremendous events of the rescue from Egypt, the tender care God showed His people in the desert, and finally by the very voice of God Himself speaking to them from out of the fire on the mountain.

You and I are always in a hurry, anxious to get on with the work, to move forward. This is because we are creatures of time, and we hear always in our ears the relentless rush of passing days and weeks. But it is exactly because we are creatures of time that God speaks to us as He does. For God's great saving acts are not idle stories written down on paper. They are *acts,* which take place in history, and history is always something that happens in time, that moves forward. In history one event flows out of another, just as a baby grows to be a child, the child becomes a young man or woman, the young man becomes a father, and then a grandfather. You have to be a child before you can be a young man; you have to be young before you can be old.

When you are a child, sometimes you feel the time will never come when you are at last grown up. The days crawl past you so slowly that time seems to stand still. But it does not. Each day is an important part of growing up, and each day brings you one day closer to being an adult — to graduation, and a job, and getting married, and making your own decisions.

So the four hundred years which follow the rebuilding of the temple are not really a dead end. In this seeming desert there are really two paths marked out, and in the end the two paths converge and become one.

The first path is a path which leads to a cross. Adam was the first to set his steps on the early, faint markings of this road. He did not see the cross which stood at the end of the road. He did not understand how God could save him. He had only the promise, and he trusted blindly in this as he went forward.

Gradually the path became clearer. When God provided a ram to serve as a sacrifice in the place of Abraham's son, Abraham caught a faint glimpse of that cross. When the first Passover was celebrated, and every Israelite family that had painted the blood of a lamb on its front door escaped death, the road became still clearer. And when God's people despaired because of God's heavy judgments on their sins, then Isaiah, the great prophet, spoke a word to encourage them as he glimpsed that cross clearly, though only for a moment:

> *Surely he hath borne our griefs, and carried our sorrows. He was wounded for our transgressions, and God hath laid on him the iniquity of us all.*

The other path ends in a day called Pentecost, when tongues of fire rested on the heads of Jesus' disciples. This path starts in the days of Abraham. For on that very day when God chose Abraham from among all the people then on earth, on that day He promised, "In you all the families of the earth shall be blessed." How? When? Where? Abraham had no idea. He set his feet on the path God showed him without any knowledge of its end. This road, unlike the first road, was a road God's people did not like to travel. They resented the suggestion that God cared about other peoples beyond their own camp where His tent was pitched. And so God continually reminded them. Over and over He set their feet back on this path. He chose Rahab, out of Jericho, to remind them. He welcomed Ruth, who came from Moab. He chose a widow in the heathen land of Sidon to look after Elijah during the terrible years of famine. And when her little boy died, God raised that child from the dead back to life — one of only two such wonderful deeds in the whole Old Testament. So, too, there were many lepers in the land of Israel, but not one of them was healed, only Naaman, the Syrian general. And when Jonah refused to walk in this path, and ran away instead, to what great pains God went to set him back where he belonged!

But this path becomes clearest of all in the great deeds God did when His people were once again captives in the land of Babylon. Over, and over, and over, the message is repeated in God's marvelous acts: It is God who rules the whole earth, who sets up kings, who gives them power and glory. And each man, whether Israelite of Babylonian, must give an account to God of what he has done.

And then the people return to Jerusalem, and there is a long silence when God does not speak. But they are not left without signposts to guide their journey in these years. For they have the history of what God has done. They have all around them the great cloud of those who tried God and found Him faithful, and who now bear witness to this fact: *God is trustworthy!* And they have the signs pointing forward to something even more wonderful to come. For when everything was ready, God actually *became* flesh. He was born as a man. He lived among His people where they could see and touch Him. Not in a tent of fine linen embroidered with cherubim, but in the tent of human nature itself: "And the Word became flesh, and pitched his tent among us, and we beheld his glory, glory as of the only-begotten from the Father." He was a king, but He did not live in a palace in Jerusalem. No, once again, as so long ago in the wilderness around Mt. Sinai, He was a wanderer, sharing the life His people lived. "The foxes have holes," He told us, "and the birds of the heaven have nests, but I have no place to lay my head."

And then He returned to His Father in heaven. But He took with Him our human nature, so that even now, as He rules our lives from His throne, He remembers the long, weary journey we must travel, and the temptations that we meet.

Is it possible for God to come closer to us than this? To share our lives more completely? Yes, even this does not exhaust all that God planned for His people.

"I will not leave you alone," Jesus said just before He died. "I will ask the Father, and he will give you another Helper, the Spirit, to stay with you forever. He remains with you, and lives in you forever." The tent of God is gone, and the golden temple long since destroyed. And even the living tent, our Saviour Jesus, has returned to heaven. But you and I are not alone. God has made our hearts into His temple; He has chosen to live *within* us. "For we are a temple of the living God; even as God said, I will dwell in them and walk in them; and I will be their God, and they shall be my people." Closer than that it is not possible to come.

You and I are on a journey, a journey back to God. God does not watch our stumbling steps indifferently. He does not merely call us to return. No, our God goes with us. He walks within our very hearts.